How to Write a Thesis

How to Write a Thesis

UMBERTO ECO

translated by Caterina Mongiat Farina and Geoff Farina
foreword by Francesco Erspamer

The MIT Press
Cambridge, Massachusetts
London, England

Translated from the original Italian, *Come si fa una tesi di laurea: le materie umanistiche*, © 1977/2012 Bompiani/RCS Libri S.p.A., Via Angelo Rizzoli 8 – 20132 Milano

This book was set in Chapparal Pro by the MIT Press. Printed and bound in the United States of America.

Library of Congress Cataloging-in-Publication Data is available.

ISBN: 978-0-262-52713-2

10   9   8

CONTENTS

FOREWORD

How to Write a Thesis was first published in 1977 in Italy, where it has remained in print ever since. Not only has the book provided instruction and inspiration for generations of Italian students, but it has been translated into seventeen languages, including Persian (1996), Russian (2001), and Chinese (2003). Remarkably, given the book's success, in an era when editorial facelifts, sequels, and new editions have become publishing norms, the book has not been revised or updated, apart from an augmented introduction that Umberto Eco wrote for the 1985 edition. Its durable rules and sound advice have remained constant, despite passing trends and changing technologies.

I am not sure whether this qualifies it as a classic. A classic, Italo Calvino wrote, is a work which relegates the noise of the present to a background hum—but without rendering that hum inaudible. Indeed, at first glance, this book may seem incompatible with our present, considering that chapter 6 is typewritten rather than word-processed (with underlining to render italics!) and that chapter 4 includes reproductions of index cards with handwritten corrections and additions. As unfamiliar as this way of taking notes may be to today's students, it evokes nostalgic memories for those of us who attended college before the 1990s. The persistence of *How to Write a Thesis* is not due to nostalgia, however, nor do I think it is because it renders the noise of the present remote. I believe the book's staying power has to do with the very essence of the humanities.

The humanities are not a body of texts, objects, and information that we inherited from the past—either a remote past or one so recent that we perceive it as our present, although as soon as we examine it we understand that it is irrevocably gone. The humanities are the process of preservation and appropriation of that *pastness*, a process that requires specific skills acquired through practice, as all skills are. This book teaches a *techne*, in the Greek sense of applied and context-related knowledge—a sort of craftsmanship. This is why its title is not, say, *What Is a Thesis?*, an ontological question. Its avowed objective, the thesis, is actually less important than the occurrence of writing it, of "making" it: how to *write* a thesis. Umberto Eco takes us back to the original purpose of theses and dissertations as defining events that conclude a program of study. They are not a test or an exam, nor should they be. They are not meant to prove that the student did his or her homework. Rather, they prove that students can *make* something out of their education.

This is particularly important today, when we are more accustomed to thinking in compliance with the software of our laptop or doing research according to the logic of a tablet than to thinking and researching in a personal and independent way. Written in the age of typewriters, card catalogs, and writing pads, *How to Write a Thesis* is less about the final outcome than about the path and method of arriving there. For Aristotle, knowledge was pursued for its own sake, and such a pursuit could be justified only by an instinctive drive and the intellectual pleasure generated by the fulfillment of that instinct. For Kant, aesthetics and judgment were based on disinterestedness: they could not be programmed, only experienced. The humanities are intrinsically creative and innovative. They are about originality and invention, not discovery. This is precisely Eco's testimony; even more than a technical manual, this book is an invitation to ingenuity, a tribute to imagination.

By exposing twenty-first-century students to long-established practices of scholarly research, this book will introduce them to the core skills that constitute the writing of a thesis: finding an important and intriguing topic, being thorough, taking pride in one's work, giving thoughts time to develop, identifying with a subject, and being resourceful in locating information about it. That is exactly what this book did for me, as a student and young scholar. *How to Write a Thesis* was first published just as I was beginning to think about writing my own thesis, and it was from the Italian edition of this book (*Come si fa una tesi di laurea*) that I learned how to choose a topic, how to look for sources and prepare a bibliography, how to use my library's research systems, how to organize and prioritize information, and finally how to write a captivating and professional dissertation. It remained an indispensable reference source to me for years, long after I had defended and published my thesis. When I began working at the University of Rome, I recommended it to my own students. Many professors in Italy today still refer their students to it, and many university websites in other countries quote long passages from the book as part of the protocol for students to become familiar with before they write a thesis.

And yet, when I moved to the United States in 1993, I was not sure whether it made sense to bring *How to Write a Thesis* with me. Moving one's library to a new place always involves questions about one's future priorities: I distinctly remember taking up the book, turning over a few pages, balancing it in my hand, and hesitating. Things were changing quickly. Eco's methods of organizing and filing information were still effective, but word processors and the Internet were beginning to offer exciting alternatives to long-established research and writing techniques. "Use colors," Eco insisted, when marking a passage. "Use abbreviations to emphasize the relevance of information," "Use abbreviations to designate the passages you must reread," "Supplement the underlining with adhesive page markers"—did this kind of advice still make sense? Moreover, the country in which I was going to live was the one where the standardization of research methodology and citation style had been codified as early as 1906 with the publication of the first edition of the *Chicago Manual of Style*.

Eco himself may have been inspired by the profoundly renovated 12th edition of that manual; published in 1969, it sold more copies than the first eleven editions combined. This was a time, in the United States as well as in Europe, when higher education was undergoing significant expansion. *How to Write a Thesis* sanctioned an extensive diffusion of the humanities into society. It was a momentous transformation, as Eco recognized in his introduction to the book: "Today the Italian university is a university for the masses. Students of all social classes arrive from a variety of high schools." An unprecedented number of young people were enrolling in universities to pursue the study of literature, history, and philosophy—often lacking and failing to acquire the cultural background necessary for careers as teachers, professors, editors, and journalists.

Eco was aware of this predicament. As a university professor, he knew that the majority of students in Italian universities seldom attended classes, that very few of them would continue to write and do research, and that the degree they eventually earned would not necessarily improve their social conditions. It would have been easy to call for the system to be reformed so as not to require a thesis from students ill-equipped to write one, and for whom the benefit of spending several months working on a thesis might be difficult to justify in cold economic terms.

But Eco did not believe that education belonged to an elite, or that it should lower its standards in including the non-elite. He understood that the writing of a thesis forced many students outside of their cultural comfort zone, and that if the shock was too sudden or strong, they would give up. For him, it was about tailoring the challenge to students' needs and capabilities, but without giving up thoroughness, complexity, and rigor. If students' interests and ambitions could be met, while the limits of their sense of security were stretched, education would be achieved. "Writing a thesis," Eco wrote, "requires a student to organize ideas and data, to work methodically, and to build an 'object' that in principle will serve others. In reality, the research experience matters more than the topic."

So I did bring *How to Write a Thesis* with me to the United States, and for the past twenty years have continued to use it and to recommend it to students who read Italian, or Spanish, or one of the many other languages into which it has been translated. As it ages, its usefulness only increases.

The translation of *How to Write a Thesis* into English is long overdue.

Among the many causes of today's crisis in the humanities is the fact that there is a loss of concrete practices and capabilities—of experiences where one must "work methodically," of opportunities "to build an object." It is a crisis long in the making. I suspect that soon after the publication of *How to Write a Thesis*, Eco himself sensed that the cultural and political centrality that criticism had enjoyed since the postwar period was about to end. While he did not give up his scholarly research, he became engaged with fiction. In the fall of 1980, his first novel, *The Name of the Rose*, was published. The society of the spectacle had truly started, with its emphasis on ratings, market surveys, and opinion polls.

But the pendulum may be swinging back. The digital humanities, for example, have revitalized archival research, philology, and curation. Today, Eco's book represents a similar invitation to rediscover the material foundation of knowledge, ideas, and research. Consider the complex filing system that he recommends: "Each type of index card should have a different color, and should include in the top right corner abbreviations that cross-reference one series of cards to another, and to the general plan. The result is something majestic." The same information could have been recorded in a notebook or on slips of paper and then heaped together haphazardly, but this would not have accomplished the same thing. Eco's ordering is principally an ordering of the mind and therefore a pleasure in itself: "something majestic." In fact, it constitutes a proposal for a sort of *slow research*, legitimized not by its results but by its procedures. An experience, a training in accuracy and responsibility. And one in innovation as well. Eco stresses the advantages of what he defines as academic humility, that is, the willingness to "listen with respect to anyone, without this exempting us from pronouncing our value judgments." Both elements are indispensable: openness *and* judgment. There is a moment for listening and a moment for intervening.

Another lesson that we can draw from *How to Write a Thesis* is that no discourse in the humanities can exist without intriguing an audience. The humanities deal with serious issues, but it is the responsibility of those who produce discourse on those issues to make them exciting to others. Eco has acknowledged this throughout his career. Whether writing about Thomas Aquinas, James Bond, fascism, or semiotics, he has consistently succeeded in entertaining and informing his readers at the same time. This book is no exception. Millions of readers have consulted the *Chicago Manual of Style* and followed its rules, but very few have read it from beginning to end. In the late 1970s I did read every page of *How to Write a Thesis*, and I did so again recently, when Roger Conover told me he was considering having the book translated into English for publication by the MIT Press. It's interesting to think, almost 40 years after its publication in Italian, that reading this book from beginning to end in English could now become a natural exercise again.

Francesco Erspamer
Harvard University

TRANSLATORS' FOREWORD

> If you consult any dictionary you will see that the word
> "exactitude" is not among the synonyms of faithfulness.
> There are rather loyalty, honesty, respect, and devotion.
>
> *Umberto Eco*[1]

Although Eco was referring to the translation of literary
texts in the lines above, his principle of faithfulness has provided the foundation for our translation of *Come si fa una tesi
di laurea*. We have striven to create a translation that is loyal
to the original text but also useful and enjoyable to contemporary English readers.

Although most of the students for whom Eco wrote this
book in 1977 shared a genuine desire for the challenges
and rewards of a university education, many lacked the
time, resources, and experience to navigate a university
system embroiled in the social and economic crisis that Eco
describes in his original introduction to the book. Because
these unique circumstances define the book's ethos, we have
preserved evidence of the book's historical context whenever
possible. We have anglicized only the most obtrusive Italian
references. We have replaced Italian expressions with close
English equivalents only when necessary, and we have preserved others when the meaning was clear in English, despite
their probable unfamiliarity to English readers. Most importantly, we have made every effort to preserve Eco's stern but
nurturing tone (including his precise lists of didactic rules,

copious use of italics for emphasis, and deadpan ironies) that so stimulated and inspired his original readers. The author of *Come si fa una tesi di laurea* held his students to a single, high standard; but he also demonstrated unfailing empathy and genuine commitment to their progress. We hope the same will be said of the author of *How to Write a Thesis*.

This book contains references to a great number of foreign books and articles, many of which have not been translated into English. We have indicated that there is no published English translation of a work by including our translation of the title after the original title, in sentence style and enclosed in parentheses. Where a published English translation does exist, we have used its title alone, unless the context also required the original title (in which case we have included the English title after the original, in parentheses and with standard formatting). Although this system may occasionally seem cumbersome, we feel that it achieves the best balance between readability and bibliographical accuracy, since it indicates the cited work's original language where the context fails to do so.

For the most part, English readers need not be familiar with the literature that Eco cites to follow his argument, and the references themselves provide a rare glimpse of Eco's diverse interests. In fact many of the works were obscure to his Italian readers in the 1970s, and they are infinitely more accessible to today's wired readers than they were to Eco's hypothetical Italian student whose only resource was the card catalog in his modest hometown library. And speaking of this student who reappears throughout the book, instead of replacing him with a contemporary English equivalent, we have left him unequivocally Italian, and in his original context of what may seem to us like the dawn of information technology. We hope English-speaking students will not only relate to his struggles and successes, but also gain valuable perspective from his unique situation, a situation that originally necessitated this book.

Early drafts of our translation occasionally suffered from the exactitude against which Eco warns, primarily on a sentence and paragraph level, and for this reason we have made many cosmetic changes. These include adding context, omitting redundancies, updating archaisms, clarifying obscure references, correcting typos and other errors, Americanizing distances and currencies,[2] and making other functional and stylistic choices that we hope have liberated Eco's nuanced ideas for a new generation of English-speaking readers.

Additionally, we envisioned a translation that would serve English-speaking students as well as the original has served students in Italy. Rather than take an overarching approach to translating all of Eco's writing instructions, we have approached them on a case-by-case basis. We have omitted certain instructions that do not apply to English, and that would have held only trivial value for the English reader. We have revised other instructions to conform to current English usage whenever we could do so without undue violence to the original text, and whenever the results would be relevant to English-speaking students. (Where appropriate, we have altered these instructions to be consistent with the *Chicago Manual of Style*, the manual that provides the editorial foundation for this book.) Finally, Eco occasionally provides instructions that do not reflect current English usage, but that are nonetheless valuable because of the perspective or argument they contain; these we have kept and noted as such.

Finally, we have preserved Eco's handwritten index card research system in all its detail, precisely because it is the soul of *How to Write a Thesis*. Obviously the card catalog of the small town library is primitive compared to today's online research systems, but the research skills that Eco teaches are perhaps even more relevant today. Eco's system demands critical thinking, resourcefulness, creativity, attention to detail, and academic pride and humility; these are precisely the skills that aid students overwhelmed by the ever-growing demands made on their time and resources, and confused by the seemingly endless torrents of information available to them. Much as today's college students lug laptops to the library in their backpacks, Eco's students lugged their files of index cards. Today's students carry access to boundless information that Eco's students could not have begun to fathom, but Eco's students owned every word they carried. They meticulously curated every byte of information, and they enjoyed the profound rewards of both the process and the product.

Our sincerest thanks to: Matthew Abbate, Pascale-Anne Brault, Fabrizio Cariani, Gary Cestaro, Roger Conover, Michael Naas, and Anna Souchuk.

Caterina Mongiat Farina and Geoff Farina
DePaul University

INTRODUCTION TO THE ORIGINAL 1977 EDITION

In the past, the Italian university was an elite institution. Only the children of university graduates attended, and with rare exceptions, students had all the time they needed at their disposal. The university allowed students to proceed slowly, with time allotted for study, for "healthy" fraternal pastimes, or for the activities of student government. Classes took the form of prestigious lectures, after which the most interested students would convene with professors and their teaching assistants in unhurried seminars, consisting of 10 or 15 people at the most.

This is still the case in many American universities, where a course never exceeds 10 or 20 students who pay generously for unlimited access to their professors. In Oxford and other British universities, there is a professor who advises the research thesis of as few as one or two students each year, and who follows their work on a daily basis. If the situation in Italian universities were similar, there would be no need to write this book, although some of its advice may also be useful in the ideal academic situation I describe above.

But today the Italian university is a university for the masses. Students of all social classes arrive from a variety of high schools. Perhaps they enroll in philosophy or classics, even if they come from a technical high school where they have never studied ancient Greek or Latin. (It may be true that Latin is of little use for many activities, but it is of great service to students of philosophy and literature.) Some Italian university courses have thousands of enrolled students, and are taught by a professor who knows only the 30 or so who attend most frequently. Even with the help of teaching assistants, the professor may be able to engage only 100 students with some regularity during the semester.

Among these students, there are many affluent young men and women who were raised in cultivated families and exposed to lively cultural environments, who were able to take educational trips, attend art and theater festivals, and go abroad. Then there are "the others," students who, for example, work in the city clerk's office in their hometown of only 10,000 inhabitants, a town where there are perhaps only newsstands that substitute for proper booksellers. Other such students, disappointed by their university experience, become radicalized and seek education through political action, but they too must eventually meet their thesis obligations. Still others are forced to choose their courses by calculating the cost of required textbooks. These students may refer to a "$13 course" by cost rather than by topic, and choose the less expensive of two electives. And finally there are students who have never learned how to take advantage of the resources of their hometown libraries, how to sign up for a library card, how to search for a book, or in which libraries to look.

The advice in this book is especially useful for these students, as well as for high school graduates who are about to embark on their college studies and who wish to understand the alchemy of the university thesis. With this book, I would like to convince these students of two points:

1. One can write a *decent* thesis despite being in a difficult situation resulting from inequity past and present.

2. Regardless of the disappointment and frustration that these students may experience at the university, their thesis provides an opportunity to regain a positive and progressive notion of study. According to this notion, studying is not simply gathering information, but is the critical elaboration of an experience. Through study, students acquire the capacity to identify problems, confront them methodically, and articulate them systematically in expository detail. These skills will serve students for a lifetime.

That said, this book is not an attempt to fully explain how to carry out academic research, nor is it a theoretical dissertation on the value of study. It is only a series of considerations on how to present oneself before a committee with a physical object, prescribed by Italian law, and constituted by a certain quantity of typewritten pages, that is supposed to have some relationship to the discipline of one's major, and that will not plunge one's thesis advisor into a state of painful stupor.

Let it be clear that this book will not tell you what to put into your thesis. That is *your* job. This book will tell you:

1. What constitutes a thesis,
2. How to choose the topic and organize a work schedule,
3. How to conduct bibliographical research,
4. How to organize the material you find,
5. How to format the thesis.

Inevitably, this book will provide the most precise instruction on the final task in this list, even if it seems to be the least important, because it is the only one with a fairly exact set of rules.

This book deals with a thesis in the humanities. Since my experience relates to studies in literature and philosophy, the majority of the examples in this book naturally concern such topics. However, within the limits set by this book, the criteria I suggest are also applicable to a thesis in political science, education, or law. If you adopt a historical or theoretical approach, rather than an experimental or applicative one, you should be able to use the model I propose for a thesis in architecture, economics, business, or some scientific topics; but do not trust me too much on those.

At the time of this book's publication, the reform of the Italian university is being debated, and there is talk of introducing two or three different levels of university degrees. It remains to be seen if this reform will radically change the concept of the thesis. If this reform creates various levels of university degrees, as is the case in most foreign countries, we will have a situation similar to what I describe in the first chapter (section 1.1), and there will be a PhD thesis in addition to the thesis already required for the *laurea*, currently the terminal humanities degree offered by Italian universities. The advice I provide in this book applies to both of these, and I will clarify when there are differences between them. Therefore, I believe that the following pages can guide students through the long transition toward prospective reform.

Cesare Segre read the manuscript of this book and has provided advice. Since I heeded some and disregarded some, he is not responsible for the final product. Naturally, I wholeheartedly thank him.

Finally, the following pages address both male and female students, and they refer to both male and female professors. However, when the language doesn't provide a gender-neutral expression, I have chosen to use the male, and I mean no gender discrimination with this grammatical usage.[1]

INTRODUCTION TO THE 1985 EDITION

This new edition of my book has been published eight years after the first. I initially wrote this book to avoid repeating time and again the same recommendations to my students, and since then the book has circulated widely. I am grateful to those colleagues who still recommend it to their students. I am most grateful to those students who discovered it by chance, after years of trying unsuccessfully to complete their college degree, and who wrote to me and said that these pages had finally encouraged them to start their thesis, or to finish one they had started. I must take some responsibility for facilitating an increase in the number of Italian college graduates, although I am not sure that this is a good thing.

Although I wrote this book based on my personal university teaching experience, and with the humanities in mind, I discovered that it was useful to almost everyone, since it focuses on the spirit, mentality, and research methods required to write a good thesis, rather than on its content. Therefore, this book has been read by people not pursuing or not yet pursuing university studies, and even by middle school students preparing research projects or reports.

This book has been translated into the languages of foreign countries that have different thesis requirements. Naturally, editors in those countries have made some adjustments, yet it seems that on the whole they have been able to retain the general argument. This does not surprise me, since the methods necessary to conduct high-quality research, at any level of complexity, are the same all over the world.

When I was writing this book, the reform of the Italian university had not yet been implemented. In the original introduction, I suggested that this book was appropriate not only for the traditional *laurea* thesis but also for the PhD thesis that was about to be implemented as part of these reforms. I believe my prediction was sensible, and today I feel I can present these pages even to a PhD student. (Although I hope that a PhD student has already learned these things, one never knows.)

In the introduction to the first edition, I talked about the shortcomings of the Italian university, shortcomings that made my little book useful to the many thousands of students who otherwise lacked the instruction to success-fully complete their thesis. Today, I would happily send the remaining copies of this book to the recycling bin rather than have to republish it. Alas, these shortcomings remain, and my original argument is as relevant today as it was in 1977.

Strange things have happened to me since this book first appeared. For example, periodically I receive letters from stu-dents who write, "I must write a thesis on such-and-such a topic." (The list of topics is immense. Some of them, I must admit, bewilder me.) They ask, "Would you be so kind as to send me a complete bibliography so that I can proceed with my work?" Evidently these students have not understood the purpose of the book, or have mistaken me for a wizard. This book tries to teach one how to work independently, not how and where to find, as Italians say, the prepared meal. More-over, these students have not understood that compiling a bibliography is a time-consuming project, and if I were to complete even one of these students' requests, I would have to work a few months, if not longer. If I had all that time avail-able, I swear to you that I would find a better way to spend it.

Here I would like to recount the most curious thing that happened to me. It regards a section of this book, specifi-cally section 4.2.4 on the topic of "Academic Humility." In this section I attempted to show that the best ideas do not always come from major authors, and that no intellectual contribution should be shunned because of the author's sta-tus. As an example, I recounted the writing of my own *laurea* thesis, during which I found a decisive idea that resolved a

thorny theoretical problem, in a small book of little originality written in 1887 by a certain abbot Vallet, a book that I
found by chance in a market stall.

After the book you are reading appeared, Beniamino Placido wrote a charming review in *La Repubblica* (September
22, 1977). In it he likened this story of my research adventure with the abbot Vallet to the fairy tale in which a character becomes lost in the woods. As happens in fairy tales, and
as has been theorized by the Soviet formalist V. Y. Propp, the
lost character meets a "donor" who gives him a "magic key."
Placido's interpretation of my story was not that bizarre,
considering that research is after all an adventure, but Placido implied that, to tell my fairy tale, I had invented the
abbot Vallet. When I met Placido, I told him:

> You are wrong; the abbot Vallet exists, or rather he existed,
> and I still have his book at home. It has been more than
> twenty years since I have opened it, but since I have a good
> visual memory, to this day I remember the page on which I
> found that idea, and the red exclamation point that I wrote
> in the margin. Come to my home and I will show you the
> infamous book of the abbot Vallet.

No sooner said than done: we go to my home, we pour ourselves two glasses of whiskey, I climb a small ladder to reach
the high shelf where, as I remembered, the fated book had
rested for twenty years. I find it, dust it, open it once again
with a certain trepidation, look for the equally fated page,
which I find with its beautiful exclamation point in the
margin.

I show the page to Placido, and then I read him the excerpt
that had helped me so much. I read it, I read it again, and I
am astonished. The abbot Vallet had never formulated the
idea that I attributed to him; that is to say he had never made
the connection that seemed so brilliant to me, a connection
between the theory of judgment and the theory of beauty.

Vallet wrote of something else. Stimulated in some mysterious way by what he was saying, I made that connection myself and, and as I identified the idea with the text
I was underlining, I attributed it to Vallet. And for more
than twenty years I had been grateful to the old abbot for

something he had never given me. I had produced the magic key on my own.

But is this really how it is? Is the merit of that idea truly mine? Had I never read Vallet, I would never have had that idea. He may not have been the father of that idea, but he certainly was, so to speak, its obstetrician. He did not gift me with anything, but he kept my mind in shape, and he somehow stimulated my thinking. Is this not also what we ask from a teacher, to provoke us to invent ideas?

As I recalled this episode, I became aware that many times over the course of my readings, I had attributed to others ideas that they had simply inspired me to look for; and many other times I remained convinced that an idea was mine until, after revisiting some books read many years before, I discovered that the idea, or its core, had come to me from a certain author. One (unnecessary) credit I had given to Vallet made me realize how many debts I had forgotten to pay. I believe the meaning of this story, not dissonant with the other ideas in this book, is that research is a mysterious adventure that inspires passion and holds many surprises. Not just an individual but also an entire culture participates, as ideas sometimes travel freely, migrate, disappear, and reappear. In this sense, ideas are similar to jokes that become better as each person tells them.

Therefore, I decided that I must preserve my gratitude to the abbot Vallet, precisely because he *had* been a magical donor. This is why, as maybe some have already noticed, I introduced him as a main character in my novel *The Name of the Rose*. He first appears in the second line of the introduction, this time as a literal (yet still mysterious and magical) donor of a lost manuscript, and a symbol of a library in which books speak among themselves.

I am not sure what the moral of this story is, but I know there is at least one, and it is very beautiful. I wish my readers to find many abbots Vallet over the course of their lives, and I aspire to become someone else's abbot Vallet.

1 THE DEFINITION AND PURPOSE OF THE THESIS

1.1 What Is a Thesis, and Why Is It Required?

A thesis is a typewritten manuscript, usually 100 to 400 pages in length, in which the student addresses a particular problem in his chosen field. Italian law requires students to successfully complete a thesis before they are granted the *laurea*, currently the terminal humanities degree offered by Italian universities. Once the student has passed all required exams and finished writing his thesis, he defends it in front of a committee. During this defense, the thesis advisor and one or more readers give a report that may include objections to the candidate's thesis. This report sparks a discussion in which other professors participate as members of the committee. The advisor and a second professor identify the strengths and weaknesses of the thesis and evaluate the candidate's capacity to defend the opinions he expressed in his thesis, and these influence the committee's final evaluation. After calculating the student's grade point average, the committee evaluates the thesis on a numeric scale of 66 to 110 points. The committee may also grant a score of 110 *cum laude*, and designate the thesis as worthy of publication. This process applies to a *laurea* in the humanities, as other fields of study may have different requirements.

As you may know, most universities around the world do not require a thesis for a first-level degree. In some universities, there are also certain higher-level degrees that are obtainable without a thesis. In others, there is a first-level degree that has similar requirements to the Italian *laurea*, obtainable through a series of exams and, in some cases, through completion of a less demanding research project. Still other universities offer various second-level degrees that require thesis-like research projects of varying complexity. Some universities outside of Italy also confer a certificate degree, called a licentiate, that shares certain affinities with the Italian *laurea*. The licentiate in its various forms verifies a graduate's competence within a certain profession.

However, outside of Italy, the thesis proper generally applies to the doctorate, a degree pursued by those students who wish to specialize and pursue academic research in a particular discipline. Although the doctorate has various designations in different parts of the world, we will use the common abbreviation "PhD." Although this is an abbreviation for "doctor of philosophy," it is generally used internationally to refer to anyone with a doctorate in the humanities, from the sociologist to the ancient Greek scholar. (Scientific disciplines use other abbreviations, such as MD, or doctor of medicine.) The PhD certifies competence in academic research, and most PhD graduates appropriately pursue academic careers.

In universities around the world that traditionally grant the PhD, the thesis usually refers to a doctoral thesis, known as a "dissertation." This is a piece of original research through which the candidate must demonstrate his scholarly capability of furthering his discipline. Although there are very young PhDs, the dissertation is generally not undertaken as an Italian student undertakes a *laurea* thesis, at the age of 22, but rather when he is older, sometimes as old as 40 or 50.

Why wait so long? Because the dissertation is a piece of original research, in which one must not only know the work of other scholars but also "discover" something that other scholars have not yet said. In the humanities, this "discovery" will rarely be a sweeping invention such as atomic scission, the theory of relativity, or a medicine that cures cancer. PhD candidates in the humanities make more modest scholarly discoveries: a new way to interpret and understand a classic text, the attribution of a manuscript that illuminates an author's biography, a reassessment of secondary studies that ripens ideas once wandering lost in various other texts.

In any case, the scholar must produce a work that, in theory, other scholars in the field should not ignore, because it says something new (see section 2.6.1).

Is the "Italian-style" *laurea* thesis of the same kind? Rarely. In fact, since students undertake it in their early twenties while they are still completing their course work, a *laurea* thesis cannot represent the conclusion of long research and contemplation, or provide evidence of full scholarly maturation. Therefore, although there may be an occasional *laurea* thesis (completed by a particularly gifted student) that attains the quality of a PhD thesis, most do not, nor does the university encourage such an accomplishment. In fact a good *laurea* thesis need not be a research thesis in the traditional sense; instead it can take the form of a "literature review."

In a literature review, the student simply demonstrates that he has critically read the majority of the existing "critical literature," or the published writings on a particular topic. The student explains the literature clearly, connects the various points of view of its authors, and thus offers an intelligent review, perhaps useful even to a specialist in the field who had never conducted an in-depth study on that specific topic.

Therefore, the student seeking a *laurea* has a choice: he can write a literature review appropriate for a *laurea* degree; or he can undertake a research thesis, one that could even attain the level of scholarship appropriate for a PhD. A research thesis is always more time-consuming, laborious, and demanding. A literature review can also be laborious and time-consuming (some have taken many years), but will usually require less time and present less risk. Writing a literature review in no way precludes a student from later taking the avenue of research; the review can constitute an act of diligence on the part of the young scholar who, before beginning independent research, wants to clarify for himself a few ideas by gathering background information on the topic. This is certainly preferable to producing a hastily finished work that claims to represent research but is in fact just a bad thesis that annoys readers and does no good for its author.

Accordingly, the choice between a literature review and a research thesis is linked to the student's ability and maturity. And regrettably, it is often linked to financial factors, because a working student certainly has less time and energy to dedicate to long hours of research and trips to foreign research institutes or libraries, and often lacks money for the purchase of rare and expensive books and other resources.

Sadly, this book will not offer advice on financial matters. Until a short time ago, research was the privilege of rich students around the world. Today, academic scholarships, travel scholarships, and foreign research grants have hardly solved this problem. A more just society would be one in which research was a profession funded by the state, and only people with true aspirations to study were compensated. It would be a society in which a piece of paper was not required to find employment or to obtain a promotion in the public sector, and a university graduate would not surpass other qualified applicants simply because the graduate had earned a *laurea*.[1]

But this is not the case in the Italian university, nor in the Italian society in which it was born. We can only hope that students of all social classes can attend the university without stressful sacrifices, and then proceed to explain the many ways in which one can write a decent thesis, taking into account one's available time, energy, and specific aspirations.

1.2 For Whom Is This Book Written?

Given the situation described above, we must assume that there are many students who are *forced* to write a thesis so that they may graduate quickly and obtain the career advancement that originally motivated their university enrollment. Some of these students may be as old as 40. They will ask for instructions on how to write a thesis *in a month*, in such a way as to receive a passing grade and graduate quickly. We should then say resolutely, *this book is not for them*. If these are their needs, if they are the victims of paradoxical legal circumstances that force them to graduate so they may resolve painful financial matters, they would be much better served by the following options: (a) Invest a reasonable amount of money in having a thesis written by a second party. (b) Copy a thesis that was written a few years prior for another institution. (It is better not to copy a book currently in print, even if it was written in a foreign language.

If the professor is even minimally informed on the topic, he will be aware of the book's existence. However, submitting in Milan a thesis written in Catania limits the probability of being caught, although it is obviously necessary to ascertain whether the thesis's advisor held a position in Catania before teaching in Milan. Consequently, even plagiarizing a thesis requires an intelligent research effort.)

Clearly the two pieces of advice we have just offered are *illegal*. They are similar to advising an emergency room patient to put a knife to the throat of a doctor who refuses to treat him. These are desperate acts. We give this paradoxical advice to emphasize that this book does not attempt to resolve the serious temporal and financial problems that many university students currently face.

However, this book does not require that the student be a millionaire or have a decade available to commit to his studies after having traveled the world. This book is for students who want to do rigorous work, despite the fact that they can only dedicate a few hours each day to study. This book is also for students who want to write a thesis that will provide a certain intellectual satisfaction, and that will also prove useful after graduation.

As we will see, the rigor of a thesis is more important than its scope. One can even collect soccer trading cards with rigor, as long as he identifies the topic of the collection, the criteria for cataloguing it, and its historical limits. It is acceptable for him to limit his collection to players active after 1960, provided that his collection is complete after this date. There will always be a difference between his collection and the Louvre, but it is better to build a serious trading card collection from 1960 to the present than to create a cursory art collection. The thesis shares this same criterion.

1.3 The Usefulness of a Thesis after Graduation

There are two ways to write a thesis that is useful after graduation. A student can write a thesis that becomes the foundation of a broader research project that will continue into the years ahead, if he has the means and desire to do so. Additionally, writing a thesis develops valuable professional skills that are useful after graduation. For example, the director of a local tourist office who authored a thesis titled "From *Stephen Hero* to *A Portrait of the Artist as a Young Man*" will have developed skills needed for his profession. He will have done the following:

1. Identified a precise topic,

2. Collected documents on that topic,

3. Ordered these documents,

4. Reexamined the topic in light of the documents collected,

5. Organized all this work into an organic form,

6. Ensured that his readers have understood him,

7. Provided the necessary documentation so that readers may reexamine the topic through his sources.

Writing a thesis requires a student to organize ideas and data, to work methodically, and to build an "object" that in principle will serve others. In reality, the research experience matters more than the topic. The student who was able to carefully research these two versions of Joyce's novel will have trained himself to methodically collect, organize, and present information, and for other professional responsibilities he will encounter working at the tourist office.

As a writer myself, I have already published ten books on different topics, but I was able to write the last nine because of the experience of the first, which happened to be a revision of my own *laurea* thesis. Without that first effort, I would never have acquired the skills I needed for the others. And, for better or for worse, the other books still show traces of the first. With time, a writer becomes more astute and knowledgeable, but how he uses his knowledge will always depend on how he originally researched the many things he did not know.

At the very least, writing a thesis is like training the memory. One will retain a good memory when he is old if he has trained it when he was young. It doesn't matter if the training involved memorizing the players of every Italian A-series soccer team, Dante's poetry, or every Roman emperor from Augustus to Romulus Augustulus. Since we are training our own memory, it is certainly better to serve our interests and needs; but sometimes it is even good exercise to learn useless things. Therefore, even if it is better to research an appealing topic, the topic is secondary to the research method and the actual experience of writing the thesis. If a student works rigorously, no topic is truly foolish, and the student can draw useful conclusions even from a remote or peripheral topic.

In fact, Marx wrote his thesis on the two ancient Greek philosophers Epicurus and Democritus, not on political economy, and this was no accident. Perhaps Marx was able to approach the theoretical questions of history and economy with such rigor precisely because of his scrupulous work on these ancient Greek philosophers. Also, considering that so many students start with an ambitious thesis on Marx and then end up working at the personnel office of a big capitalist business, we might begin to question the utility, topicality, and political relevance of thesis topics.

1.4   Four Obvious Rules for Choosing a Thesis Topic

Although we will discuss thesis topics in greater detail in the next chapter, the following rules will help you get started. They do not apply if the professor pressures you to choose a particular topic (see section 2.7, "How to Avoid Being Exploited by Your Advisor"), or if you lack interest and are willing to choose any topic so as to graduate quickly. If you are inspired by a particular interest, and your advisor is willing to facilitate this interest, the following rules will guide you:

1. *The topic should reflect your previous studies and experience.* It should be related to your completed courses; your other research; and your political, cultural, or religious experience.

2. *The necessary sources should be materially accessible.* You should be near enough to the sources for convenient access, and you should have the permission you need to access them.

3. *The necessary sources should be manageable.* In other words, you should have the ability, experience, and background knowledge needed to understand the sources.

4. *You should have some experience with the methodological framework that you will use in the thesis.* For example, if your thesis topic requires you to analyze a Bach violin sonata, you should be versed in music theory and analysis.

Put this way, these four rules seem banal. We could summarize them in this single rule: "You must write a thesis that you are able to write." This rule may seem trivial, but it is true, and many a thesis has been dramatically aborted precisely because this rule was broken.[2] The following chapters will provide instruction on how to write a thesis that is both manageable and feasible.

CHOOSING THE TOPIC

2.1 Monograph or Survey?

The first temptation of any student is to write a thesis that is too broad. For example, the first impulse of a literature student is to write a thesis titled "Literature Today." If advised to narrow the scope, the student might choose "Italian Literature from the Postwar Period to the Sixties," a topic with slightly more focus, but one that is still impossibly vast.

A thesis like this is dangerous. Such a topic will make a seasoned scholar tremble, and will present an impossible challenge for a young student. Presented with this challenge, a student will either write a tedious survey consisting only of author's names and current scholarly opinions, or will try to imitate the approach of a mature critic and will inevitably be accused of unforgivable omissions. In 1957 the great contemporary Italian critic Gianfranco Contini published a survey titled *Letteratura italiana. Ottocento-Novecento* (Italian literature: The nineteenth and twentieth centuries). Had the survey been a thesis, it would have earned a failing grade, despite its 472 pages in length. Contini dedicated entire chapters to so-called "minor" authors, and relegated certain "major" authors to mentions in short footnotes or omitted them altogether. The committee would have attributed these choices to carelessness or ignorance. Naturally, since Contini is a scholar of recognized historical knowledge and critical acumen, readers understood that the omissions and disproportions were intentional, and that the absence of a particular author was a more eloquent expression of

Contini's disfavor than a hostile review. But if a student in
his twenties plays the same trick, who guarantees that there
is shrewdness behind his silence? Do the omissions replace
criticism that the student has written elsewhere, or that he
would be capable of writing?

Usually, with a thesis of this kind, the student later accuses
the committee members of having failed to understand him.
But a thesis that is too broad cannot be understood, and
therefore is always an act of pride. It is not that intellectual
pride in a thesis should be rejected a priori. A student can
even argue that Dante was a lousy poet, but only after at least
300 pages of rigorous analysis of Dante's texts. However, the
necessary breadth of a topic like "Italian Literature from
the Postwar Period to the Sixties" leaves no space for these
demonstrations, and this is why the student should aptly
choose something more modest. Not "The Novels of Beppe
Fenoglio," but "The Different Versions of *Johnny the Partisan*." Boring? Maybe, but the challenge it presents is ultimately more interesting.

If you think about it, specificity is also an act of shrewdness. A survey of 40 years of literature is vulnerable to all
kinds of objections. How can the advisor or another committee member resist the temptation to show his knowledge of
a minor author absent from the student's work? If each committee member jots down even two or three omissions in the
margins of the table of contents, the thesis will end up looking like a missing persons list, and the student will become
the target of a burst of charges. If instead the student works
diligently on a specific topic, he will find himself mastering
material unknown to most of the committee members. I am
not suggesting a cheap trick. (It may be a trick, but it takes
hard work, so it is certainly not cheap.) The candidate simply
presents himself as "expert" in front of a less expert audience, and since he worked hard to gain his expertise, it is fair
that he benefits from the situation.

Between these two extremes of a 40-year literature survey and a strict monograph on the variants of a short text,
there are thesis topics of varying scope. We can find topics like "The New Literary Avant-garde of the Sixties," or
"The Image of the Langhe in Pavese and Fenoglio," or even

"Similarities and Differences in Three Writers of the Fantastic: Savinio, Buzzati, and Landolfi."

As for the sciences, a little book on the same topic as ours gives advice that is valid for all subjects:

> The subject "Geology," for instance, is much too broad a topic. "Vulcanology," as a branch of geology, is still too comprehensive. "Volcanoes in Mexico" might be developed into a good but superficial paper. However, a further limitation to "The History of Popocatepetl" (which one of Cortéz's conquistadores probably climbed in 1519 and which erupted violently as late as 1702) would make for a more valuable study. Another limited topic, spanning fewer years, would be "The Birth and Apparent Death of Paricutín" (February 20, 1943, to March 4, 1952).[1]

Here, I would suggest the last topic, but only if the candidate really says all there is to say about that damned volcano.

Some time ago a student approached me with the impossibly broad topic "The Symbol in Contemporary Thought." At the very least, I did not understand what the student meant by "symbol," a term that has different meanings to different authors, meanings that are sometimes directly opposed. Consider that formal logicians and mathematicians designate with the term "symbol" certain expressions without meaning that occupy a specific place with a specific function in a given formalized calculus (such as the a and b or x and y of algebraic formulas), whereas other authors use the term to mean a form full of ambiguous meanings, such as images in dreams, in which a tree can refer to a sex organ, the desire of growth, and so on. So how can anybody write a thesis with this title? One would have to analyze all of the meanings of "symbol" in all of contemporary culture, list their similarities and differences, determine whether there is an underlying fundamental unitary concept in each author and each theory, and whether the differences nevertheless make the theories in question incompatible. Well then, no contemporary philosopher, linguist, or psychoanalyst has yet been able to complete such a work satisfactorily. How can a neophyte succeed? How can we expect such a work from a young student who, albeit precocious, has no more than six or seven years of academic reading behind him? Even if he could intelligently write at least part of an argument, he would still face the problems of Contini's history of Italian literature. Alternatively, he could neglect the work of other authors and propose his own theory of the symbol, but we will discuss this questionable choice in section 2.2.

I spoke with the student in question. We discussed the possibility of a thesis on symbol in Freud and Jung, one that would have excluded all other definitions of the term and would have compared only the meanings given to it by these two authors. Then I learned that the student's only foreign language was English. (We will return to the question of foreign language skills in section 2.5.) We then settled on "The Concept of Symbol in Peirce," a thesis that would require only English-language skills. Naturally over the course of the thesis the student would have described how Peirce's definition of the term differed from that of authors such as Freud and Jung, but these German-speaking authors would not be central to the thesis. Nobody could object that the student had read these authors only in translation, since the thesis proposed to study only the American author fully and in the original language. In this way, we managed to limit the survey to a medium length, while not changing it into a strict monograph. This solution was acceptable to all.

I should also clarify that the term "monograph" can have a broader meaning than the one we have used here. A monograph is the study of a single topic, and as such it is opposed to a "history of," a manual, and an encyclopedia. A monograph can analyze many writers, but only from the perspective of a specific theme. For example, a monograph could appropriately be titled "The Theme of 'The World Turned Upside Down' in Medieval Writers," and it could explore the paradox in which fish can fly, birds can swim, and so on. The student could write an excellent monograph on this topic if he worked rigorously. However, this topic would include a vast amount of readings, as the student would need to familiarize himself with all the writers who treated the subject, however minor or obscure. The student might do well to narrow his scope to "The Theme of 'The World Turned Upside Down' in Carolingian Poets."

A student may consider a survey more exciting than a monograph, if only because focusing on the same author for one, two, or more years may seem boring. But the student should understand that a strict monograph also involves the author's cultural and historical context. A thesis on Beppe Fenoglio's fiction requires reading related writers such as Cesare Pavese or Elio Vittorini, reading the American writers whom Fenoglio read and translated, and examining Italian realism in general. It is only possible to understand and interpret an author within his wider cultural context. However, it is one thing for a portraitist to paint a landscape for his subject's background, and it is another thing to paint a complete, detailed landscape painting. The portrait of a gentleman might contain the countryside with a river in the background, but a landscape contains fields, valleys, and rivers, all in fine detail. The technique or, in photographic terms, the focus must change between the two. In a monograph, the landscape can even be somewhat out of focus, incomplete, or unoriginal.

Finally, remember this fundamental principle: *the more you narrow the field, the better and more safely you will work.* Always prefer a monograph to a survey. It is better for your thesis to resemble an essay than a complete history or an encyclopedia.

2.2 Historical or Theoretical?

This choice only applies to certain subjects. A thesis in history of mathematics, Romance philology, history of German literature, and other similar subjects can only be historical. A thesis on experimental subjects such as architectural composition, nuclear reactor physics, or comparative anatomy is usually theoretical. But there are other subjects such as theoretical philosophy, sociology, cultural anthropology, aesthetics, philosophy of law, pedagogy, or international law that allow a thesis of both kinds.

In a theoretical thesis, a student confronts an abstract problem upon which other works may or may not have already reflected: the nature of human will, the concept of freedom, the notion of social role, the existence of God, or the genetic code. Considered together, such topics may elicit smiles, as they require the writer to compose what Antonio Gramsci called "brief notes on the universe." And yet illustrious thinkers have devoted themselves to such topics. However, they usually did so after decades of reflection.

In the hands of less experienced students, these topics can generate two outcomes. The first and less worrisome is a survey like the one defined in the previous section, on which I have already provided observations. For example, the student tackles the concept of social role as it appears in the writings of a chosen set of authors. The second outcome is more tragic, because the candidate presumes he can solve the question of God or define the concept of freedom, within only a few pages. My experience is that a thesis like this usually turns out to be short and unorganized, and resembles more a lyric poem than an academic study. Usually, when the committee objects to the candidate's argument as too personalized, generic, informal, and lacking in historiographic verification and evidence, the candidate responds that he has been misunderstood, and that his thesis is more intelligent than other banal literature surveys. This may be true, but this answer usually comes from a candidate with confused ideas, one who lacks academic humility and communicative skills. I will define academic humility (which requires pride, and is not a virtue for the weak) in section 4.2.4. This candidate may indeed be a genius who has acquired a lifetime of knowledge in a mere 22 years, and let it be clear that I am presenting this hypothesis without any shade of irony. However, it takes a long time for mankind to notice that such a genius has appeared on the Earth's crust, and his work must be read and digested for a certain number of years before its greatness is grasped. How can we expect that the busy committee, responsible for so many students, should grasp at first sight the greatness of this lone runner?

Let us hypothesize that the student believes he has understood an important problem. Since nothing is born from nothing, the student must have developed his thoughts under a particular author's influence. In this case, he should transform his theoretical thesis into a historiographic thesis. In other words, he should not discuss the problem of being, the notion of freedom, or the concept of social action;

but develop a topic such as "The Question of Being in Early Heidegger," "The Notion of Freedom in Kant," or "The Concept of Social Action in Parsons." His original ideas will emerge as he grapples with his author's ideas, as it is possible to say new things about freedom while studying an author's work on the concept. If he is ambitious, he can transform the theoretical thesis that he originally conceived into the final chapter of his historiographic thesis. Consequently, readers will understand his original ideas in the context of a previous thinker, and the concepts he proposes will gain support from their proper frame of reference.

Even the brightest young writer will find it difficult to work in a vacuum and establish an argument *ab initio*. He must find a foothold in past scholarship, especially for questions as vague as the notions of being and freedom. Even if someone is a genius, and especially if someone is a genius, he will never be diminished by starting from another author's work. Building on a previous author's work does not mean a student must fetishize, adore, or swear by that author, and in fact the student can demonstrate the author's errors and limits. Medieval writers saw themselves as "dwarves" compared to the "giant" ancients they revered, and yet they could see further than the ancients because they were "dwarves standing on the shoulders of giants."

Not all of these observations are valid for applied and laboratory-based subjects. In psychology for example, the alternative to "The Question of Perception in Piaget" is not "The Question of Perception," even if there were a student reckless enough to attempt such a dangerously generic topic. The alternative to the first topic's historiographic approach is rather an experimental approach, such as "The Perception of Colors in a Group of Handicapped Children." This is a different story, because the student has the right to approach a question through experimentation, provided he has a sound research method, adequate laboratory conditions, and the necessary assistance. But a good laboratory researcher will not begin an experiment without having compiled a literature review that examines the results of similar experiments. He would otherwise risk reinventing the wheel by proving something that has already been amply proven, or by applying methods that have already failed (although the new verification of a heretofore unsuccessful method could provide the foundation for a successful thesis). Therefore an experimental thesis requires library research, laboratory work, and an established research method. Here the student should follow the examples of the medieval authors and climb onto the shoulders of a giant, at least one of modest height, or even onto another dwarf. The student will always have the chance to develop his own original ideas later in his career.

2.3   Ancient or Contemporary?

Here I am not attempting to revive the age-old quarrel of the Ancients and the Moderns.

Instead I am here using the term "ancient" in the most general sense of "very old," referring to authors whose works have survived and been studied by scholars. The choice between an ancient and a contemporary author does not apply to subjects such as the history of contemporary Italian literature, although even a thesis in Latin could involve both Horace and the state of Horatian studies in the last two decades. Nevertheless, Italian students frequently prefer contemporary authors, like Cesare Pavese, Giorgio Bassani, and Edoardo Sanguineti, to the sixteenth-century Petrarchan or the eighteenth-century Arcadian poets suggested by their advisors. Sometimes the student chooses a poet out of an authentic love for his work, and this is a choice that is difficult to challenge. Other times the student is under the false conviction that a contemporary author is easier and more fun.

Let us state from the outset that *a thesis on a contemporary author is always more difficult*. It may be true that scholarship on a contemporary author generally involves a smaller bibliography of easily accessible texts, and that the student can accomplish the first phase of the research by reading a good novel on the beach, rather than sitting in a library. The problem arises when the student begins to comment on the author, considering that the thesis will be flawed if he simply repeats what other critics have said. (If the student is to write a flawed thesis, he could do so more easily on a sixteenth-century Petrarchan poet.) Since opinions on most contemporary authors are still vague and divided, the student's critical skills will be hindered by a lack of perspective, and the project will become enormously difficult. On the other hand, the texts of ancient authors are usually supported by a solid foundation of interpretation upon which the student can build. Certainly a thesis on an ancient author involves more laborious reading, and more careful bibliographical research, but the titles are more organized, and complete bibliographies are common. Moreover, if the student approaches his thesis as a chance to learn how to properly conduct research, a thesis on a past author will provide better training. And even if the student has a flair for contemporary criticism, the thesis can provide a final opportunity for him to challenge himself with literature of the past, and to exercise his taste and reading skills. He would be in good company, for many great contemporary authors, even avant-garde authors, wrote their thesis on Dante or Foscolo rather than Montale or Pound.

To be sure, there are no precise rules, and a good researcher can historically or stylistically analyze a contemporary or past author with equal philological acumen and precision. The problem also varies among disciplines: in philosophy, a thesis on Husserl might provide the student with a more challenging research experience than one on Descartes; and the fact that it is easier to read Pascal than Carnap shows that a modern author may require more laborious reading than an ancient. Therefore, I can confidently provide only this advice: *work on a contemporary author as if he were ancient, and an ancient one as if he were contemporary.* You will have more fun and write a better thesis.

2.4   How Long Does It Take to Write a Thesis?

Let us state from the outset: *no longer than three years and no less than six months*. This period includes not just the time necessary to write the final draft, which may take only a month or two weeks, depending on the student's work habits. Instead, this period begins at the genesis of the first idea and ends at the delivery of the final work. For example, a student may only work on his thesis for a year, but he may use ideas and readings accumulated in the two preceding years, even though he initially did not know what would come from this preliminary research.

A thesis should take *no more than three years* because, if the student has failed to delimit his topic and find the necessary sources after this period, he has one of the following problems:

1. The student has chosen an overwhelming topic that is beyond his skill level.

2. The student is one of those insatiable persons who would like to write about everything, and who will continue to work on his thesis for 20 years. (A clever scholar will instead set limits, however modest, and produce something definitive within those limits.)

3. The "thesis neurosis" has begun: the student abandons the thesis, returns to it, feels unfulfilled, loses focus, and uses his thesis as an alibi to avoid other challenges in his life that he is too cowardly to address. This student will never graduate.

A thesis should take *no less than six months* because, even if the student's goal is a modest journal article of less than 60 typewritten pages, six months pass in a flash. This may not be sufficient time for the student to structure the work, research the bibliography, catalog the sources, and draft the text. Surely a more experienced scholar can compose an essay in less time, but only because he has years of reading behind him, complete with cataloged notes. The student must instead start from scratch.

Ideally the student will choose his thesis topic and thesis advisor toward the end of his sophomore year. By then the student has already become familiar with various subjects, and he even has a general understanding of disciplines he has not yet studied, their focus, and the difficulties they present. Such a timely choice is neither compromising nor irreversible. The student has an entire year to assess the choice, and if need be, to change the topic, the advisor, or even the discipline. Note that even if the student spends a year researching ancient Greek literature and later realizes that he prefers contemporary history, he has not wasted his time, as he will have learned how to create a preliminary bibliography, how to take notes on a text, and how to organize a table of contents. Remember the point we made in section 1.3: first and foremost, a thesis teaches one to coordinate ideas, and the topic is secondary.

If the student chooses his topic toward the end of his sophomore year, he will have until the spring of the fourth year to graduate well within the time frame outlined above. He will have two complete years to finish his thesis and two summers to devote to research and, if he has the resources, to research trips. During this period, he can also choose courses and readings that are appropriate for his thesis. To be sure, if the student is writing a thesis on experimental psychology, he will still be required to take Latin or other unrelated courses. However, in courses related to philosophy and sociology, the student may be able to arrange with the professor to substitute texts related to the thesis for course texts (even required ones), as long as this is done without dialectical contortions or puerile tricks. In this case, an intelligent professor will prefer a motivated student taking his course purposefully to one taking his course without passion, randomly, or out of an obligation to fulfill a requirement.

In any case, nothing forbids the student from choosing a thesis topic earlier. And nothing forbids the student from choosing it later, if he is willing to take more than the prescribed four years to graduate. But the biggest mistake he can make is to fail to allow sufficient time for his thesis.

If the student is to write a good thesis, he must discuss his work incrementally with his advisor, at least within reason. This is not to put the professor on a pedestal. Instead, because writing a thesis is like writing a book, working incrementally with the professor is a communication exercise that assumes the existence of an audience, and the advisor is the only competent audience available to the student during the course of his work. If the student completes the thesis hastily, the advisor will only have time to skim the text. Moreover, if the student presents the thesis to his advisor at the last minute, and if the advisor is dissatisfied with the results, he will challenge the candidate at the defense. This will produce unpleasant results not only for the student but also for the advisor, who should never arrive at a defense with a thesis he does not support. In this case, the advisor shares in the defeat. Early in the process, if the advisor notices that the candidate is having trouble, he must immediately inform the candidate, and suggest either that the student pursue another topic or that he postpone his thesis until he is better prepared. If the student ignores this advice, and if he is in a rush to graduate or if he simply believes that his advisor is wrong, he will again face a stormy defense, but he will do so deliberately.

Considering these risks, a six-month thesis is certainly not the optimum choice, even though it is within our range of acceptability. But as we have implied, it may prove successful if the topic, chosen in the last six months, builds on research and experience gained in the years before. Also, sometimes a student must complete a thesis in six months because of some external necessity. In these cases, the student must find a topic that he can research thoroughly and that will yield a decent product in that short period of time. Here I do not want to sound too much like a salesman, as if I were selling an inexpensive "six-month thesis" and a pricier "three-year thesis," a thesis to satisfy every kind of customer. Instead my point is that, without a doubt, a student can produce a decent thesis in as little as six months. There are three requirements for a six-month thesis:

1. The topic should be clearly defined.

2. The topic should be contemporary (notwithstanding the advice given in section 2.3), eliminating the need to explore a bibliography that goes back to the ancient Greeks. Alternatively, it should be a marginal subject on which little has been written.

3. The primary and secondary sources must be locally available and easily accessible.

Let us look at some examples. If I choose the topic "The Church of Santa Maria di Castello in Alessandria," I can hope to find everything I need to reconstruct its history and the events of its restoration in the municipal library of Alessandria, and also in the city's civic archives. I use the word "hope" because I am speaking hypothetically, and putting myself in the shoes of a student who hopes to complete a thesis in six months. Before I begin the project, I should test the validity of my hypothesis. First, I should verify that I will reside in or near Alessandria during the process; if I live 930 miles south in Caltanissetta, I have made a bad choice. Additionally, if some of the available sources are unpublished medieval manuscripts, I should know something of paleography and have the skills necessary to decipher these manuscripts. Here you can see how a seemingly easy topic can quickly become difficult. If I determine, instead, that all of the secondary sources have been published no earlier than the nineteenth century, I am safe to proceed on solid ground.

Here is another example: Raffaele La Capria is a contemporary Italian writer who has written only three novels and a single book of essays, all published by the Italian publisher Bompiani. Let us imagine a thesis with the title "The Fortunes of Raffaele La Capria in Contemporary Italian Criticism." Since publishers commonly archive all of the critical essays and articles written about their authors, I can hope to find almost all the texts I need in a series of visits to the publisher in Milan. Since the author is living, I can write to him or interview him in person, ask him for other bibliographic suggestions, and probably even obtain photocopies of these relevant texts. Surely a certain critical essay will refer us to other authors to whom La Capria is compared or contrasted, widening the research field a bit, but in a manageable way. This project will pose no problem if I have chosen La Capria out of a more general interest in Italian contemporary literature. If this is not the case, I have probably chosen cynically, coldly, and recklessly.

Here is another example of a six-month thesis: "The Interpretation of World War II in Middle School History Books Published in the Last Five Years." The student may have some difficulty locating all of the Italian middle school history books in circulation, but in fact there are only a few scholastic presses. Once the student has acquired or photocopied the texts, he will find that the treatments of World War II occupy a few pages in each, and that he can quickly do good comparative work. However, in order to judge a book's treatment of World War II, the student must compare it to half a dozen reputable histories of the war, and also

assess the book's treatment of history in general. Thus he
must widen his scope. Surely, without these forms of critical
examination, the student could write the thesis in a week
rather than in six months, but it would take the form of a
newspaper article instead of a thesis. The article may even
be sharp and brilliant, yet it would still be unfit to document
the candidate's research abilities.

Ultimately, if you want to write a six-month thesis but are
only willing to commit an hour each day, there is no point in
continuing our discussion. Please refer to the advice given in
section 1.2: copy a thesis and call it quits.

2.5   Is It Necessary to Know Foreign Languages?

This section does not concern those students writing a thesis on a foreign language or on foreign literature. One would
hope that these students know the language *on which* they
write their thesis. Better still, one would hope that a student studying a French author writes his thesis *in* French,
as many universities around the world rightfully require.
Also, the observations below are no substitute for learning
the language by spending time in the country in question.
However, this is an expensive solution, and here I would like
to advise students who do not have this option.

Let us pose the problem of an Italian student who writes
his thesis in philosophy, sociology, law, political science, history, or natural sciences. Even if the thesis involves Italian
history, Dante, or the Renaissance, the student will inevitably have to read a book in a foreign language, since illustrious scholars of Dante and the Renaissance have written in
English, German, and other languages foreign to our Italian
student. In these cases, the student generally uses the thesis
as an excuse to start reading in a new language. If the student is motivated by the topic and up to the challenge, he will
begin to gain understanding. Often this is how the student
first learns a foreign language. Although he will not learn
to speak the new language, he will learn to read it, which is
better than nothing. If there is *only* one book in German on a
specific topic, and if the student does not know German, he
can ask someone to read him the most important chapters.
He will have the decency not to rely on that particular book

too much, but at least he will be able to legitimately include it in his bibliography.

But these are all secondary issues. The main tenet is this: *we should not choose a topic that involves foreign language skills that we do not currently possess, or that we are not willing to acquire.* For now, let us examine some essential requirements:

1. *We cannot write a thesis on a foreign author if we do not read his texts in the original language.* This seems self-evident if the author is a poet, but many students do not see this as a prerequisite for a thesis on Kant, Freud, or Marx. However, it is required for three reasons. First, not *all* of the author's works may be available in translation, and sometimes neglecting even a minor work can lead to a misrepresentation of the author's intellectual background, or his work in general. Second, most of the secondary sources on a given author are usually in the author's original language. Even if the author is available in translation, his critics may not be. Finally, the translation does not always do justice to an author's thought, and writing a thesis involves the act of restoring the author's original thought from the distortions of translations, and from vulgarizations of various kinds. Writing a thesis requires going beyond the easy formulas of school textbooks, such as "Foscolo is a classicist while Leopardi is a romantic," or "Plato is an idealist and Aristotle is a realist," or "Pascal favors the heart and Descartes favors reason."

2. *We cannot write a thesis on a topic on which the most important secondary sources are in a language we do not know.* For example, since some of the past decade's most groundbreaking reassessments of Nietzsche's German texts have been written in French, a student whose only foreign language was German could not write a thesis on Nietzsche. The same applies to Freud; it would be difficult to reinterpret the Viennese master without considering the American Freudian "revisionists" or the French structuralists.

3. *We cannot write a thesis on an author or a topic by reading only the sources written in familiar languages.* How can we know beforehand that the most influential secondary

source on our author or topic is written in a language in
which we are fluent? Surely questions like this can lead to
paralysis, so here we should use common sense: rules of
academic rigor allow a Western student to acknowledge a
secondary source written in Japanese, and to admit that
he has not read it. This "license to ignore" usually extends
to non-Western languages and Slavic languages, so that
a student can complete a rigorous study on Marx and
still admit his ignorance of Russian sources. But in these
cases, the rigorous scholar will demonstrate that he has
explored these sources through reviews or abstracts. For
example, Soviet, Bulgarian, Czechoslovakian, and Israeli
academic journals usually provide abstracts of their articles in English or French. Therefore, if the student works
on a French author, he may manage with no knowledge
of Russian, but he must read at least English. In any case,
before the student chooses a topic, he must have the good
sense to consult the existing bibliography in order to
avoid considerable linguistic difficulties. In some cases,
this is easy to determine: it is unthinkable to write a thesis in Greek philology without knowing German, the language in which there is a flood of important studies on
the subject.

Additionally, the thesis will inevitably introduce the student to a smattering of general terminology in all Western
languages. For example, even if the student does not read
Russian, he must at least be able to recognize the Cyrillic
alphabet enough to determine whether a quoted book speaks
of art or science. It takes an evening to gain this familiarity,
and after comparing a few titles the student will know that
iskusstvo means "art" and *nauka* means "science." Do not let
this terrorize you. You should consider your thesis a unique
chance to learn skills that will serve you for a lifetime.

Let us form a final, conciliatory hypothesis. Suppose an
Italian student is interested in the problem of visual perception pertaining to the topic of art. This student *does not
know any foreign languages, nor does he have the time to learn
them.* (Or the student may have some kind of psychological
block; there are people who learn Swedish in a week, and

others who can barely speak French after ten years of practice.) In addition to these limitations, let us suppose that the student must write a six-month thesis for economic reasons. Although the student must graduate quickly and find employment, he is sincerely interested in his topic, and he eventually plans to study it more deeply when time permits. (We must think of this kind of student as well.)

In this case, the student may narrow his topic to "The Problems of Visual Perception in Relation to Figurative Arts in Particular Contemporary Authors." First, he must paint a picture of the psychological question, and on this topic there is a series of works translated into Italian, from Richard L. Gregory's *Eye and Brain* to major texts on the psychology of perception and transactional psychology. Then the student can bring the theme into focus in three authors: he can use Rudolf Arnheim for the *Gestalt* approach, Ernst Gombrich for the semiological-informational approach, and Erwin Panofsky for his essays on perspective from an iconological point of view. After all, from three different points of view, these three authors discuss the role of nature and culture in the perception of images. There are some works, for example the books of Gillo Dorfles, that will help the student contextualize and link these authors. Once the student has traced these three perspectives, he can also attempt to apply their criteria to a specific painting, perhaps by revising an already classic interpretation (for example drawing from Roberto Longhi's analysis of Piero della Francesca's paintings) and integrating it with the more "contemporary" data that he has gathered from these authors. The final product will be nothing original, and it will fall between the survey and the monograph, but the student will be able to develop it on the basis of Italian translations. The student will avoid reproach for not having read *all* Panofsky, including work available only in German or English, because the thesis is not *on* Panofsky. Panofsky is relevant only to a specific aspect of the topic, and is useful as a reference only for some questions presented by the thesis. As I said in section 2.1, this type of thesis is not the best choice, because it risks becoming incomplete and generic. To be clear, this is an example of a six-month thesis for a student who wishes to gather preliminary data on a problem about which he truly cares. It is a makeshift solution, yet it can produce a decent thesis.

In any case, if our Italian student does not know any foreign languages, and if he cannot seize this precious opportunity that the thesis provides to acquire them, the most reasonable solution is for the student to choose a specifically Italian topic, so that he can eliminate the need for foreign sources completely, or at least rely on the few sources that have been translated into Italian. Therefore, if the student wishes to write a thesis on "The Models of the Historical Novel in Giuseppe Garibaldi's Prose," he should have some basic knowledge of Walter Scott and his role as the originator of the modern historical novel, in addition to the nineteenth-century Italian polemic on the same subject. He could also find some reference works in Italian, and he could find at least the major works of Walter Scott in translation, especially if he searched the library for the nineteenth-century Italian translations. A topic such as "Francesco Domenico Guerrazzi's Influence on the Italian Culture of the Risorgimento" would pose even fewer problems. Obviously, the student should never begin his work based on such optimistic assumptions, and he should always consult available bibliographies to determine which foreign authors have written on his topic.

2.6 "Scientific" or Political?

After the student protests in 1968,[2] a widespread opinion emerged that students should write a thesis that is linked to political and social interests, rather than on "cultural" or bookish topics. If we believe this, then the title of this section becomes provocative and deceitful, because it suggests that a "political" thesis is not "scientific." Nowadays we often hear about "science," "being scientific," "scientific research," and "the scientific value" of a thesis, and these terms can cause unintentional misunderstandings, mystifications, as well as unfounded suspicions of cultural conservatism.

2.6.1 *What Does It Mean to Be Scientific?*

Some identify science with natural sciences or quantitative research. In other words, they believe research is only scientific if it contains formulas and diagrams. From this perspective, research on Aristotle's ethics would not be scientific, nor would a thesis on class consciousness and the peasant revolts during the Protestant Reformation. Clearly this is not the meaning that academia assigns to the term "scientific."

Let us try to understand by what reasoning we can call a work scientific. We can still take as a model the natural sciences as they have been defined since the beginning of the modern period. In this sense, research is scientific when it fulfills the following conditions:

1. *The research deals with a specific object, defined so that others can identify it.* The term "object" need not necessarily have a physical meaning. Even the square root of a number is an object, though it cannot actually be seen or touched. Social class is also an object of research, despite the objection that we can only know individuals or statistical means and not actual classes. In this sense, the class of all integers above 3,725 also lacks physical reality, though a mathematician could study it. Defining the object therefore means defining the conditions by which we can talk about it, based on rules that we establish, or that others have established before us. If we establish the conditions that allow anyone to discern an integer above 3,725 when he encounters it, we have established our object's rules of identification.

Obviously, problems arise if we must speak, for example, of a fictional being such as the centaur, commonly understood to be nonexistent. At this point we have three alternatives. First, we can decide to talk about centaurs as they are presented in classical mythology. Here our object becomes publicly recognizable and identifiable, because we are dealing with the *texts* (verbal or visual) in which these mythical creatures appear. We will then have to determine the characteristics that an object being described in classical mythology must possess for it to be recognized as a centaur. Second, we can conduct a hypothetical investigation to determine which characteristics a creature living in a possible world (that is, not the real world) should possess in order to be a centaur. Then we would have to define the conditions of existence of this possible world, taking care to inform our readers that all of our discussion is developed within this hypothesis. If we remain rigorously faithful to the initial assumption, we have defined an object appropriate for scientific investigation. Third, we can produce sufficient evidence to prove that centaurs are in fact real. In this case, to build a realistic object of discussion, we should present evidence (skeletons, bone remains, tracks petrified in lava, infrared photographs from Greek woodlands, and whatever else might support our case) so that others might agree that, regardless of the correctness of our hypothesis, there is something we can talk about. Obviously this example is paradoxical, and I can't believe that anyone would want to write a thesis on centaurs, especially by way of the third alternative. Instead, my purpose is to show how it is always possible, given certain conditions, to constitute a publicly recognizable object of research. And if it is possible with centaurs, it will surely be possible with notions such as moral behavior, desires, values, or the concept of historical progress.

2. *The research says things that have not yet been said about this object, or it revises the things that have already been said from a different perspective.* A mathematically correct thesis that proved the Pythagorean theorem with traditional methods would not be a scientific work, because it would not add anything to our knowledge. At best, it would provide clear instruction on how to solve the theorem, much as a manual provides instruction on how to build a doghouse using wood, nails, a plane, a saw, and a hammer. As we have already said in section 1.1, a literature review can also be scientifically useful because the author has collected and organically linked together the opinions expressed by others on a particular topic. Similarly, an instruction manual on how to build a doghouse is not a scientific work, but a work that discusses and compares all known doghouse-building methods can make a modest claim of scientific value. However, bear in mind that a literature review has scientific value only if something

similar does not already exist in a given field. If someone has already written a work comparing the systems used to build a doghouse, writing a similar manual is at best a waste of time, at worst plagiarism (see section 5.3.2).

3. *The research is useful to others.* An article that presents a new finding on the behavior of the elementary particles of physics is useful. An article that presents a transcription of an unpublished letter by the Italian romantic poet Giacomo Leopardi, and that recounts the circumstances of its discovery, is useful. A work is scientific if, in addition to fulfilling the two conditions above, it advances the knowledge of the community, and if all future works on the topic will have to take it into consideration, at least in theory.

Naturally the scientific relevance is commensurate with the contribution's significance. Scholars must take certain contributions into account in order to say anything relevant on a particular topic, while they can leave others behind without serious consequences. Recently, a number of letters from James Joyce to his wife have been published, specifically letters that deal with explicit sexual matters. People studying the origin of Molly Bloom's character in Joyce's *Ulysses* may find it useful to know that, in his private life, Joyce attributed to his wife a sexuality as vivacious and developed as Molly's. Therefore, the publication of these letters is a useful scientific contribution. On the other hand, some superb interpretations of *Ulysses* present a keen analysis of Molly's character without this data. Therefore this contribution is not indispensable. We can find an example of a more important scientific contribution in the publication of *Stephen Hero*, the first version of Joyce's novel *A Portrait of the Artist as a Young Man*. *Stephen Hero* is generally considered fundamental for understanding the development of the Irish writer, and is therefore a fundamental scientific contribution.

Here we should address the so-called "laundry lists" often associated with extremely meticulous German philologists. These might include an author's shopping list, to-do list, and other incidental texts that are generally of low value. Occasionally these kinds of data are useful because they shed the light of humanity on a reclusive author, or they reveal that during a certain period he lived in extreme poverty. Other times these texts do not add anything to what we already know. They are small biographical curiosities with no scientific value, even if there are people who build reputations as indefatigable researchers by bringing these trifles to light. We should not discourage those who enjoy pursuing this type of research, but we also should understand that they are not advancing human knowledge. From a pedagogical perspective, if not from a scientific one, it would be more fruitful for them to write an entertaining popular biography that recounted the author's life and works.

4. *The research provides the elements required to verify or disprove the hypotheses it presents, and therefore it provides the foundation for future research.* This is a fundamental requirement. For example, to prove that centaurs live in Peloponnesus I must do the following with precision: (a) produce proof (as we have already said, at least a tail bone); (b) recount exactly how I discovered and exhumed the archaeological find; (c) instruct readers on how more evidence can be unearthed; and (d) if possible, give examples of the precise type of bone (or other archaeological find) that would disprove my hypothesis, were it to be discovered in the future. If I accomplish these four goals, I have not only provided the evidence to support my hypothesis, but I have facilitated the continuation of research that may confirm or challenge it.

The same is true for any topic. Suppose I am writing a thesis on an Italian extraparliamentary movement that took place in 1969, and that is generally believed to have been politically homogeneous. In my thesis, I wish to prove that there were in fact two factions, one Leninist and the other Trotskyist. For my thesis to be successful, I must produce documents (flyers, audio recordings of meetings, articles, etc.) that verify my hypothesis; recount the circumstances of the acquisition of this material to provide a foundation for further research; and present the criteria by which I attribute the supporting documents to the members of the 1969 movement. For example, if the group was dissolved in 1970, I must weigh the relevance of material produced by members while the group was active against that produced by former members of the group after its dissolution, considering that they may have cultivated their ideas while the group was still active. I must also define the criteria for group membership, such as actual registration, participation in meetings, and presumptions of the police. In doing this, I provide the foundation for further investigation, even if it may eventually invalidate my own conclusions. For example, let us suppose that I consider a person a member of the group based on evidence from the police, but future research exposes evidence that other members never considered the person in question as a member, and therefore he should not be judged as such. In this way, I have presented not only a hypothesis and supporting evidence, but also methods for its verification or falsification.

The various examples that we have discussed demonstrate that a student can apply the requirements for scientific validity to any topic. They also illustrate the artificial opposition between a "scientific" and a "political" thesis. *In fact a political thesis can observe all the rules necessary for scientific validity.* For example, I could write a thesis that is both scientific and political, and that would analyze my experience as an activist establishing an independent radio station in a working-class community. The thesis will be scientific to the extent to which it documents my experience in a public and verifiable manner, and allows future researchers to reproduce the experience either to obtain the same results or to discover that my results were accidental and not linked to my intervention, but to other factors I failed to consider. The beauty of a scientific approach is that it does not waste the time of future researchers. If a future researcher is working in the wake of my scientific hypothesis and discovers that it is incorrect, my initial hypothesis has still proven useful. In this example, if my thesis inspires a future researcher to also become an activist in a working-class community, my work has had a positive result, even if my original assumptions were naïve.

In these terms, there is clearly no opposition between a scientific and a political thesis, and as we have seen, one can write a "scientific" thesis without using logarithms and test tubes. On one hand, every scientific work has a positive political value in that it contributes to the development of knowledge (every action that aims at stopping the process of knowledge has a negative political value); but on the other hand, every political enterprise with a chance of success must be grounded in the scientific diligence I have described.

2.6.2   Writing about Direct Social Experience

Here our initial question returns in a new form: is it more useful to write an erudite thesis on an established, scholarly topic, or one tied to practical experiences and direct social activities? In other words, is it more useful to write a thesis that involves famous authors or ancient texts, or one that calls for a direct participation in the contemporary world, be it of a theoretical nature ("The Concept of Exploitation in Neocapitalist Ideology") or of a practical nature ("The Conditions of Slum Dwellers on the Outskirts of Rome")?

In itself the question is pointless. A student will gravitate toward his interest and experience, and if he has spent four years studying Romance philology we cannot expect him to write on Roman slum dwellers. Similarly, it would be absurd to require an act of "academic humility" from someone who has studied for four years with the Italian social activist and sociologist Danilo Dolci, by asking the student to write a thesis on the royal family of France.

But suppose the person who asks the question is a student in crisis, one who is wondering about the usefulness of his university studies, and especially about what to expect from the thesis experience. Suppose this student has strong political and social interests, and that he is afraid of betraying his calling by choosing a "bookish" topic. Now, if this student is already immersed in a political-social experience that suggests the possibility of building a conclusive argument, he should consider how he could treat his experience in a scientific manner. But if he has not yet had such an experience, then it seems to me that his fear is naïve, albeit noble. As we have already said, the experience of writing a thesis is always useful for our future work (be it professional or political) not so much for the chosen topic, but instead for the training that it demands, for the experience of rigor it provides, and for the skills required to organize the material.

Paradoxically, we could then say that a student with political aspirations will not betray his ideals if he writes a thesis on the recurrence of demonstrative pronouns in the writings of an eighteenth-century botanist. Or on the theory of *impetus* in pre-Galilean science; or on non-Euclidean geometries; or on the dawn of ecclesiastical law; or on the mystical sect of the Hesychasts; or on medieval Arabic medicine; or on the article of criminal law on bid rigging in public auctions. A student can cultivate a political interest in unions, for example, by writing a historical thesis on workers' movements in the past century. A student can even understand the contemporary need for independent information among the subaltern classes by studying the style, circulation, and modes of production of popular xylographic prints in the Renaissance period. In fact, if I wanted to be controversial, I would advise a student whose only experience was in political and social activism to choose precisely one of these topics, rather than narrate his own experience. This is because the thesis will provide his last opportunity to acquire historical, theoretical, and technical knowledge; to learn systems of documentation; and to reflect in a more dispassionate manner on the theoretical and historical assumptions of his political work.

Obviously this is just my opinion. Since I wish to respect points of view different from my own, I will now address this question of someone who is immersed in political activity, someone who wishes to orient his thesis toward his work, and to orient his political experience to the writing of his thesis. It is certainly possible to do this, and to do it well. But to make such an endeavor respectable, it is necessary to clarify a few points.

Occasionally a student will hastily prepare a hundred pages of flyers, debate recordings, activity reports, and statistics (perhaps borrowed from some previous study) and present his work as a "political" thesis. And sometimes the committee will even accept the work, out of laziness, demagogy, or incompetence. But this work is a joke, not only because it betrays the university's thesis criteria, but precisely because it does a disservice to the political cause. There is a serious way and an irresponsible way to participate in politics. A politician who approves a development plan without sufficient information on the community's situation is simply a fool, if not a criminal. Similarly, one can betray his political party by writing a political thesis that lacks scientific rigor.

Once I encountered a student defending a thesis that dealt with a topic related to mass communication. He claimed that he had conducted a "survey" of the TV audience among workers in a certain region. In reality, he had tape-recorded a dozen interviews of commuters during two train trips. Naturally the resulting transcriptions of these opinions could not constitute a survey, not only because they lacked standards of verifiability, but also because of the banality of the results. (For example, it is predictable that the majority of 12 Italians will declare that they enjoy watching a live soccer game.) Consequently, a 30-page pseudo-survey that concludes with such predictable results is a joke. It also constitutes self-deception for the student, who believes he has acquired "objective" data, while he has only superficially supported his own preconceived opinions.

A political thesis in particular risks superficiality for two reasons. First, unlike a historical or philological thesis that requires traditional methods of investigation, a thesis on a specific current social phenomenon often requires the student to invent his methodology. (For this reason, the process of writing a historical thesis may seem serene compared to that of a good political thesis.) Secondly, a political thesis risks superficiality because a large segment of "American-style" social research methodology has fetishized quantitative statistical methods, producing enormous studies that are dense with data but not useful for understanding real phenomena. Consequently, many young politicized people are skeptical of this "sociometry," and they accuse it of simply serving the system by providing ideological cover. But people who react this way often end up doing no research at all, and their thesis becomes a sequence of flyers, appeals, or purely theoretical statements.

We can avoid this risk in various ways, including consulting "serious" works on similar topics, following the practices of an experienced group of activists, mastering proven methods of gathering and analyzing data, realizing that surveys are long and expensive and cannot be conducted in just a few weeks, etc. But since the problems presented by a historical thesis vary according to different fields, different topics, and students' skills, it is impossible to give generic advice. I will therefore limit myself to one example. I will choose a brand-new subject on which no research has previously been done; that is of great topical interest; that has unquestionable political, ideological, and practical implications; and that many traditional professors would define as "purely journalistic": the phenomenon of "free radio" stations.[3]

2.6.3 Treating a "Journalistic" Topic with Scientific Accuracy

As most Italians know, scores of these stations have appeared in large Italian cities. There are a few even in centers of a hundred thousand inhabitants, and more continue to appear across Italy. They can be political or commercial in nature. They often have legal problems, but the legislation regarding these stations is ambiguous and evolving. In the period between the genesis of this book and its publication, the situation will already have changed; as it would change during the time it would take for a student to complete this hypothetical thesis.

Therefore, I first must define the exact geographical and chronological limits of my investigation. It could be as limited as "Free Radio Stations from 1975 to 1976," but within those limits the investigation must be thorough and complete. If I choose to examine only those radio stations located in Milan, I must examine *all* the radio stations in Milan. Otherwise I risk neglecting the most significant radio station in terms of its programs, ratings, location (suburb, neighborhood, city center), and the cultural composition of its hosts. If I decide to work on a national sample of 30 radio stations, so be it. However, I must establish the selection criteria for this sample. If nationally there are in fact three commercial stations for every five political radio stations, or one extreme right-wing station for every five left-wing stations, my sample must reflect this reality. I cannot choose a sample of 30 stations in which 29 are left-wing or 29 are right-wing. If I do so, I will represent the phenomenon in proportion to my hopes and fears, instead of to the facts.

I could also decide to renounce the investigation of radio stations as they appear in reality and propose an ideal radio station, much as I tried to prove the existence of centaurs in a possible world. But in this case, the project must not only be organic and realistic (I cannot assume the existence of broadcasting equipment that does not exist, or that is inaccessible to a small private group), but it must also consider the trends of the actual phenomenon. Therefore, a preliminary investigation is indispensable, even in this case.

After I determine the limits of my investigation, I must define exactly what I mean by "free radio station," so that the object of my investigation is publicly recognizable. When I use the term "free radio station," do I mean only a left-wing radio station? Or a radio station built by a small group of people under semilegal circumstances? Or a radio station that is independent of the state monopoly, even if it happens to be well organized and has solely commercial purposes? Or should I consider territorial boundaries, and include only those stations located in the Republic of San Marino or Monte Carlo? However I choose to define the term, I must clarify my criteria and explain why I exclude certain phenomena from the field of inquiry. Obviously the criteria must be defined unequivocally; if I define a free radio station as one that expresses an extreme left-wing political position, I must consider that the term is commonly used in a broader sense. In this case, I must either clarify to my readers that I challenge the common definition of the term, and defend my exclusion of the stations it refers to; or I must choose a less generic term for the radio stations I wish to examine.

At this point, I will have to describe the structure of a free radio station from an organizational, economic, and legal point of view. If full-time professionals staff some stations, and part-time volunteers staff others, I will have to build an organizational typology. I must determine whether these types share common characteristics that can serve as an abstract model of a free radio station, or whether the term covers a series of heterogeneous experiences. Here you can see how the scientific rigor of this analysis is useful also from a practical perspective; if I wanted to open a free radio station myself, I would need to understand the optimal conditions for it to function well.

To build a reliable typology, I could draw a table that compared the possible characteristics as they appear in the stations I have examined. I could present the characteristics of a given radio station vertically, and the statistical frequency of the given characteristic horizontally. Below, I provide a simplified and purely hypothetical example with only four parameters: the presence of professional staff, the music-speech ratio, the presence of commercials, and the ideological characterization. Each is applied to seven fictional radio stations.

This table tells me that a nonprofessional, ideologically explicit group runs Radio Pop, that the station broadcasts more music than speech, and that it accepts commercials. It also tells me that the presence of commercials and the abundant music content are not necessarily in contrast with the station's ideology, since we find two radio stations with similar characteristics, and only one ideological station that broadcasts more speech than music. On the other hand, the

Table 2.1

	Radio Beta	Radio Gamma	Radio Delta	Radio Aurora	Radio Centro	Radio Pop	Radio Canale 100
professional staff	−	+	−	−	−	−	−
prevalence of music	+	+	−	+	+	+	+
presence of commercials	+	+	−	−	+	+	+
explicit ideological characterization	+	−	+	+	−	+	−

presence of commercials and abundant music characterize all nonideological stations. And so on. This table is purely hypothetical and considers only a few parameters and a few stations. Therefore it does not allow us to draw reliable statistical conclusions, and it is only a suggested starting point.

And how then do we obtain this data? We can imagine three sources: official records, managers' statements, and listening protocols that we will establish below.

Official records: These always provide the most dependable information, but few exist for independent radio stations. I might first look for an organization's registration documents at the local public safety authority. I might also find the organization's constitutive act or a similar document at the local notary, although these documents may not be publicly accessible. In the future, more precise regulation may facilitate more accessible data, but for now this is the extent of what I can expect to find. However, consider that the name of the station, the broadcasting frequency, and the hours of operation are among the official data. A thesis that provided at least these three elements for each station would already be a useful contribution.

Managers' statements: We can interview each station's manager. Their words constitute objective data, provided that the interview transcriptions are accurate, and that we use homogeneous criteria for conducting the interviews. We must devise a single questionnaire, so that all managers respond to the questions that we deem important, and so that the refusal to answer a question becomes a matter of record. The questionnaire need not necessarily be black and white, requiring only answers of "yes" or "no." If each station manager releases a statement of intent, these statements together could constitute a useful document. Let us clarify the notion of "objective data" in this case: If the director of a particular station states, "We have no political agenda, and we do not accept outside financing," this may or may not be true. However, the fact that that radio station publicly presents itself in that light is an objective piece of information. Additionally, we may refute this statement based on our critical analysis of the contents of the station's broadcasts, and this brings us to the third source of information.

Listening protocols: This aspect of the thesis will determine the difference between rigorous and amateurish work. To thoroughly investigate the activity of an independent radio station, we must listen hour after hour for a few days or a week, and devise a sort of "program guide" that indicates what content is broadcast at what time, the length of each program, and the ratio of music to talk. If there are debates, the schedule should indicate the topics, participants, and so on. You will not be able to present all of the data you have collected, but you can include meaningful examples (commentary on the music, witty debate remarks, particular styles of news delivery) that define the artistic, linguistic, and ideological profile of the station you are scrutinizing. It may help to consult the models for radio and TV listening protocols developed over some years by the ARCI Bologna,[4] in which listeners determined the duration of news presentation, the recurrence of certain terms, and so on.

Once you have completed this investigation for various radio stations, you could compare your data. For example, you could compare the manner in which two or more radio stations introduced the same song or presented a recent event. You could also compare state-owned radio shows to those of independent stations, noting differences in the ratios of music to speech, news to entertainment, programs to commercials, classical to pop music, Italian to foreign music, traditional pop music to "youth-oriented" pop music, and so on. With a tape recorder and pencil in hand, you will be able to draw many more conclusions through systematic listening than from your interviews with station managers. Sometimes even a simple comparison of commercial sponsors (the ratios between restaurants, cinemas, publishers, etc.) can clarify the obscure financing sources of a given station.

The only condition is that you must not follow impressions or make imprudent conclusions such as, "At noon a particular radio station broadcast pop music and a

Pan American commercial, so the station must be pro-American." You must also consider what the station broadcast at one o'clock, two o'clock, three o'clock, and on Monday, Tuesday, and Wednesday.

If you are investigating many stations, your listening protocol should take one of the following two approaches. The first is to listen to all the stations simultaneously for one week. You can do this by organizing a group of researchers, each one listening to a different station simultaneously. This is the most rigorous solution because you will be able to compare the various radio stations during the same period. Your other choice is to listen to the stations sequentially, one station per week. This will require hard work, and you must proceed directly from one station to the next so that the listening period is consistent. The total listening time for all stations should not exceed six months or a year at most, since changes are fast and frequent in this sector, and since it would make no sense to compare the programs of Radio Beta in January with those of Radio Aurora in August.

When you have compiled the data from the three sources outlined above, there is still much left to do. For example, you can do the following:

Establish the size of each station's audience. Unfortunately, there are no official ratings data, and you cannot trust the station managers' figures. The only alternative is a random sample telephone survey in which you ask participants to which stations they listen. This is the method followed by RAI, Italy's national broadcasting company, but it requires an organization that is both specialized and expensive. This is a good example of the difficulty involved in a scientific treatment of a contemporary, topical phenomenon. You cannot rely on personal impressions and conclude, for example, that "the majority of listeners choose Radio Delta" simply because this station is popular among four or five of your friends. (Perhaps a thesis on a subject like Roman history might be a better choice after all, and it will certainly pose fewer research problems.)

Search newspapers and magazines for mentions of the stations you are scrutinizing. Record any opinions of the stations that you find, and describe any controversies.

Record the specific laws relevant to the stations' operations, and explain how various stations follow or elude them. Describe the legal issues that arise. Document the relevant positions of the political parties on the stations you are scrutinizing, and on free radio stations in general.

Attempt to establish comparative tables of commercial fees. The managers may not disclose these, or they may provide erroneous data, but you may be able to gather the data elsewhere. For example, if Radio Delta broadcasts advertisements for a particular restaurant, you may be able to solicit data from the restaurant owner.

Record specifically how different radio stations cover a specific event. (For example, the Italian national elections of June 1976 would have provided a perfect opportunity for this part of the project.)

Analyze the linguistic style of the broadcasters. (The ways that they imitate American DJs or public radio hosts, their use of the terminology of specific political groups, their use of dialects, etc.)

Analyze the influence that free radio programs have had on certain public radio programs. Compare the nature of the programming, the linguistic usage, etc.

Thoroughly collect and catalog the opinions that jurists, political leaders, and other public figures express about the stations you are scrutinizing. (Remember that three opinions are only enough for a newspaper article, and that a thorough investigation may require a hundred.)

Collect the existing bibliography on the subject of free radio stations. Collect everything from books and journal articles on analogous experiments in other countries to the articles in the most remote local newspapers or smallest Italian magazines, so that you assemble the most complete bibliography possible.

Let it be clear that you do not have to complete *all* of these things. Even one of them, if done correctly and exhaustively, can constitute the subject of a thesis. Nor is this the only work to be done. I have only presented these examples to show how, even on a topic as "unscholarly" and devoid of critical literature as this one, a student can write a scientific work that is useful to others, that can be inserted into broader research, that is indispensable to anyone wishing to investigate the subject, and that is free of subjectivity, random observations, and imprudent conclusions.

As we have established, the dichotomy between a scientific and a political thesis is false. It is equally scientific to write a thesis on "The Doctrine of Ideas in Plato" and on "The Politics of 'Lotta Continua' from 1974 to 1976."[5] If you intend to do rigorous work, think hard before choosing the second topic, for it is undoubtedly more difficult. It will require superior research skills and scholarly maturity; if nothing else, you will not have a library on which to rely, but instead must effectively create your own.

In any case, we have seen that a student can write scientifically on a subject that others would judge as purely "journalistic," just as a student can write a journalistic thesis on a topic that most would qualify as scientific, at least from its title.

2.7   How to Avoid Being Exploited by Your Advisor

As I've mentioned earlier, often a student chooses a topic based on his own interests, but other times a student wishes to work with a particular professor who suggests a topic to the student. Professors tend to follow two different criteria when suggesting a topic: a professor can recommend a familiar topic on which he can easily advise the student, or a professor can recommend an unfamiliar topic on which he would like to know more.

Contrary as it may seem, the second criterion is the more honest and generous. The professor believes that his ability to effectively judge and assist the candidate will require him to devote himself to something new, and thus the professor will expand his horizons. When the professor chooses this second path, it is because he trusts the candidate, and he usually tells the candidate explicitly that the topic is new and interesting to him. Even though universities currently require professors to advise many students, and therefore

2.7 | How to Avoid Being Exploited by Your Advisor   **43**

incline professors to cater to students' interests, some professors still refuse to advise a thesis on a banal topic.

There are also specific cases in which a professor is conducting a wide-ranging research project that requires vast amounts of data, and he decides to engage graduating students as members of a team. In other words, he orients the students' work in a specific direction for a certain number of years. He will assign topics that work together to establish a complete picture of his research question. This approach is not only legitimate but also scientifically useful, as each thesis contributes to a larger project that is more important for the collective interest. This approach is also useful from a teaching perspective, because each candidate will benefit from the advice of a professor who is well informed on the question, and each student can use as background and comparative material the theses that other students have already written on related topics. If the candidate does good work, he can hope to publish the results, at least as part of a larger collective work.

However, this approach does pose some possible risks:

1. The professor is absorbed by his own topic to such an extent that he imposes it on a candidate who has no interest in the subject. The student becomes a lackey who wearily gathers material for others to interpret. Although the student will have written a modest thesis, he risks not being credited for his work. When the professor writes the final research project, he will perhaps fish out some parts of the student's work from the material he has gathered, but he may use them without citing the student, if only because the student's specific contribution to the final product is difficult to delineate.

2. The professor is dishonest, requires the student to work on his project, approves the thesis, and then unscrupulously uses the work as if it were his own. Sometimes this dishonesty is *almost* in good faith; the professor may have followed the thesis with passion and suggested many ideas, but over time he loses the ability to distinguish his students' ideas from his own, in the same way that, after a passionate group discussion on a certain topic, we are

unable to discern the ideas we introduced from those inspired by others.

How can you avoid these risks? Before approaching the professor, you should assess the professor's honesty from the opinions of friends and the experiences of graduates whom the professor advised. You should read his books, and pay particular attention to citations of his collaborators. This investigation will take you so far, but you must also intuitively feel some sense of trust and respect toward the professor.

On the other hand, you should not become so paranoid that you believe you have been plagiarized every time a professor or another student addresses a topic related to your thesis. For example, if you did a thesis on the relationship of Darwinism and Lamarckism, your research would show that many scholars have treated the same topic, and have shared many common ideas. Therefore, you should not feel like a defrauded genius if the professor, one of his teaching assistants, or one of your classmates writes on the same topic. The actual theft of scientific work means something different altogether: using specific data from your experiments, appropriating your original transcriptions of rare manuscripts, using statistical data that you were the first to collect, or using your original translations of texts that were either never translated or translated differently by others. These constitute theft only if you have not been cited as a source, because once you publish your thesis, others have the right to cite it.

So, without slipping into paranoia, consider your willingness to join a collective project, and consider whether the risks are worth it.

3   CONDUCTING RESEARCH

3.1   The Availability of Primary and Secondary Sources

3.1.1   What Are the Sources of a Scientific Work?

A thesis studies an *object* by making use of specific *instruments*. Often the object is a book and the instruments are other books. For a thesis on "Adam Smith's Economic Thought," the object is Adam Smith's bibliography, and the instruments are other books on Adam Smith. In this case, we can say that Adam Smith's writings constitute the *primary sources* and the writings about Adam Smith are the *secondary sources* or the *critical literature*. Naturally, if the topic were "The Sources of Adam Smith's Economic Thought," the primary sources would then be the books or other writings that inspired Adam Smith. Certainly historical events (and particular discussions on certain concrete phenomena that Smith may have witnessed) may also have inspired Adam Smith's work, but these events are nevertheless accessible to us in the form of written material, that is, in the form of other texts.

But there are also cases in which the object is a real phenomenon. This would be true for a thesis on the internal migrations of Italians in the twentieth century, the behavior of a group of handicapped children, or an audience's opinion of a current TV program. In these cases, primary sources may not yet exist in an organized written form. Instead you must gather and create your primary documents, including statistical data, interview transcriptions, and sometimes photographs or even audiovisual documents. The critical literature in these cases will not differ greatly from that of our thesis on Adam Smith, although it may consist of newspaper articles and other kinds of documents, instead of books and journal articles.

You must be able to clearly distinguish primary sources from critical literature. The critical literature often reproduces quotes from primary sources, but—as we will see in the next paragraph—these are *indirect sources*. Moreover, a student conducting hasty and disorderly research can easily mistake the arguments contained in primary sources with those of the critical literature. For example, if I am writing a thesis on "Adam Smith's Economic Thought" and I notice that I am dwelling on a certain author's interpretations more than my own direct reading of Smith, I must either return to the source or change my topic to "The Interpretations of Adam Smith in Contemporary English Liberal Thought." The latter topic will not exempt me from understanding Smith's work, but my primary interest will be the interpretations of Smith's work by others. Obviously, an in-depth study of Smith's critics will require a comparison of their work to the original text.

However, there could be a case in which the original object matters little to me. Suppose I begin a thesis on traditional Japanese Zen philosophy. Clearly I must be able to read Japanese, and I cannot trust the few available Western translations. Now suppose that, in examining the critical literature, I become interested in how certain literary and artistic avant-garde movements in the United States made use of Zen in the fifties. At this point, I am no longer interested in understanding the meaning of Zen thought with absolute theological and philological accuracy. Instead, I am now interested in how original Oriental ideas have become elements of a Western artistic ideology. I will change my topic to "Zen Principles in the 'San Francisco Renaissance' of the 1950s," and my primary sources will become the texts of Kerouac, Ginsberg, Ferlinghetti, and so on. As for my understanding of original Zen philosophy, some reliable critical works and good translations will now suffice. Naturally, this approach assumes that I do not wish to demonstrate that the Californians misinterpreted the original Zen thought, which would require me to make comparisons with the Japanese originals. But because the Californians loosely based their work on Western translations, I am more interested in their interpretations than in the original philosophy.

This example also illustrates that I should promptly define the true object of my thesis so that I can determine the availability of my sources from the outset. In section 3.2.4, I will demonstrate how to start a thesis from scratch with no pre-conceived bibliography, and how to obtain all the sources I need from a single, small library. Although this procedure is possible, the situation will rarely occur, because realistically I would not choose a topic unless I already knew: (a) where I could find the sources, (b) whether they were easily accessible, and (c) whether I was capable of fully understanding them. It would be imprudent of me to accept a thesis on a particular set of James Joyce's manuscripts without knowing that they reside at the University of Buffalo, or (if I knew their location) knowing full well that I would never be able to travel to New York. It would be equally unwise to enthusiastically accept a topic on a private collection of documents belonging to a family that is overly protective of them, and that reveals them only to renowned scholars. And I should not accept a topic that deals with medieval manuscripts, no matter how accessible they are, if I lack the proper training needed to read them.

More realistically, I might agree to study an author only to learn that his original texts are very rare, and that I must travel like a maniac from library to library, or even from country to country. Or I may rely on the fact that microfilms of his complete oeuvre are readily available, forgetting that my department does not own the apparatus to read them, or that I suffer from conjunctivitis and cannot endure such exhausting work. And it would be quite useless for me, if I were studying film at an Italian university, to plan a thesis on a minor work of a director from the 1920s, if I then discover that the only copy of this work resides in the Library of Congress in Washington.

Once the problem of the primary sources is resolved, the same questions arise for the critical literature. I could choose a thesis on a minor eighteenth-century author because the first edition of his work coincidentally resides in my city's library, but I may then learn that the best critical works on my author are not available at any library to which I have access, and are very expensive to purchase. You cannot avoid this problem by deciding to work only on the sources to which you have access. You must read all of the critical literature, or at least all of it that matters, and you must access the sources *directly* (see the following paragraph). Otherwise, you should choose another topic according to the criteria described in chapter 2, rather than irresponsibly complete a thesis with unforgivable omissions.

Let us look at some concrete examples from thesis defenses that I have recently attended. In each of these, the authors precisely identified sources that were unquestionably within their range of expertise, verified the availability of these sources, and used them effectively. The first thesis was on "The Clerical-Moderate Experience in the City Hall Administration of Modena (1889–1910)." As the title indicates, the candidate (or the advisor) had precisely defined the scope of the project. The candidate was from Modena, so he could work locally. He discriminated between a general bibliography and bibliography specifically on the subject of Modena. He may have traveled to other cities for the former, and I assume he was able to work in the city libraries of Modena on the latter. He also divided the primary sources into *archival* sources and *journalistic* sources, the latter including relevant articles from contemporary newspapers.

The second thesis was on "The Scholastic Policy of the Italian Communist Party (P.C.I.) from the Formation of the Center-Left (1963) to the Student Protests (1968)." Here too, the student specified the topic with precision and, I would say, prudence, because conducting research on the period after 1968 would have been difficult due to the sheer quantity of sources. The student judiciously chose to focus on the period before 1968, limiting his sources to the official press of the Communist Party, the parliamentary acts, the party's archives, and the general press. I have to imagine that, no matter how precisely the student researched the general press, some information must have slipped through the cracks due to the amount of coverage involved. Nevertheless, the general press was unquestionably a valid secondary source of opinions and criticisms. As for the other sources, the official declarations were sufficient to define the Communist Party's scholastic policy. Had the thesis dealt with the scholastic policy of the Christian Democracy, a party in the government coalition, this would have been a very different story, and the research would surely have assumed dramatic proportions. On one hand there would have been the official statements, on the other the actual governmental acts that may have contradicted these statements. Take also into account that, if the period had extended beyond 1968, the student would have had to include, among the sources of unofficial opinions, all the publications of the extraparliamentary movements that began to proliferate after that period. Once again, the research would have been far more difficult. Finally, I imagine that the candidate had the opportunity to work in Rome, or he was able to have the required material photocopied and sent to him.

The third thesis dealt with medieval history, and was on a seemingly difficult topic. It examined the vicissitudes of the San Zeno Abbey's estate in Verona during the High Middle Ages. The heart of the work consisted of a transcription, previously never attempted, of certain folios from the San Zeno Abbey's registry in the thirteenth century. Naturally, the project required some knowledge of paleography, but once the candidate acquired this technique, he only needed to diligently execute the transcription and comment on the results. Nevertheless, the thesis included a bibliography of 30 titles, a sign that the student had historically contextualized the specific problem on the basis of previous literature. I assume that the candidate was from Verona and had chosen a project that did not involve much travel.

The fourth thesis was titled "Contemporary Drama Performances in Trentino." The candidate, who lived in that region of Italy, knew that there had been a limited number of performances, and he reconstructed them by consulting newspapers, city archives, and statistical surveys on the audience's frequency. The fifth thesis, "Aspects of Cultural Policy in the City of Budrio with Particular Reference to the City Library's Activity," was similar. These are two examples of projects whose sources are easily available, but that are nevertheless useful because they require a compilation of statistical-socio-logical documentation that will serve future researchers.

A sixth thesis required more time and effort than the others. It illustrates how a student can treat with scientific rigor a topic that at first seems appropriate only for an honest literature survey. The title was "The Question of the Actor in Adolphe Appia's Oeuvre." Appia is a well-known Swiss author and the subject of abundant historical and theoretical theater studies that, it would seem, have exhausted all there is to say about him. But the candidate painstakingly researched the Swiss archives, along with countless libraries, and explored each and every place where Appia had worked. The student was able to compile an exhaustive bibliography of works on the author, along with the author's own writings, including minor articles that had been forgotten shortly after their original publication. This gave the thesis a breadth and precision that, according to the advisor, qualified it as a definitive contribution. The student thus went beyond the literature survey by making these obscure sources accessible.

3.1.2   Direct and Indirect Sources

Regarding books, a *direct source* is an original edition or a critical edition of the work in question.

A translation is not a direct source: it is instead a prosthetic like dentures or a pair of glasses. It is a means by which I gain limited access to something that lies outside my range.

An anthology is not a direct source: it is a stew of sources, useful only for a first approach to the topic. If I write a thesis on a particular author, my goal is to see in him what others have not, and an anthology only provides someone else's view.

The critical works of other authors, no matter how rich with quotations, are not direct sources: at best, they are indirect sources.

Indirect sources can take many forms. If the subject of my thesis is the Italian communist politician Palmiro Togliatti, the parliamentary speeches published by the newspaper *Unità* constitute an indirect source, because there is no assurance that the newspaper has not made edits or mistakes. Instead, the parliamentary acts themselves constitute a direct source. If I could locate an actual text written by Togliatti himself, I would have the ultimate direct source. If I want to study the Declaration of Independence of the United States of America, the only direct source is the original document. However, a good photocopy can also be considered a direct source. I can also use as a direct source the critical edition by a historiographer of undisputed rigor, if I define "undisputed" to mean that his edition has never been challenged by other critical works. Clearly the concepts of "direct" and "indirect" sources depend on my perspective and the approach that I take for my thesis. If I wish to discuss the political meaning of the Declaration of Independence in my thesis, a good critical edition will be more than adequate. If I want to write a thesis on "The Narrative Structures in *The Betrothed*," any edition of Alessandro Manzoni's novel will suffice. Instead, my thesis might be called "Manzoni's Linguistic Transformation from Milan to Florence." It would explore the novel's linguistic change from the blend of Lombard vernacular and traditional literary language of the 1827 edition to the contemporary Florentine of the 1840 edition. In this case, my thesis would require a good critical edition of each version of the novel.

Let us then say that my sources should always be direct, *within the limits set by the object of my research*. The only absolute rule is that I should not quote my author through another quote. In theory, a rigorous scientific work should never quote from *any* quote, even if the material that I wish to quote is from someone other than the object of my thesis. Nevertheless, there are reasonable exceptions, especially for a thesis. For example, if you choose "The Question of the Transcendental Nature of Beauty in Thomas Aquinas's *Summa theologiae*," your primary source will be Thomas Aquinas's *Summa*. Let us say that Marietti's currently available edition is sufficient, unless you suspect that it betrays the original, in which case you must return to other editions. (In this case your thesis will have a philological character, instead of an aesthetic/philosophical character.) You will soon discover that Aquinas also addresses the transcendental nature of beauty in his Commentary to Pseudo-Dionysius's *De divinis nominibus* (*The Divine Names*), and you must address this

work as well, despite your thesis's restrictive title. Finally you
will discover that Aquinas's work on this theme drew from
an entire religious tradition, and that researching all of the
original sources would take a scholar his entire career. You
will also discover that such a work already exists, and that its
author is Dom Henry Pouillon who, in this vast work of his,
quotes large passages from all the authors who commented
on Pseudo-Dionysius and illuminates the relationships, ori-
gins, and contradictions of these commentaries. Within the
scope of your thesis, you can certainly use the material Pouillon gathered each time you refer to Alexander of Hales or
Hilduin. If you come to realize that Alexander of Hales' text
becomes essential for the development of your argument,
then you can consult the Quaracchi edition of the direct text,
but if you only need to refer to a short quote, it will suffice to
declare that you found the source through Pouillon. Nobody
will fault you because Pouillon is a rigorous scholar, and
because the text you quoted indirectly through him was not
central to your thesis.

What you should *never* do is quote from an indirect source
pretending that you have read the original. This is not just a
matter of professional ethics. Imagine if someone asked how
you were able to read a certain manuscript directly, when it is
common knowledge that it was destroyed in 1944! This being
said, you need not get caught up in "direct source neurosis."
The fact that Napoleon died on May 5, 1821 is common
knowledge, usually acquired through indirect sources, such
as history books written on the basis of other history books.
If you wish to study the precise date of Napoleon's death, you
would need to locate original documentation. But if you wish
to address the influence of Napoleon's death on the psychology of European liberal youth, you can trust the date that
appears in any history book. After you declare that you are
citing an indirect source in your thesis, it may be prudent to
check other indirect sources to determine the accuracy of a
certain quote, or the reference to a certain fact or opinion. If
you find inconsistencies that raise suspicion, you can either
choose not to quote the data, or search for the direct source.

For example, since we have already mentioned St. Thomas's aesthetic thought, let us note that a number of recent

texts that discuss this topic assume that St. Thomas said the following: "pulchrum est id quod visum placet." Since I wrote my own thesis on this topic, I consulted the original texts and noticed that St. Thomas *had never said that*. Instead, he said, "pulchra dicuntur quae visa placent," and I will not go into the details of why the two formulations can lead to very different interpretations. What had happened? Many years ago the philosopher Jacques Maritain had proposed the first formulation, thinking he was faithfully summarizing St. Thomas's thought. Since then, other scholars have referred to Maritain's formulation (which Maritain had drawn from an indirect source), without bothering to check the original.[1]

The same issue arises in regard to bibliographical entries. In a rush, you may decide to include in your bibliography sources you have not read; you may discuss these works in footnotes, or what's worse, in the body of the text, all along drawing from information that you gathered indirectly. For example, you may find yourself writing a thesis on the baroque; having read Luciano Anceschi's article "Bacone tra Rinascimento e Barocco" (Bacon between the Renaissance and baroque), in *Da Bacone a Kant* (From Bacon to Kant) (Bologna: Il Mulino, 1972), you cite this article in a note and then, to make a good impression, you add the following comment: "For other acute and stimulating observations on the same topic see Id., 'L'estetica di Bacone' (Bacon's aesthetics), in *L'estetica dell'empirismo inglese* (The aesthetic of English empiricism) (Bologna: Alfa, 1959)." However, since you have not actually read "L'estetica di Bacone," and you are simply mentioning a text that you saw referenced in a note, you will make a terrible impression when a professor points out that the two articles are one and the same, "L'estetica di Bacone" having been published 13 years before "Bacone tra Rinascimento e Barocco" in a more limited edition.

These observations are also valid if the object of your thesis is a current event rather than a series of texts. If I want to address the reactions of farmers from Romagna to a particular set of TV news programs, a primary source will be the survey I conduct *in the field*, interviewing a reliable and adequate sample of farmers according to defined rules. If not this, I should at least use as my primary source a recent analogous survey published by a reliable source. Clearly I would be at fault if I relied on ten-year-old research, if nothing else because both the farmers and the TV news programs have changed significantly over the past decade. However, this research might be appropriate for a thesis titled "Studies on the Relationship between the Audience and Television in the Sixties."

3.2   Bibliographical Research

3.2.1   *How to Use the Library*

How should a student conduct preliminary research in the library? If he already has a reliable bibliography, he can obviously search the author catalog to discover what a particular library has to offer. If the library lacks some of the titles in his bibliography, he can search another library, and so on. But this method assumes that he already has a bibliography, and that he is able to access a series of libraries, maybe one in Rome and another in London. But as we have previously discussed, readers of this book may not have such opportunities. Nor do many professional scholars. Furthermore, although we sometimes go to the library to find a book that we already know exists, we often go to the library to find out *if* a book exists, or to discover books about which we have no previous knowledge. In other words, we often go to the library to compile a bibliography, and this means searching for sources that we do not yet know exist. A good researcher can enter a library without having the faintest idea about scholarship on a particular topic, and exit knowing more about it, if only a little more.

The catalog   The library offers some resources that allow us to find relevant sources about which we have no previous knowledge. Naturally, the first is called the *subject catalog*. Of course there is also an alphabetically arranged *author catalog* that is useful to those who already know what they want, but the subject catalog is for those who do not yet know. Here, a good library tells me everything that I can find in its stacks, for example, on the fall of the Western Roman Empire.

But querying the subject catalog requires some skill. Clearly we cannot find the entry "Fall of the Roman Empire"

under the letter "F," unless we are dealing with a library with
a very sophisticated indexing system. We will have to look
under "Roman Empire," and then under "Rome," and then
under "(Roman) History." And if we have retained some preliminary knowledge from primary school, we will have the
foresight to consult "Romulus Augustulus" or "Augustulus (Romulus)," "Orestes," "Odoacer," "Barbarians," and
"Roman-barbarian (regna)."

Our problems do not end there. In many libraries there
are two author catalogs and two subject catalogs: old ones
that stop at a certain date, and the new ones that are works
in progress and that will absorb the old ones only at some
future date. And we will not necessarily find information
on the fall of the Roman Empire in the old catalog simply
because that event took place centuries ago. In fact there
could be recent books on the subject that are only indexed
in the new catalog. Also, in certain libraries there are separate catalogs for different collections. In other libraries, subjects and authors are indexed together. There also may be
separate catalogs for books and journals, divided by subject
and author; and we may even encounter a library that stores
books on the first floor and journals on the second. Consequently, we must study the system used by the library in
which we are working, and make our decisions accordingly.
Also, some intuition is usually necessary. For example, if the
older of the two catalogs is very old, and I am researching the
Greek region of Laconia, I should also search for the obsolete
spelling "Lacedaemonia," because an overly diligent librarian
may have indexed this entry separately.

Also note that the author catalog is always more reliable
than the subject catalog because the act of compiling it does
not depend on the librarian's interpretation, as is the case
with the subject catalog. In fact, if the library has a book by
John Smith, you will invariably find "Smith, John" under "S"
in the author catalog. But if John Smith has written an article on "The Role of Odoacer in the Fall of the Western Roman
Empire and the Advent of the Roman-Barbarian Regna," the
librarian may have recorded it under the subject "(Roman)
History" or "Odoacer," but not necessarily under the entry
"Western Roman Empire" where you are currently looking.

Finally, the author and subject catalogs simply may not provide the information you require, and in this case you must settle for a more elementary approach. In every library there is a reference section (or an entire room) that contains a collection of encyclopedias, general histories, and bibliographical indexes. If you are looking for works on the Western Roman Empire, you can search the subject of Roman history, compile a basic bibliography starting from the reference works you find, and then search for the authors in the author catalog.

Bibliographical indexes These are the safest resources for a student who already has clearly defined ideas about a topic. For some disciplines there are famous manuals where the student can find all the necessary bibliographical information. For other disciplines there are periodical indexes that contain updates in each issue, and even journals dedicated solely to a subject's bibliography. For others still, there are journals that include an appendix in every issue that documents the most recent publications in the field. Bibliographical indexes are essential supplements to catalog research, as long as they are *updated*. In fact, some libraries may have an extensive collection of the oldest publications, but little or no updated work. Or they may offer histories or manuals of the discipline in question that were published in 1960, and that provide useful bibliographical information, but will not tell you if an interesting work was published in 1975. (The library may actually contain these recent works, but may have indexed them under a subject that you have not thought of.) An updated bibliographical index gives you exactly this kind of information on the latest contributions to a particular field.

The most convenient way to learn about bibliographical indexes is to ask your advisor. You can also ask the librarian (or a staff person at the reference desk) who can direct you to the room or the section of the stacks that contains the bibliographical indexes. Again here, the issue changes from discipline to discipline, so I cannot offer further advice.

The librarian You must overcome any shyness and have a conversation with the librarian, because he can offer you

reliable advice that will save you much time. You must consider that the librarian (if not overworked or neurotic) is
happy when he can demonstrate two things: the quality of
his memory and erudition and the richness of his library,
especially if it is small. The more isolated and disregarded
the library, the more the librarian is consumed with sorrow
for its underestimation. A person who asks for help makes
the librarian happy.

Although you must rely on the librarian's assistance, you
should not trust him blindly. Listen to his advice, but then
search deeply and independently. The librarian is not an
expert on every subject, and he is also unaware of the particular perspective you wish to adopt for your research. He
may deem fundamental a particular book that you end up
barely consulting, and may disregard another that you find
very useful. Additionally, there is no such thing as a prede-
termined hierarchy of useful and important works. An idea
contained almost by mistake on a page of an otherwise useless (and widely ignored) book may prove decisive for your
research. You must discover this page on your own, with
your own intuition and a little luck, and without anybody
serving it to you on a silver platter.

Union catalogs, electronic catalogs, and interlibrary loan
Many libraries publish updated inventories of their holdings.
Therefore, in some libraries it is possible to consult catalogs
that list the holdings of other national and foreign libraries,
at least for some particular disciplines. Asking for information from the librarian is also useful in this case. There are
certain specialized libraries linked via computer to a central
memory that can quickly inform you whether and where you
can find a certain book. For example, the Venice Biennale
instituted the Historical Archives of Contemporary Arts that
are linked via computer to the National Central Library's archive in Rome. You can search the catalog by author, title,
subject, series, publisher, year of publication, etc.

If you have located a book in a national or foreign library,
keep in mind that a library usually has an *interlibrary loan*
service that may be national or international. It may take
some time to get what you need, but it is worth trying if you

need sources that are difficult to find. Even if there is such a service, the library that has the book may not lend it, as some libraries will only lend duplicate copies. Here again you should consult your advisor about all the possibilities of locating needed sources. In any case, remember that the services we need often do exist, but they only work if they are patronized often.

Also remember that many libraries keep a list of their new arrivals, their most recent acquisitions that have not yet been indexed. Finally do not forget that, if you are working rigorously on a project that interests your advisor, you may be able to convince your institution to *purchase* some important texts that you cannot obtain otherwise.

3.2.2   *Managing Your Sources with the Bibliographical Index Card File*

Naturally, to compile a basic bibliography you must consult many books. Many librarians will only lend one or two books at a time, are slow to find each book for you, and will grumble if you quickly return for new books. This is why you should not try to immediately read every book you find, but rather compile a basic bibliography of sources pertaining to your topic. A preliminary inspection of the catalogs allows you to prepare a list of books that you can then begin borrowing. However, the list you derive from the catalogs does not say much about each book's contents, and it is sometimes difficult to determine which books you should borrow first. For this reason, in addition to consulting the catalogs in the reference room, you should preliminarily inspect each book. When you find a chapter and its accompanying bibliography that pertain to your topic, you can skim the chapter (you will return to it later), but be sure to copy *all* of that chapter's bibliography. Together with the chapter that you have skimmed, its bibliography (and if it is annotated, the bibliography's comments) will show which books the author considers fundamental among those he cites, and you can begin by borrowing those. Additionally, if you cross-check the bibliographies with some reference works, you will determine which books are cited most often, and you can begin to establish a first hierarchy of sources for your topic.

This hierarchy may change as you proceed in your work, but for now it constitutes a starting point.

Now, you may object to the idea of copying the entire bibliography from ten different sources. In fact, your research may lead you to as many as a few hundred books, even though your cross-check will eliminate doubles. (Organizing your bibliography in alphabetical order will also help you eliminate doubles.) Fortunately, these days every legitimate library has a copy machine, and each copy costs about a dime. A specific bibliography contained in a reference work, except in very rare cases, occupies only a few pages. With a few dollars you can photocopy a series of bibliographies that you can easily organize once you return home. Once you have finished the bibliography, you can return to the library to determine which sources are actually available.

At this point it will be useful to begin to document your bibliography. You might at first be tempted to record the titles in a notebook as you encounter them. Later, after determining if the titles are available in the library, you might finish each notebook entry by writing the call number near the title. The problem with this approach is that it becomes more difficult to locate the titles in your notebook as your bibliography grows. Also consider that your preliminary research might generate a bibliography of hundreds of titles, even if only some of them will ultimately be useful to your thesis.

A better system is to create a *bibliographical index card* for each book. On each card you can record an abbreviation that signifies the library where the book is available, as well as the call number of the book. A single card might contain many library abbreviations and call numbers, indicating that the book is widely available in different locations. (There will also be index cards with no abbreviations—this is trouble!) You can then file your cards in a small *index card box*. You can purchase a small box of this kind inexpensively from the stationer, or you can make one yourself. You can fit one or two hundred index cards into one small box, and you can take the box with you to the library. This is your *bibliography file*, and if your documentation is well organized, it will give you a clear picture of the sources you have found, and those you still need to locate. Additionally, everything will be in alphabetical order and easy to find. If you wish, you could standardize your index cards so that the call number is in the top right, and a conventional abbreviation in the top left that indicates if the book is a good general reference, a source for a specific chapter, and so on.

Naturally, if you do not have the patience to organize and use this system, you can resort to using a notebook. But the disadvantages are evident: you may note the "A" authors on the first page and the "B" authors on the second, but your first page may fill up before you find an article by Federico Azzimonti or Gian Saverio Abbati. You are better off buying an address book, in which you might not record Abbati before Azzimonti if you found the latter author first, but at least they will both be in the four pages dedicated to the letter "A." The virtue of the index card system is that you can easily reorganize the cards as the bibliography grows and changes, and your cards will always be in true alphabetical order. You may also thank yourself for using this system when you need to use your bibliography file to pursue a related project later (although you will certainly need to supplement it with new sources), and you will have an organized system to lend to someone who is working on a similar topic.

In chapter 4 we will talk about some other types of index card files: the *readings file*, the *idea file*, and the *quote file*; and we will address the applications of each. For now, a brief introduction to the readings file and some preliminary remarks about the difference between it and the bibliography file will suffice. Your readings file should contain index cards dedicated only to the books (or articles) that you have actually read. Here you can document summaries, assessments, and quotes, although you may wish to dedicate an entire file exclusively to quotations. In short, on each card in your readings file you can document everything you will need when you actually begin writing your thesis and your *final bibliography*, bearing in mind that the book may not be available to you at that time. Unlike your bibliography file, you do not have to carry your readings file with you on every trip to the library. Also, your readings file may require larger sheets of paper, although a system of index cards is always the most manageable.

Unlike the readings file, the bibliography file must also contain index cards for *all the books you must find*, not only for the ones you have already located and read. It would even be possible for a bibliography file to contain ten thousand titles and a readings file a mere ten, although this would clearly illustrate a thesis that began extraordinarily well but ended very badly. In any case, you should take your bibliography file with you every time you go to a library. Its index cards contain only a book's essential information, and the libraries and call numbers under which the book can be found. At most, you can annotate "very important according to author X," "absolutely must find," "so-and-so says this is a worthless work," or even "buy this." But any further annotation should be left for the readings file. An entry in the readings file can absorb multiple index cards (one book may generate many notes), whereas each item in the bibliography file comprises one and only one index card.

Finally, construct your bibliography file with care. Do not hastily scribble down titles in stenographic characters, a process prone to error. The better you make your bibliography file, the easier it will be to preserve and supplement for future research. It will also be more valuable to lend or even sell, and therefore it is worth ensuring that it is legible and well organized. Most importantly, *the bibliography file will provide the foundation for the final bibliography*, provided that it contains thorough documentation on the books you have found, read, and archived in the readings file.

For this reason, in the following section I will provide *documentation guidelines*, the instructions to correctly document your sources so that others can easily find them. Use these guidelines for each of the following:

1. The bibliography file,
2. The readings file,
3. References in notes,
4. The final bibliography.

Although I will return to these guidelines in the chapters in which I discuss these four different stages in preparing the thesis, I will establish them definitively in the following section. These guidelines are of the utmost importance, and you must have the patience to become familiar with them. You will realize that they are primarily *functional* guidelines, because they allow you and your reader to identify the exact book to which you are referring. But they are also rules, so to speak, of *erudite etiquette.* Their observance reveals a scholar who is familiar with the discipline, and their violation betrays the academic parvenu, and sometimes casts a shadow of discredit on an otherwise rigorous work. These rules of etiquette matter, and they should not be disparaged as a formalist's weakness. There is a similar dynamic in sports, stamp collecting, billiards, and political life. If a participant misuses key expressions, he raises suspicion, like an outsider who is not "one of us." Thus, you must heed the rules of the company you want to join. As the Italian proverb goes, "If in company you don't pee, a spy or a thief you may be." And if you wish to violate or oppose rules, you must first know them well enough to expose their inconsistencies or repressive functions. So, for example, before you can declare that it is unnecessary to italicize a book's title, you must first know that this is in fact the convention, and you must understand the reasons for this convention.

3.2.3   Documentation Guidelines

Books   Here is an example of an incorrect reference:

Wilson, J. "Philosophy and religion." Oxford, 1961.

This reference is incorrect for the following reasons:

1. It provides only the initial of the author's first name. The first initial is not enough, first of all, because readers may want to know the full name; and second of all, because there can be two authors with the same last name and first initial. If I read that the author of the book *Logic and the Art of Memory: The Quest for a Universal Language* is P. Rossi, I cannot determine whether the author is the philosopher Paolo Rossi of the University of Florence or the philosopher Pietro Rossi of the University of Turin. And who is J. Cohen? Is he the French critic and aesthetician Jean Cohen or the English philosopher Jonathan Cohen?

2. The book title is in quotation marks. However you choose to format a reference, never use quotation marks for book titles, because this is the method used almost universally to refer to journal articles or book chapters. Also, in the title in question the word "Religion" should also be capitalized. English titles capitalize nouns, adjectives, verbs, and adverbs; but not articles, particles, and prepositions (unless they are the last word of the title, as in *The Logical Use of It*).

3. It is hideous to say *where* the book has been published and not *by whom*. Suppose you find an Italian book that seems important, and that you would like to purchase, but the only publication information in the reference is "Milan, 1975." Which press published this book? Mondadori, Rizzoli, Rusconi, Bompiani, Feltrinelli, or Vallardi? How can the bookseller help you? And if you find "Paris, 1976," to whom do you address your letter of inquiry? And if the book has been published in "Cambridge," which Cambridge is it, the one in England or the one in the United States? In fact, many important authors cite books this way. Know that, except when they are writing an encyclopedia entry (where brevity is a virtue that saves space), these authors are snobs who despise their audience. References like these are sufficient only in the case of books published before 1900 ("Amsterdam, 1678") that you will only find in a library, or in a limited number of antique booksellers.

4. Despite what this reference would lead you to believe, this book was not published in Oxford. As noted on the title page, the book was published by Oxford University Press, and this press has locations in London, New York, and Toronto. What's more, it was printed in Glasgow. The reference should indicate *where the book was published, not where it was printed*. (Here again we make an exception in the case of very old books: because printers were also publishers and booksellers, books then were published, printed, and sold in the same location.) I once encountered a reference in a thesis for a particular book that included "Farigliano: Bompiani." Knowing that Bompiani

is in Milan, I turned to the copyright page (usually located directly after the title page) and learned that by chance the book was printed at a printer located in the town of Farigliano. The person concocting such references gives the impression that he has never seen a book in his life. To be safe, never look for the publishing information only on the title page, but also on the copyright page, where you will find the real place of publication, as well as the date and number of the edition. If you only look briefly on the title page, you may incur other pathetic mistakes, such as leading your readers to believe that the quaint beach town of Cattolica on the Adriatic Sea is the place of publication for a book published by the prestigious Università Cattolica in Milan. It would be as if an Italian student found books published by Yale University Press, Harvard University Press, or Cornell University Press and indicated that they were published in Yale, Harvard, or Cornell. These are of course not names of places, but the proper nouns of those famous private universities, located in the cities of New Haven, Cambridge (Massachusetts), and Ithaca respectively.

5. As for the date, it is correct only by chance. The date marked on the title page is not always the actual date of the book's first publication. It can be that of the latest edition. Only on the copyright page will you find the date of the first edition (and you may even discover that the first edition was published by another press). Sometimes the difference between these dates is very important. Suppose for example that you find the following reference:

Searle, J. *Speech Acts*. Cambridge, 1974.

On top of the other inaccuracies, by checking the copyright page you discover that the date of the first edition is 1969. Now, the point of your thesis may be to establish whether Searle talked about these "speech acts" before or after other authors, and so the date of the first edition is fundamental. Besides, if you thoroughly read the book's preface, you discover that he presented this fundamental thesis as his PhD dissertation in Oxford in 1959 (ten years earlier than the book's first publication), and that during that ten-year period various parts of the book appeared in a number of philosophical journals. And nobody would ever think to cite Herman Melville's nineteenth-century classic as follows, simply because he is holding a recent edition that was published in Indianapolis:

Melville, Herman. *Moby Dick, or, The Whale*. Indianapolis, 1976.

Whether you are studying Searle or Melville, you must never spread wrong ideas about an author's work. If you worked on a later, revised, or augmented edition by Melville, Searle, Wilson, you must specify both the date of the first publication and that of the edition you quote.

Now that we have seen how *not* to cite a book, I will show you five ways to correctly cite these works by Searle and Wilson.[2] Let it be clear that there are other methods, and that each method could be valid provided it does the following: (a) distinguishes the book from articles or the chapters of other books; (b) indicates unequivocally both the author's name and the title; and (c) indicates the place of publication, the name of the publisher, and the edition. Therefore each of the following five examples works. Each has its pros and cons; however, for a number of reasons that will soon become clear, we will prefer the first example:

1.

Searle, John R. *Speech Acts: An Essay in the Philosophy of Language.* 5th ed. Cambridge: Cambridge University Press, 1974. First published 1969.

Wilson, John. *Philosophy and Religion: The Logic of Religious Belief.* London: Oxford University Press, 1961.

2.

Searle, John R., *Speech Acts* (Cambridge: Cambridge, 1969).

Wilson, John, *Philosophy and Religion* (London: Oxford, 1961).

3.

Searle, John R., S p e e c h   A c t s, 5th ed., Cambridge, Cambridge University Press, 1974. First published 1969.

Wilson, John, P h i l o s o p h y   a n d   R e l i g i o n, London, Oxford University Press, 1961.

4.

Searle, John R., Speech Acts. Cambridge: Cambridge University Press, 1969.

Wilson, John, Philosophy and Religion. London: Oxford University Press, 1961.

5.

Searle, John R. 1969. *Speech Acts: An Essay in the Philosophy of Language*. 5th ed. Cambridge: Cambridge University Press, 1974.

Wilson, John. 1961. *Philosophy and Religion: The Logic of Religious Belief*. London: Oxford University Press.

Naturally there are also hybrid solutions. For instance, the fourth example could contain the subtitle as do the first and fifth. As we shall see, there are even more complex systems that include, for example, the title of the series. In any case, we can consider all five of these examples to be valid. For now, let us disregard the fifth (the author-date system), because it applies to a specialized bibliography that we will discuss later when we address the subjects of notes and the final bibliography. The second example is typically American, and it is more common in footnotes than in the final bibliography. The third example, typically German, is nowadays fairly rare, and in my opinion does not offer any advantage. The fourth is also quite popular in the United States, and I find it quite annoying because it does not allow us to immediately distinguish the book's title. The first system tells us all we need to know, and that we are in fact referring to a book and not an article.

Journals   Consider these three different ways to cite a journal article:

Anceschi, Luciano. "Orizzonte della poesia" (Horizon of poetry). *Il Verri*, n.s., 1 (February 1962): 6–21.

Anceschi, Luciano. "Orizzonte della poesia." *Il Verri*, n.s., 1:6–21.

Anceschi, Luciano. *Orizzonte della poesia*. In "Il Verri" (February 1962): 6–21.

There are other systems also, but let us immediately turn to the first and the third examples. The first presents the article in quotation marks and the journal in italics; the third presents the article in italics and the journal in quotation marks. *Why is the first preferable?* Because it allows us at a glance to understand that "Orizzonte della poesia" is a short text and not a book. As we shall see, journal articles are included in the same category as book chapters and conference proceedings. Clearly the second example is a variation of the first, but it eliminates the reference to the date of publication, and is therefore defective—it would have been better to at least include: *Il Verri* 1 (1962).

You will note that both the first and second examples include the indication "n.s." or "new series." This designation is quite important because a previous series of *Il Verri* appeared in 1956 with another first issue. If I had to cite a reference from the first issue of volume one of the previous series, I would specify the volume in addition to the issue number, as follows:

Gorlier, Claudio. "L'Apocalisse di Dylan Thomas" (The apocalypse of Dylan Thomas). *Il Verri* 1, no. 1 (Fall 1956): 39–46.

In addition, note that some journals number the pages progressively over the year. Therefore, if I wanted, for these journals I could omit the issue number and record only the year and the pages. For example:

Guglielmi, Guido. "Tecnica e letteratura" (Tecnique and literature). *Lingua e stile*, 1966:323–340.

If I then find this journal in the library, I will realize that page 323 is in the third issue of the first volume. But I do not see why I should subject my reader to this exercise (even if other authors subject theirs) when it would have been so much more convenient to write:

Guglielmi, Guido. "Tecnica e letteratura." *Lingua e stile* 1, no. 3 (1966).

This reference makes the article easier to find, even though it lacks page numbers. Also, consider that if I wanted to order the journal from the publisher as a back issue, I would care only about the issue number, not the pages. However,

I do need to know the first and last pages to determine the
length of the article, and for this reason it is recommended
to include the page numbers:

Guglielmi, Guido. "Tecnica e letteratura." *Lingua e stile* 1, no. 3
    (1966): 323–340.

Multiple authors and an editor   Let us move on to the chapters of larger works, be they collections of essays by the same
author or miscellaneous volumes. Here is a simple example:

Morpurgo-Tagliabue, Guido. "Aristotelismo e Barocco" (Aristotelian-
    ism and the baroque). In *Retorica e Barocco: Atti del III Congresso
    Internazionale di Studi Umanistici, Venezia, 15–18 giugno 1954*
    (Rhetoric and the baroque: Proceedings of the third international
    conference on humanism, Venice, June 15–18, 1954), ed. Enrico
    Castelli, 119–196. Rome: Bocca, 1955.

This reference tells me everything I need to know. First,
it tells me that Morpurgo-Tagliabue's text is part of a collection of other texts. Although it is not a book, the number of
pages his article occupies (77) tells me that it is quite a substantial study. Second, it tells me that the volume is a collection of conference proceedings by various authors titled
Retorica e Barocco. This is important information because I
may discover that some bibliographies list it under the head-
ing of "Convention and Conference Proceedings." Finally, it
tells me that the editor of the collection is Enrico Castelli.
This information is also important, not only because some
libraries may catalog the volume under his name, but also
because bibliographies alphabetize multiauthor volumes
under the name of the editor (ed.) or editors (eds.), as
follows:

Castelli, Enrico, ed. *Retorica e Barocco*. Rome: Bocca, 1955.

These distinctions are important for locating a book in a
library catalog or in a bibliography.

As we shall see when we conduct an actual experiment
of bibliographical research in section 3.2.4, I will find Morpurgo-Tagliabue's essay cited in the *Storia della letteratura
italiana* (History of Italian literature) published by Garzanti
in the following terms:

On this topic see the miscellaneous volume *Retorica e Barocco: Atti del III Congresso Internazionale di Studi Umanistici* (Milan, 1955), and in particular Morpurgo-Tagliabue's important essay "Aristotelismo e Barocco."

This is a terrible reference because (a) it does not tell us the author's first name; (b) it makes us think that either the conference was in Milan or the publisher is in Milan (neither is true); (c) it does not indicate the publisher; (d) it does not indicate the length of the essay; and (e) it does not indicate the editor of the volume, even though the designation of "miscellaneous" would seem to imply that the volume is a collection of essays from various authors requiring an editor. Shame on us if we wrote such a reference on our bibliographical index card. Instead, we should write our reference so that there is free space for the missing information:

Morpurgo-Tagliabue, G_____. "Aristotelismo e Barocco." In *Retorica e Barocco: Atti del III Congresso Internazionale di Studi Umanistici* _____, edited by_____, _____. Milan: _____, 1955.

This way, we can later fill in the blanks with the missing information, once we find it in another bibliography, in the library catalog, or on the title page of the book itself.

Multiple authors and no editor Suppose I want to index an essay that appeared in a book written by four different authors, none of whom is the editor. For example, let us cite a German book with four essays by T. A. van Dijk, Jens Ihwe, Janos S. Petöfi, and Hannes Rieser. In this case, we should note the names of all four authors because we must include them in the bibliographical entry. But in a note, we should indicate only the first author followed by et al. or "and others" for convenience:

T. A. van Djik et al., *Zur Bestimmung narrativer Strukturen auf der Grundlage von Textgrammatiken* (On the determination of narrative structures based on textual grammar), etc.

Let us consider the more complex example of the essay "Anthropology and Sociology" by Dell Hymes. This essay appears in the third book of the twelfth volume of a multiauthor work, in which each volume has a title different from that of the entire work. Cite the essay as follows:

Hymes, Dell. "Anthropology and Sociology." In *Current Trends in Linguistics*, ed. Thomas A. Sebeok, 1445–1475, vol. 12, bk. 3, *Linguistics and Adjacent Arts and Sciences*. The Hague: Mouton, 1974.

If instead we must cite the entire work, the information the reader expects is no longer in *which* volume Dell Hymes's essay resides, but of *how many* volumes the entire work consists:

Sebeok, Thomas A., ed. *Current Trends in Linguistics*. 12 vols. The Hague: Mouton, 1967–1976.

When we must cite an essay belonging to a collection of essays by the same author, the reference is similar to that of a multiauthor book, except for the fact that we omit the name of the author before the book:

Rossi-Landi, Ferruccio. "Ideologia come progettazione sociale." In *Il linguaggio come lavoro e come mercato*, 193–224. Milan: Bompiani, 1968. Trans. Martha Adams et al. as "Ideology as Social Planning," in *Language as Work and Trade* (South Hadley, MA: Bergin and Garvey, 1983), 83–106.

You may have noticed that usually the title of a chapter is cited as being "in" a given book, while the article of a journal is not "in" a journal, and the name of the journal directly follows the title of the article.

The series   A more perfect reference system might require the series in which a volume appears. I do not consider this an indispensable piece of information, as it is easy enough to find a book if you know its author, title, publisher, and the year of publication. But in some disciplines, the series may guarantee or indicate a specific scientific trend. In this case, the series is noted without quotation marks or parentheses after the book title, and is followed directly by the number of the volume in the series:

Rossi-Landi, Ferruccio. *Il linguaggio come lavoro e come mercato*. Nuovi Saggi Italiani 2. Milan: Bompiani, 1968.

Anonymous authors and pseudonyms   If you are dealing with an anonymous author, begin the entry with the title and alphabetize the entry accordingly, ignoring any initial article. If the author has a pseudonym, begin the entry with the pseudonym followed by the author's real name (if known) in brackets. After the author's real name, place a question mark if the attribution is still a hypothesis, no matter how reliable the source. If you are dealing with an author whose identity is established by tradition, but whose historicity scholars have recently challenged, record him as "Pseudo" in the following manner:

Pseudo-Longinus. *On the Sublime* ...

Reprints in collections or anthologies   A work that originally appeared in a journal may have been reprinted in a collection of essays by the same author, or in a popular anthology. If this work is of marginal interest with respect to your thesis topic, you can cite the most convenient source. If instead your thesis specifically addresses the work, then you must cite the *first* publication for reasons of historical accuracy. Nothing forbids you from using the most accessible edition, but if the anthology or the collection of essays is well prepared, it should contain a reference to the work's first edition. This information should allow you to create references such as this:

Fodor, Jerry A., and Jerold J. Katz. "The Structure of a Semantic Theory." In *The Structure of Language*, ed. Jerry A. Fodor and Jerold J. Katz, 479–518. Englewood Cliffs, NJ: Prentice-Hall, 1964. Originally published as "The Structure of a Semantic Theory." *Language* 39 (1963): 170–210.

When you use the author-date system for your bibliography (which I will discuss in section 5.4.3), include the date of the first publication, as follows:

Fodor, Jerry A., and Jerold J. Katz. 1963. "The Structure of a Semantic Theory." In *The Structure of Language*, ed. Jerry A. Fodor and Jerold J. Katz, 479–518. Englewood Cliffs, NJ: Prentice-Hall, 1964.

Citing newspapers   References to newspapers and magazines are similar to those for journals, except that it is more

appropriate to put the date rather than the issue number,
since it makes the source easier to find:

Nascimbeni, Giulio. "Come l'Italiano santo e navigatore è diventato
   bipolare" (How the Italian saint and sailor became bipolar). *Cor-
   riere della Sera* (Milan), June 25, 1976.

For foreign newspapers it may be useful to specify the city:
Times (London).

Citing official documents or monumental works   References to official documents require shortened forms and
initialisms that vary from discipline to discipline, just as
there are typical abbreviations for works on ancient manuscripts. Here your best source is the critical literature in
the specific discipline you are studying. Bear in mind that
certain abbreviations are commonly used within a discipline
and you need not explain them to your audience. For a study
on U.S. Senate resolutions, an American manual suggests
the following reference:

S. Res. 218, 83d Cong., 2d Sess., 100 Cong. Rec. 2972 (1954).

Specialists are able to read this as, "Senate Resolution number 218 adopted at the second session of the Eighty-Third
Congress, 1954, as recorded in volume 100 of the *Congres-
sional Record,* beginning on page 2972."[3] Similarly, when
you indicate that a text is available in *PL* 175.948 in a study
on medieval philosophy, anyone in the field will know that
you are referring to column 948 of the 175th volume of
Jacques-Paul Migne's *Patrologia Latina*, a classic collection
of Latin texts of the Christian Middle Ages. However, if you
are building a bibliography from scratch, it is not a bad idea
to record on your index card the entire reference the first
time you find it, because in the final bibliography it would be
appropriate to give the full reference:

Patrologiae cursus completus, series latina, accurante J. P. Migne. 222
   vols. Paris: Garnier, 1844–1866 (+ *Supplementum*, Turnhout: Bre-
   pols, 1972).

Citing classic works   For the citation of classic works,
there are fairly universal conventions that indicate the title-

book-chapter, section-paragraph, or canto-line. Some works have been subdivided according to criteria dating back to antiquity, and when modern editors superimpose new subdivisions, they generally also preserve the traditional line or paragraph marks. Therefore, if you wanted to quote the definition of the principle of noncontradiction from Aristotle's *Metaphysics*, the reference will be "*Met.* 4.3.1005b18." An excerpt from Charles S. Peirce's *Collected Papers* is cited as "*CP* 2.127." A passage from the Bible is cited instead as "1 Sam. 14:6–9." References to classical (and modern) comedies and tragedies are comprised of act, scene, and if necessary the line or lines in Arabic numerals: "*Shrew*, 4.2.50–51." Naturally your reader must know that "*Shrew*" refers to Shakespeare's *The Taming of the Shrew*. If your thesis is on Elizabethan drama, there is no problem in using this short citation. If instead a mention of Shakespeare intervenes as an elegant and erudite digression in a psychology thesis, you should use a more extended reference.

In references to classic works, the first criterion should be that of practicality and intelligibility. If I refer to a Dantean line as "2.27.40," it is reasonable to guess that I am talking about the 40th line of the 27th canto of the second canticle of the *Divine Comedy*. But a Dante scholar would rather write "*Purg.* XXVII.40." It is best to follow disciplinary conventions; these are a second but no less important criterion. Naturally you must pay attention to ambiguous cases. For example, references to Pascal's *Pensées* (*Thoughts*) will differ depending on the edition from which you cite; Brunschvicg's popular edition is ordered differently from other editions. You can only learn these types of things by reading the critical literature on your topic.

Citing unpublished works and private documents Specify a thesis, a manuscript, and a private document as such. Here are two examples:

La Porta, Andrea. "Aspetti di una teoria dell'esecuzione nel linguaggio naturale" (Aspects of a performance theory in natural language). *Laurea* thesis. University of Bologna, 1975–1976.

Valesio, Paolo. "Novantiqua: Rhetorics as a Contemporary Linguistic Theory." Unpublished manuscript, courtesy of the author.

Cite private letters and personal communications similarly. If they are of marginal importance it is sufficient to mention them in a note, but if they are of decisive importance for your thesis, include them in the final bibliography:

Smith, John, personal letter to author, January 5, 1976.

As we shall see in section 5.3.1, for this kind of citation it is polite to ask permission from the person who originated the personal communication and, if it is oral, to submit our transcription for his approval.

Originals and translations   Ideally you should always consult and cite a book in its original language. If you write a thesis on Molière, it would be a serious mistake to read your author in English. But in some cases it is fine to read some books in translation. If your thesis is on romantic literature, it is acceptable to have read *The Romantic Agony*, the English translation published by Oxford University Press of Mario Praz's *La carne, la morte e il diavolo nella letteratura romantica*. You can cite the book in English with a good conscience, but for your reference to be useful also to those who wish to go back to the original edition, a double reference would be appropriate. The same is true if you read the book in Italian. It is correct to cite the book in Italian, but why not aid readers who wish to know if there is an English translation and, if so, who published it? Therefore, in either case, the best choice is the following:

Praz, Mario. *La carne, la morte e il diavolo nella letteratura romantica.* Milan and Rome: La Cultura, 1930. Trans. Angus Davidson as *The Romantic Agony* (London: Oxford University Press, 1933).

Are there exceptions? Some. For example, if you cite Plato's *Republic* in a thesis on a topic other than ancient Greek (in a thesis on law, for example), it is sufficient that you cite an English translation, provided that you specify the exact edition you used. Similarly, let us say your thesis deals with literary studies, and that you must cite the following book:

Lotman, Yu. M., G. Permyakov, P. G. Bogatyrev, and V. N. Toporov. *General Semiotics.* Ed. Lawrence Michael O'Toole and Ann Shukman. Russian Poetics in Translation 3. Oxford: Holdan Books, 1976.

In this case, it is appropriate to cite only the English translation, for two good reasons: First, it is unlikely that readers interested in your topic will have the burning desire to examine the Russian original. Second, an original version of the cited book does not even exist, because the English volume is a collection of miscellaneous Russian essays from various sources put together by the editors. Therefore, you should cite after the book title, "Ed. Lawrence Michael O'Toole and Ann Shukman." But if your thesis were on the current state of semiotic studies, then you would be obligated to proceed with more precision. Granted, you may not be able to read Russian, and readers can reasonably understand (provided your thesis is not on Soviet semiotics) that you are not referring to the collection in general but instead, for example, to the first essay in the collection. And then it would be interesting to know when and where the essay was originally published—all details that the editors provide in their notes on the essay. Therefore you will cite the essay as follows:

Lotman, Yuri M. "The Modeling Significance of the Concepts 'End' and 'Beginning' in Artistic Texts." In *General Semiotics*, ed. Lawrence Michael O'Toole and Ann Shukman, 7–11. Russian Poetics in Translation 3. Oxford: Holdan Books, 1976. Originally published in *Tezisy dokladov vo vtoroi letnei Shkole po vtorichnym modeliruyushchim sistemam*, 69–74. Tartu, 1966.

This way you have not led readers to believe you have read the original text because you indicate your English source, but you have provided all the information needed to locate the original.

Also, when there is no translation available for a work in a language that is not commonly known, it is customary to include a translation of the title in parentheses directly after the original title.

Finally, let us examine a seemingly complicated case that at first suggests an elaborate solution, though this may be simplified depending on the context. David Efron is an Argentinian Jew who in 1941 published, in English and in the United States, a study on the gestural expressiveness of Jews and Italians in New York, called *Gesture and Environment*.

In 1970 a Spanish translation appeared in Argentina with a different title, *Gesto, raza y cultura*. In 1972 a new edition in English appeared in the Netherlands with the title *Gesture, Race and Culture* (similar to the one in Spanish). From this edition derives the 1974 Italian translation titled *Gesto, razza e cultura*. How then should an Italian student cite this book?

Let us imagine two extreme cases. In the first case, the student is writing his thesis on David Efron. His final bibliography will contain a section dedicated to the author's works, in which he must create references for all the editions separately in chronological order, and for each reference, he must specify whether the book is a new edition of a previous one. We assume that the candidate has examined all the editions, because he must check whether they contain changes or omissions. In the second case, the student is writing his thesis in economics, political science, or sociology, and he is addressing the questions of emigration. In this case, he cites Efron's book only because it contains some useful information on marginal aspects of his topic. Here the student may cite only the Italian edition.

But let us also discuss an intermediate case, one in which the citation is marginal but it is important to know that the study dates back to 1941 and is not recent. The best solution would then be the following:

Efron, David. *Gesture and Environment*. New York: King's Crown Press, 1941. Trans. Michelangelo Spada as *Gesto, razza e cultura* (Milan, Bompiani, 1974).

As it happens, the Italian edition indicates in the copyright that King's Crown Press published the original in 1941, but rather than citing the original title, it gives the full reference to the Dutch 1972 edition. This is a matter of serious negligence (and I can say this because I am the editor of the Bompiani series in which Efron's book appeared) because an Italian student might mistakenly cite the 1941 edition as *Gesture, Race, and Culture*. This is why it is always necessary to check the references against more than one source. A more scrupulous student who wished to document the fortunes of Efron's volume and the rhythm of its rediscovery

by scholars might gather enough information to compile the
following reference:

Efron, David. *Gesture, Race and Culture*. 2nd ed. The Hague: Mouton,
  1972. Trans. Michelangelo Spada as *Gesto, razza e cultura* (Milan,
  Bompiani, 1974). First published as *Gesture and Environment*
  (New York: King's Crown Press, 1941).

In any case, it is evident that the extent of the required information depends on the type of thesis and the book's role in
its general argument (primary source, secondary source,
marginal or accessory source, etc.).

Although the instructions above provide a foundation
for creating a final bibliography for your thesis, here we are
only interested in creating a good bibliographical reference
in order to develop our index cards, and these instructions
are more than adequate for this purpose. We will talk in
more detail about the final bibliography in chapter 6. Also,
sections 5.4.2 and 5.4.3 describe two different citation systems and the relations between notes and the bibliography.
There you will also find two full pages of a sample bibliography (tables 5.2 and 5.3) that essentially summarize what we
have said here.

Table 3.1 summarizes this section by listing all the
information that your references should contain. Note the
required usage of italics, quotation marks, parentheses,
and punctuation. Essential information that you should
never omit is marked with an asterisk. The other information is optional and depends on the type of thesis you are
writing.

Finally, in table 3.2 you will find an example of a bibliographical index card. As you can see, in the course of my
bibliographical research I first found a citation of the Italian
translation. Then I found the book in the library catalog and
I marked on the top right corner the initialism for the name
of the library, and the call number of the volume. Finally I
located the volume and deduced from the copyright page the
original title and publisher. There was no indication of the
publication date, but I found one on the dust jacket flap and
noted it with reservations. I then indicated why the book is
worth considering.

Table 3.1

SUMMARY OF DOCUMENTATION GUIDELINES

BOOKS

* 1. Last name, first name of the author or editor [with information on pseudonyms or false attributions].
* 2. *Title: Subtitle of the Work.*
  3. Edition [if it is the second or later].
  4. Volume number [or total number of volumes in a multi-volume work cited in its entirety].
  5. Series.
* 6. Place of publication [if missing, write "n.p." which means "no place"]:
* 7. Publisher [omit if this information is missing from the book],
* 8. Date of publication [if this information is missing from the book, write "n.d." which means "no date"].
  9. Trans. [if the original title was in a foreign language and there is an English translation, specify the translator's full name, the English title, the place of publication, the publisher, and the date of publication].

JOURNAL ARTICLES

* 1. Last name, first name of the author.
* 2. "Article Title."
* 3. *Journal Title*
* 4. Volume number, issue number [indicate if it is a new series],
  5. (Month and year):
  6. Inclusive page numbers.

BOOK CHAPTERS, CONFERENCE PROCEEDINGS, AND ESSAYS FROM A MULTIAUTHOR VOLUME

* 1. Last name, first name of the author.
* 2. "Chapter or Essay Title."
* 3. In
* 4. *Title of the Multiauthor Volume,*
* 5. First name and last name of the editor.
* 6. Volume number [if it is in a multivolume work].
* 7. Chapter or essay's inclusive page numbers.
* 8. Place of publication:
* 9. Publisher,
* 10. Date of publication.

Table 3.2
EXAMPLE OF A BIBLIOGRAPHICAL INDEX CARD

BS. Con.
107 - 5171

Auerbach, Erich. Mimesis. Il realismo nella letteratura occidentale (Mimesis. The Representation of Reality in Western Literature). 2 vols. Turin: Einaudi, 1956, xxxix-284 and 350.

Original Title:
Mimesis: Dargestellte Wirklichkeit in der abendländischen Literatur. Bern: Francke, 1946?

[in the second volume, see the essay
   "The World in Pantagruel's Mouth"]

3.2.4 An Experiment in the Library of Alessandria

Some may object that the advice I have given so far may work for a specialist, but that a young person who is about to begin his thesis, and who lacks specialized expertise, may encounter many difficulties:

1. He may not have access to a well-equipped library, perhaps because he lives in a small city.

2. He may have only vague ideas of what he is looking for, and he may not know how to begin searching the subject catalog because he has not received sufficient instructions from his professor.

3. He may not be able to travel from library to library. (Perhaps he lacks the funds, the time, or he may be ill, etc.)

Let us then try to imagine the extreme situation of a working Italian student who has attended the university very little during his first three years of study. He has had sporadic contact with only one professor, let us suppose, a professor of aesthetics or of history of Italian literature. Having started his thesis late, he has only the last academic year at his disposal. Around September he managed to approach the professor or one of the professor's assistants, but in Italy final exams take place during this period, so the discussion was very brief. The professor told him, "Why don't you write a thesis on the concept of metaphor used by Italian baroque treatise authors?" Afterward, the student returned to his home in a town of a thousand inhabitants, a town without a public library. The closest city (of 90,000 inhabitants) is half an hour away, and it is home to a library that is open daily. With two half-day leaves from work, the student will travel to the library and begin to formulate his thesis, and perhaps do all the work using only the resources that he finds there. He cannot afford expensive books, and the library is not able to request microfilms from elsewhere. At best, the student will be able to travel to the university (with its better-furnished libraries) two or three times between January and April. But for the moment, he must do the best he can locally. If it is truly necessary, the student can purchase a few recent books in paperback, but he can only afford to spend about 20 dollars on these.

Now that we have imagined this hypothetical picture, I will try to put myself in this student's shoes. In fact, I am writing these very lines in a small town in southern Monferrato, 14.5 miles away from Alessandria, a city with 90,000 inhabitants, a public library, an art gallery, and a museum. The closest university is one hour away in Genoa, and in an hour and a half I can travel to Turin or Pavia, and in three to Bologna. This location already puts me in a privileged situation, but for this experiment I will not take advantage of the university libraries. I will work only in Alessandria.

I will accept the precise challenge posed to our hypothetical student by his hypothetical professor, and research the concept of metaphor in Italian baroque treatise writing. As I have never specifically studied this topic, I am adequately unprepared. However, I am not a complete virgin on this topic, because I do have experience with aesthetics and rhetoric. For example, I am aware of recent Italian publications on the baroque period by Giovanni Getto, Luciano Anceschi, and Ezio Raimondi. I also know of *Il cannocchiale aristotelico* (The Aristotelian telescope) by Emanuele Tesauro, a seventeenth-century treatise that discusses these concepts extensively. But at a minimum our student should have similar knowledge. By the end of the third year he will have completed some relevant courses and, if he had some previous contact with the aforementioned professor, he will have read some of the professor's work in which these sources are mentioned. In any case, to make the experiment more rigorous, I will presume to know nothing of what I know. I will limit myself to my high school knowledge: I know that the baroque has something to do with seventeenth-century art and literature, and that the metaphor is a rhetorical figure. That's all.

I choose to dedicate three afternoons to the preliminary research, from three to six p.m. I have a total of nine hours at my disposal. In nine hours I cannot read many books, but I can carry out a preliminary bibliographical investigation. In these nine hours, I will complete all the work that is documented in the following pages. I do not intend to offer this experiment as a model of a complete and satisfactory work, but rather to illustrate the introductory research I will need to complete my final thesis.

As I have outlined in section 3.2.1, upon entering the library I have three paths before me:

1. I can examine the subject catalog. I can look for the following entries: "Italian (literature)," "(Italian) literature," "aesthetics," "seventeenth century," "baroque period," "metaphor," "rhetoric," "treatise writers," and "poetics."[4] The library has two catalogs, one old and one updated, both divided by subject and author. They have not yet been merged, so I must search both. Here I might make an imprudent calculation: if I am looking for a nineteenth-century work, I might assume that it resides in the old catalog. This is a mistake. If the library purchased the work a year ago from an antique shop, it will be in the new catalog. The only certainty is that any book published in the last ten years will be in the new catalog.

2. I can search the reference section for encyclopedias and histories of literature. In histories of literature (or

aesthetics) I must look for the chapter on the seventeenth century or on the baroque period. I can search encyclopedias for "seventeenth century," "baroque period," "metaphor," "poetics," "aesthetics," etc., as I would in the subject catalog.

3. I can interrogate the librarian. I discard this possibility immediately both because it is the easiest and because it would compromise the integrity of this experiment. I do in fact know the librarian, and when I tell him what I am doing, he barrages me with a series of titles of bibliographical indexes available to him, even some in German and English. Were I not engaged in this experiment, I would immediately explore these possibilities. However, I do not take his advice into consideration. The librarian also offers me special borrowing privileges for a large number of books, but I refuse with courtesy, and from now on speak only with the assistants, attempting to adhere to the allotted time and challenges faced by my hypothetical student.

I decide to start from the subject catalog. Unfortunately, I am immediately exceptionally lucky, and this threatens the integrity of the experiment. Under the entry "metaphor" I find Giuseppe Conte, *La metafora barocca. Saggio sulle poetiche del Seicento* (The baroque metaphor: Essay on seventeenth-century poetics) (Milan: Mursia, 1972). This book is essentially my thesis realized. If I were dishonest, I would simply copy it, but this would be foolish because my (hypothetical) advisor probably also knows this book. This book will make it difficult to write a truly original thesis, because I am wasting my time if I fail to say something new and different. But if I want to write an honest literature review, this book could provide a straightforward starting point.

The book is defective in that it does not have a comprehensive bibliography, but it has a thick section of notes at the end of each chapter, including not only references but also descriptions and reviews of the sources. From it I find references to roughly 50 titles, even after omitting works of contemporary aesthetics and semiotics that do not strictly relate to my topic. (However, the sources I have omitted may illuminate relationships between my topic and current issues. As we shall see later, I could use them to imagine a slightly different thesis that involves the relationships between the baroque and contemporary aesthetics.) These 50 titles, all of which are specifically on the baroque, could provide a preliminary set of index cards that I could use later to explore the author catalog. *However, I decide to forgo this line of research.* The stroke of luck is too singular, and may jeopardize the integrity of my experiment. Therefore, I proceed as if the library did not own Conte's book.

To work more methodically, I decide to take the second path mentioned above. I enter the reference room and begin to explore the reference texts, specifically the *Enciclopedia Treccani* (Treccani encyclopedia). Although this encyclopedia contains an entry for "Baroque Art" that is entirely devoted to the figurative arts, there is no entry for "Baroque." The reason for this absence becomes clear when I notice that the "B" volume was published in 1930: the reassessment of the baroque had not yet commenced. I then think to search for "Secentismo," a term used to describe the elaborate style characteristic of seventeenth-century European literature. For a long time, this term had a certain negative connotation, but it could have inspired the encyclopedia listing in 1930, during a period largely influenced by the philosopher Benedetto Croce's diffidence toward the baroque period.

And here I receive a welcome surprise: a thorough, extensive, and mindful entry that documents all the questions of the period, from the Italian baroque theorists and poets such as Giambattista Marino and Emanuele Tesauro to the examples of the baroque style in other countries (B. Gracián, J. Lyly, L. de Góngora, R. Crashaw, etc.), complete with excellent quotes and a juicy bibliography. I look at the date of publication, which is 1936; I look at the author's name and discover that it is Mario Praz, the best specialist during that period (and, for many subjects, he is still the best). Even if our hypothetical student is unaware of Praz's greatness and unique critical subtlety, he will nonetheless realize that the entry is stimulating, and he will decide to index it more thoroughly later. For now, I proceed to the bibliography and notice that this Praz, who has written such an excellent entry, has also written two books on the topic: *Secentismo e marinismo in Inghilterra* (Secentismo and Marinism in England) in 1925, and *Studi sul concettismo* (*Studies in Seventeenth-Century Imagery*) in 1934. I decide to index these two books. I then find some Italian titles by Benedetto Croce and Alessandro D'Ancona that I note. I find a reference to T. S. Eliot, and finally I run into a number of works in English and German. I note them all, even if I (in the role of our hypothetical student) assume ignorance of the foreign languages. I then realize that Praz was talking about *Secentismo* in general, whereas I am looking for sources centered more specifically on the Italian application of the style. Evidently I will have to keep an eye on the foreign versions as background material, but perhaps this is not the best place to begin.

I return to the Treccani for the entries "Poetics," "Rhetoric," and "Aesthetics." The first term yields nothing; it simply cross-refers to "Rhetoric," "Aesthetics," and "Philology." "Rhetoric" is treated with some breadth. There is a paragraph on the seventeenth century worthy of investigation, but there are no specific bibliographical directions. The philosopher Guido Calogero wrote the entry on "Aesthetics," but he understood it as an eminently philosophical discipline, as was common in the 1930s. There is the philosopher Giambattista Vico (1668–1744), but there are no baroque treatise writers. This helps me envisage an avenue to follow: perhaps I will find Italian material more easily in sections on literary criticism and the history of literature than in sections that deal with the history of philosophy. (As I will see later, this is only true until recently.) Nevertheless, under Calogero's entry "Aesthetics," I find a series of classic histories of aesthetics that could tell me something: R. Zimmermann (1858), M. Schlasler (1872), B. Bosanquet (1895), and also G. Saintsbury (1900–1904), M. Menéndez y Pelayo (1890–1901), W. Knight (1895–1898), and finally B. Croce (1928). They are almost all in German and English, and very old. I should also say immediately that none of the texts I have mentioned are available in the library of Alessandria, except Croce. I note them anyway, because sooner or later I may want to locate them, depending on the direction that my research takes.

I look for the *Grande dizionario enciclopedico UTET* (UTET great encyclopedic dictionary) because I remember that it contains extensive and updated entries on "Poetics" and various other sources that I need, but apparently the library doesn't own it. So I begin paging through the *Enciclopedia filosofica* (Encyclopedia of philosophy) published by Sansoni. I find two interesting entries: one for "Metaphor" and another for "Baroque." The former does not provide any useful bibliographical direction, but it tells me that everything begins with Aristotle's theory of the metaphor (and only later will I realize the importance of this information). The latter provides citations of nineteenth- and twentieth-century critics (B. Croce, L. Venturi, G. Getto, J. Rousset, L. Anceschi, E. Raimondi) that I prudently note, and that I will later reencounter in more specialized reference works; in fact I will later discover that this source cites a fairly important study by Italian literature scholar Rocco Montano that was absent from other sources, in most cases because these sources preceded it.

At this point, I think that it might be more productive to tackle a reference work that is both more specialized and more recent, so I look for the *Storia della letteratura italiana* (History of Italian literature), edited by the literary critics Emilio Cecchi and Natalino Sapegno and published by Garzanti. In addition to chapters by various authors on poetry, prose, theater, and travel writing, I find Franco Croce's chapter "Critica e trattatistica del Barocco" (Baroque criticism and treatise writing), about 50 pages long. (Do not confuse this author with Benedetto Croce whom I have mentioned above.) I limit myself to reading this particular chapter, and in fact I only skim it. (Remember that I am not yet closely reading texts; I am only assembling a bibliography.) I learn that the seventeenth-century critical discussion on the baroque begins with Alessandro Tassoni (on Petrarch), continues with a series of authors (Tommaso Stigliani, Scipione Errico, Angelico Aprosio, Girolamo Aleandro, Nicola Villani, and others) who discuss Marino's illustrious epic poem *Adone* (Adonis), and passes through the treatise writers that Franco Croce calls "moderate baroque" (Matteo Peregrini, Pietro Sforza Pallavicino) and through Tesauro's canonical text *Il cannocchiale aristotelico* which is the foremost treatise in defense of baroque ingenuity and wit and, according to Franco Croce, "possibly the most exemplary of all baroque manuals in all of Europe."[5] Finally, the discussion finishes with the late seventeenth-century critics (Francesco Fulvio Frugoni, Giacomo Lubrano, Marco Boschini, Carlo Cesare Malvasia, Giovan Pietro Bellori, and others).

Here I realize that my interests must center on the treatise writers Sforza Pallavicino, Peregrini, and Tesauro, and I proceed to the chapter's bibliography, which includes approximately one hundred titles. It is organized by subject, and it is not in alphabetical order. My system of index cards will prove effective in putting things in order. As I've noted, Franco Croce deals with various critics, from Tassoni to Frugoni, and in the end it would be advantageous to index all the references he mentions. For the central argument of my thesis, I may only need the works on the moderate critics and on Tesauro, but for the introduction or the notes it may be useful to refer to other discussions that took place during the same period. Ideally, once our hypothetical student has completed the initial bibliography, he will discuss it with his advisor at least once. The advisor should know the subject well, so he will be able to efficiently determine which sources the student should read and which others he should ignore. If the student keeps his index cards in order, he and his advisor should be able to go through them in about an hour. In any case, let us assume that this process has taken place for my experiment, and that *I have decided to limit myself to the general works on the baroque and to the specific bibliography on the treatise writers.*

We have already explained how to index books when a bibliographical source is missing information. On the index card for E. Raimondi reproduced below, I left space to write the author's first name (Ernesto? Epaminonda? Evaristo? Elio?), as well as the publisher's name (Sansoni? Nuova Italia? Nerbini?). After the date, I left additional space for other information. I obviously added the initialism "APL" that I created for *Alessandria Public Library* after I checked for the book in Alessandria's author catalog, and I also found the call number of Ezio (!!) Raimondi's book: "Co D 119."

Table 3.3
EXAMPLE OF AN INCOMPLETE INDEX CARD
FROM A DEFECTIVE BIBLIOGRAPHICAL SOURCE

APL
CoD 119

Raimondi, E
La letteratura barocca (Baroque literature).
Florence: , 1961.

If I were truly writing my thesis, I would proceed the same way for all the other books. But for the sake of this experiment, I will instead proceed more quickly in the following pages, citing only authors and titles without adding other information.

To summarize my work up to this point, I consulted Franco Croce's essay and the entries in the *Treccani* and the *Enciclopedia filosofica*, and I decided to note only the works on Italian treatises. In tables 3.4 and 3.5 you will find the list of what I noted. Let me repeat that, while I made only succinct bibliographical entries for the purpose of this experiment, the student should ideally create an index card (complete with space allotted for missing information) that corresponds with each entry. Also, in each entry in tables 3.4 and 3.5, I have noted a "yes" before titles that exist in the author catalog of the Alessandria library. In fact, as I finished filing these first sources, I took a break and skimmed the library's card catalog. I found many of the books in my bibliography,

Table 3.4

GENERAL WORKS ON THE ITALIAN BAROQUE FOUND IN THREE
REFERENCE VOLUMES
(*TRECCANI, ENCICLOPEDIA FILOSOFICA SANSONI-GALLARATE,
STORIA DELLA LETTERATURA ITALIANA GARZANTI*)

Found in the Library	Works Searched for in the Author Catalog	Other Works by the Same Author Found in the Author Catalog
yes	Croce, B. *Saggi sulla letteratura italiana del seicento* (Essays on seventeenth-century Italian literature)	
yes		*Nuovi saggi sulla letteratura italiana del seicento* (New essays on seventeenth-century Italian literature)
yes	Croce, B. *Storia dell'età barocca in Italia* (History of the baroque period in Italy)	
yes		*Lirici marinisti* (Marinist poets); *Politici e moralisti del seicento* (Seventeenth-century writers on politics and morals)
	D'Ancona, A. "Del secentismo nella poesia cortigiana del secolo XV" (On *secentismo* in fifteenth-century courtly poetry)	
	Praz, M. *Secentismo e marinismo in Inghilterra* (*Secentismo* and Marinism in England)	
	Praz, M. *Studi sul concettismo* (*Studies in Seventeenth-Century Imagery*)	
yes	Wölfflin, H. *Renaissance und Barock* (*Renaissance and Baroque*)	
	Retorica e Barocco (Rhetoric and the baroque)	
yes	Getto, G. "La polemica sul barocco" (The polemic on the baroque)	
	Anceschi, L. *Del barocco* (On the baroque)	

Found in the Library	Works Searched for in the Author Catalog	Other Works by the Same Author Found in the Author Catalog
yes		"Le poetiche del barocco letterario in Europa" (The poetics of the literary baroque in Europe)
yes		*Da Bacone a Kant* (From Bacon to Kant)
yes		"Gusto e genio nel Bartoli" (On style and genius in Bartoli)
yes	Montano, R. "L'estetica del Rinascimento e del Barocco" (Renaissance and baroque aesthetics)	
yes	Croce, F. "Critica e trattatistica del Barocco" (Baroque criticism and treatise writing)	
yes	Croce, B. "I trattatisti italiani del concettismo e B. Gracián" (Italian treatise writers on *concettismo* and B. Gracián)	
yes	Croce, B. *Estetica come scienza dell'espressione e linguistica generale* (*Aesthetic as Science of Expression and General Linguistic*)	
yes	Flora, F. *Storia della letteratura italiana* (History of Italian literature)	
yes	Croce, F. "Le poetiche del Barocco in Italia" (Baroque poetics in Italy)	
	Calcaterra, F. *Il Parnaso in rivolta* (The rebellion of Parnassus)	
yes		"Il problema del barocco" (The question of the baroque)
	Marzot, G. *L'ingegno e il genio del seicento* (Seventeenth-century wit and genius)	
	Morpurgo-Tagliabue, G. "Aristotelismo e Barocco" (Aristotelianism and the baroque)	
	Jannaco, C. *Il seicento* (The seventeenth century)	

Table 3.5

WORKS ON INDIVIDUAL ITALIAN SEVENTEENTH-CENTURY TREATISE
WRITERS FOUND IN THREE REFERENCE VOLUMES
(*TRECCANI, ENCICLOPEDIA FILOSOFICA SANSONI-GALLARATE, STORIA DELLA
LETTERATURA ITALIANA GARZANTI*)

Found in the Library	Works Searched for in the Author Catalog	Other Works by the Same Author Found in the Author Catalog
	Biondolillo, F. "Matteo Peregrini e il secentismo" (Matteo Peregrini and *secentismo*)	
yes	Raimondi, E. *Letteratura barocca* (Baroque literature)	
yes		*Trattatisti e narratori del Seicento* (Seventeenth-century treatise and narrative prose writers)
yes	*Studi e problemi di critica testuale* (Studies and issues of textual criticism)	
	Marrocco, C. *Un precursore dell'estetica moderna: Il card. Sforza Pallavicino* (A forerunner of modern aesthetics: Cardinal Sforza Pallavicino)	
	Volpe, L. *Le idee estetiche del Cardinale Sforza Pallavicino* (The aesthetic ideas of Cardinal Sforza Pallavicino)	
	Costanzo, M. *Dallo Scaligero al Quadrio* (From Scaligero to Quadrio)	
	Cope, J. "The 1654 Edition of Emanuele Tesauro's *Il cannocchiale aristotelico*"	
	Pozzi, G. "Note prelusive allo stile del *Cannocchiale aristotelico*" (Preliminary notes on the style of the *Cannocchiale aristotelico*)	
	Bethell, S. L. "Gracián, Tesauro and the Nature of Metaphysical Wit"	

Found in the Library	Works Searched for in the Author Catalog	Other Works by the Same Author Found in the Author Catalog
	Mazzeo, J. A. "Metaphysical Poetry and the Poetics of Correspondence"	
	Menapace Brisca, L. "L'arguta et ingegnosa elocuzione" (The witty and ingenious style)	
	Vasoli, C. "Le imprese del Tesauro" (Tesauro's enterprises)	
yes		"L'estetica dell'Umanesimo e del Rinascimento" (The aesthetics of humanism and the Renaissance)
	Bianchi, D. "Intorno al *Cannocchiale aristotelico*" (On the *Cannocchiale aristotelico*)	
	Hatzfeld, H. "Three National Deformations of Aristotle: Tesauro, Gracián, Boileau"	
yes		"L'Italia, la Spagna e la Francia nello sviluppo del barocco letterario" (Italy, Spain, and France in the development of the literary baroque)
	Hocke, G. R. *Die Welt als Labyrinth* (The world as labyrinth)	
yes	Hocke, G. R. *Manierismus in der Literatur* (Mannerism in literature)	Italian translation
yes	Schlosser Magnino, J. *Die Kunstliteratur* (Art literature)	
	Ulivi, F. *Galleria di scrittori d'arte* (A gallery of art critics)	
yes		"Il manierismo del Tasso" (A note on Tasso's *manierismo*)
	Mahon, D. *Studies in Seicento Art and Theory*	

and I can consult them for the missing information on my index cards. As you will notice, I found 14 of the 38 works I cataloged, plus 11 additional works that I encountered by the authors I was researching.

Because I am limiting myself to titles referring to Italian treatise writers, I neglect, for example, Panofsky's *Idea: A Concept in Art Theory*, a text that, as I will discover later from other sources, is equally important for the theoretical problem in which I am interested. As we will see, when I consult Franco Croce's essay "Le poetiche del Barocco in Italia" (Baroque poetics in Italy) in the miscellaneous volume *Momenti e problemi di storia dell'estetica* (Moments and issues in the history of aesthetics), I will discover in that same volume an essay by literary critic Luciano Anceschi on the poetics of the European baroque, one that is three times as long. Franco Croce did not cite this essay in his chapter on the baroque, because he was limiting his study to Italian literature. This is an example of how, by discovering a text through a citation, a student can then find other citations in *that* text, and so on, potentially infinitely. You see that, even starting from a good history of Italian literature, I am making significant progress.

I will now glance at the *Storia della letteratura italiana* (History of Italian literature) written by the good old Italian literary critic Francesco Flora. He is not an author who lingers on theoretical problems. Instead, he enjoys savoring the wittiness and originality of particular passages in the texts he analyzes. In fact his book contains a chapter full of amusing quotes from Tesauro, and many other well-chosen quotes on the metaphoric techniques of seventeenth-century authors. As for the bibliography, I am not expecting much from a general work that stops at 1940, but it does confirm some of the classical texts I have already cited. The name of Eugenio D'Ors strikes me. I will have to look for him. On the subject of Tesauro, I find the names of critics C. Trabalza, T. Vallauri, E. Dervieux, and L. Vigliani, and I make a note of them.

Now I move on to consult the abovementioned miscellaneous volume *Momenti e problemi di storia dell'estetica*. When I find it, I notice that Marzorati is the publisher (Franco Croce told me only that it was published in Milan), so I

supplement the index card. Here I find Franco Croce's essay
on the poetics of Italian baroque literature ("Le poetiche del
Barocco in Italia"). It is similar to his "Critica e trattatistica
del Barocco" that I have already seen, but it was written earlier, so the bibliography is more dated. Yet the approach is
more theoretical, and I find the essay very useful. Additionally, the theme is not limited to the treatise writers, as in
the previous essay, but deals with literary poetics in general.
So, for example, "Le poetiche del Barocco in Italia" treats the
Italian poet Gabriello Chiabrera at some length. And on the
subject of Chiabrera, the name of literary critic Giovanni
Getto (a name I have already noted) comes up again.

In the Marzorati volume, together with Franco Croce's
essay I find Anceschi's essay "Le poetiche del barocco letterario in Europa" (The poetics of the literary baroque in
Europe), an essay that is almost a book in itself. I realize it is
quite an important study not only because it philosophically
contextualizes the notion of the baroque and all of its meanings, but also because it explains the dimensions of the question in European culture, including Spain, England, France,
and Germany. I again find names that were only mentioned
in Mario Praz's entry in the *Enciclopedia Treccani*. I also find
other names, from Bacon to Lyly and Sidney, Gracián, Góngora, Opitz, the theories of wit, *agudeza*, and *ingegno*. My
thesis may not deal directly with the European baroque, but
these notions must serve as context. In any case, if my bibliography is to be complete, it should reflect the baroque as
a whole.

Anceschi's extensive essay provides references to approximately 250 titles. The bibliography at the end is divided
into a concise section of general studies and a longer section of more specialized studies arranged by year from 1946
to 1958. The former section highlights the importance of
the Getto and Helmut Hatzfeld studies, and of the volume
Retorica e Barocco (Rhetoric and the baroque)—and here I
learn that it is edited by Enrico Castelli—whereas Anceschi's
essay had already brought my attention to the critical works
of Heinrich Wölfflin, Benedetto Croce, and Eugenio D'Ors.
The latter section presents a flood of titles, only a few of
which, I wish to make clear, I attempt to locate in the author

catalog, because this would have required more time than my allotted limit of three afternoons. In any case, I learn of some foreign authors who treated the question from many points of view, and for whom I will nevertheless have to search: Ernst Robert Curtius, René Wellek, Arnold Hauser, and Victor Lucien Tapié. I also find references to the work of Gustav René Hocke, and to Eugenio Battisti's *Rinascimento e Barocco* (The Renaissance and the baroque), a work that deals with the links between the literary metaphor and the poetics of art. I find more references to Morpurgo-Tagliabue that confirm his importance to my topic, and I realize that I should also see Galvano Della Volpe's work on the Renaissance commentators on Aristotelian poetics, *Poetica del Cinquecento* (Sixteenth-century poetics).

This realization also convinces me to look at Cesare Vasoli's extensive essay (in the Marzorati volume that I am still holding) "L'estetica dell'Umanesimo e del Rinascimento" (The aesthetics of humanism and the Renaissance). I have already seen Vasoli's name in Franco Croce's bibliography. In the encyclopedia entries on metaphor that I have examined, I have already noticed (and noted on the appropriate index card) that the question of metaphor had already arisen in Aristotle's *Poetics* and *Rhetoric*. Now I learn from Vasoli that during the sixteenth century there was an entire scene of commentators on Aristotle's *Poetics* and *Rhetoric*. I also learn that between these commentators and the baroque treatise writers there are the theorists of *Manierismo* who discussed the question of ingenuity as it relates to the concept of metaphor. I also notice the recurrence of similar citations, and of names like Julius von Schlosser. And before leaving Anceschi, I decide to consult his other works on the topic. I record references to *Da Bacone a Kant* (From Bacon to Kant), *L'idea del Barocco* (The idea of baroque) and an article on "Gusto e genio nel Bartoli" (On style and genius in Bartoli). However, the Alessandria library only owns this last article and the book *Da Bacone a Kant*.

Is my thesis threatening to become too vast? No, I will simply have to narrow my focus and work on a single aspect of my topic, while still consulting many of these books for background information.

At this point I consult Rocco Montano's study "L'estetica del Rinascimento e del Barocco" (Renaissance and baroque aesthetics) published in *Pensiero della Rinascenza e della Riforma* (Renaissance and Reformation thought), the eleventh volume of the *Grande antologia filosofica Marzorati* (Marzorati's great anthology of philosophy). I immediately notice that it is not only a study but also an anthology of texts, many of which are very useful for my work. And I see once again the close relationships between Renaissance scholars of Aristotle's *Poetics*, the mannerists, and the baroque treatise writers. I also find a reference to *Trattatisti d'arte tra Manierismo e Controriforma* (Art treatise writers between *Manierismo* and the Counter-Reformation), a two-volume anthology published by Laterza. As I page through the catalog to find this title, I discover that the Alessandria library owns another anthology published by Laterza, *Trattati di poetica e retorica del Cinquecento* (Sixteenth-century treatises on poetics and rhetoric). I am not sure if my topic will require firsthand sources, but I note the book just in case. Now I know where to find it.

I return to Montano and his bibliography, and here I must do some reconstructive work, because each chapter has its own bibliography. In any case, I recognize many familiar names and, as I read, it dawns on me that I should consult some classic histories of aesthetics, such as the aforementioned Bernard Bosanquet's, George Saintsbury's, Marcelino Menéndez y Pelayo's, and Katherine Gilbert and Helmut Kuhn's (1939). I also find the names of the sixteenth-century commentators of Aristotle's *Poetics* that I've mentioned above (Robortello, Castelvetro, Scaligero, Segni, Cavalcanti, Maggi, Varchi, Vettori, Speroni, Minturno, Piccolomini, Giraldi Cinzio, etc.). I note these just in case, and I will later learn that Montano anthologized some of them, Della Volpe others, and the Laterza anthology others yet.

Montano's bibliography refers me once again to *Manierismo*. Panofky's *Idea* continues to reappear as a pressing critical reference, and so does Morpurgo-Tagliabue's essay "Aristotelismo e Barocco." I wonder if I should become more informed on mannerist treatise writers like Sebastiano Serlio, Lodovico Dolce, Federico Zuccari, Giovanni Paolo

Lomazzo, and Giorgio Vasari; but this would lead me to the figurative arts and architecture. Perhaps some classic critical texts like Wölfflin's, Panofsky's, Schlosser's, or Battisti's more recent one would suffice. I must also note the importance of non-Italian authors like Sidney, Shakespeare, and Cervantes. Finally, I find in Montano's bibliography familiar names cited as having authored fundamental critical studies: Curtius, Schlosser, and Hauser, as well as Italians like Calcaterra, Getto, Anceschi, Praz, Ulivi, Marzot, and Raimondi. The circle is tightening. Some names are cited everywhere.

To catch my breath, I return to the author catalog and begin to page through it. I find important books in German, most of which are also available in English translation: Panofsky's *Idea,* Ernst Curtius's famous *European Literature and the Latin Middle Ages,* Schlosser's *Die Kunstliteratur* (Art literature), and, while I am looking for Hauser's *The Social History of Art,* Hauser's fundamental volume *Mannerism: The Crisis of the Renaissance and the Origin of Modern Art.*

Realizing that I must somehow read Aristotle's *Rhetoric* and *Poetics,* I look for Aristotle in the author catalog. I am surprised to find 15 antiquarian editions of the *Rhetoric* published between 1515 and 1837: one with Ermolao Barbaro's commentary; another, Bernardo Segni's translation; another with Averroes and Alessandro Piccolomini's paraphrases; and the Loeb English edition with the parallel Greek text. The Italian edition published by Laterza is absent. As far as the *Poetics* goes, there are also various editions, including one with Castelvetro's and Robortello's sixteenth-century commentaries, the Loeb edition with the parallel Greek text, and Augusto Rostagni's and Manara Valgimigli's two modern Italian translations. This is more than enough. In fact, it is enough for a thesis about Renaissance commentaries on the *Poetics.* But let us not digress.

From various hints in the texts I have consulted, I realize that some observations made by historians Francesco Milizia and Lodovico Antonio Muratori, and by the humanist Girolamo Fracastoro, are also relevant to my thesis. I search for their names in the author catalog, and I learn that the Alessandria library owns antiquarian editions of these authors. I then find Della Volpe's *Poetica del Cinquecento*

(Sixteenth-century poetics), Santangelo's *Il secentismo nella critica* (Criticism on *secentismo*), and Zonta's article "Rinascimento, aristotelismo e barocco" (A note on the Renaissance, Aristotelianism, and the baroque). Through the name of Helmuth Hatzfeld, I find a multiauthor volume that is interesting in many other respects, *La critica stilistica e il barocco letterario. Atti del secondo Congresso internazionale di studi italiani* (Stylistic criticism and the literary baroque. Proceedings of the second international conference of Italian studies), that was published in Florence in 1957. I am disappointed to find that the Alessandria library does not own one of Carmine Jannaco's apparently important works, and also *Il Seicento* (The seventeenth century), a volume of the history of literature published by Vallardi. The library also does not own Praz's books, Rousset's and Tapié's studies, the oft-quoted volume *Retorica e Barocco* with Morpurgo-Tagliabue's essay, and the works of Eugenio D'Ors and Menéndez y Pelayo. In a nutshell, the Alessandria library is not the Library of Congress in Washington, nor the Braidense Library in Milan, but all in all I have already secured 35 books, a decent beginning. Nor is this the end of my research.

In fact, sometimes a single text can solve a whole series of problems. As I continue checking the author catalog, I decide (since it is there, and since it appears to be a fundamental reference work) to take a look at Giovanni Getto's "La polemica sul barocco" (The polemic on the baroque), in the first volume of the 1956 miscellaneous work *Letteratura italiana. Le correnti* (The currents of Italian literature). I quickly notice that the study is almost a hundred pages long and exceptionally important, because it narrates the entire controversy on baroque style. I notice the names of major Italian writers and intellectuals who have been discussing the baroque from the seventeenth to the twentieth century: Giovanni Vincenzo Gravina, Ludovico Antonio Muratori, Girolamo Tiraboschi, Saverio Bettinelli, Giuseppe Baretti, Vittorio Alfieri, Melchiorre Cesarotti, Cesare Cantù, Vincenzo Gioberti, Francesco De Sanctis, Alessandro Manzoni, Giuseppe Mazzini, Giacomo Leopardi, Giosuè Carducci, up to the twentieth-century writer Curzio Malaparte and the other authors that I have already noted. And Getto quotes long excerpts from many of these authors, which clarifies an issue for me: if I am to write a thesis on the historical controversy on the baroque, it should be of high scientific originality, it will require many years of work, and its purpose must be precisely to prove that Getto's inquiry has been insufficient, or was carried out from a faulty perspective. For a thesis of this kind, I must explore all of these authors. However, works of this kind generally require more experience than that of our hypothetical student in this experiment. If instead I work on the baroque texts, or the contemporary interpretations of these texts, I will not be expected to complete such an immense project (a project that Getto has already done, and done excellently).

Now, Getto's work provides me with sufficient documentation for the background of my thesis, if not on its specific topic. Extensive works such as Getto's must generate a series of separate index cards. In other words, I will write an index card on Muratori, one on Cesarotti, one on Leopardi, and so on. I will record the work in which they expressed their opinions on the baroque, and I will copy Getto's summary onto each index card, with relevant quotes. (Naturally, I will also note that I took the material from Getto's essay.) If I eventually choose to use this material in my thesis, I must honestly and prudently indicate in a footnote "as quoted in Getto" because I will be using secondhand information. In fact, since we are modeling research done with few means and little time, I will not have time to check the quote against its original source. Therefore, I will not be responsible for the quote's possible imperfections. I will faithfully declare that I took it from another scholar, I will not pretend that I have seen the original information, and I will not have to worry. However, ideally the student would have the means to check each quote with the original text.

Having altered my course, the only authors I must not ignore at this point are the baroque authors *on whom* I will write my thesis. I must now search for these baroque authors because, as we have said in section 3.1.2, a thesis must also have primary sources. I cannot write about the treatise writers if I do not read them in their original form. I can trust the critical studies on the mannerist theorists of the figurative arts because they do not constitute the focus of my research, but I cannot ignore a central figure of baroque poetics such as Tesauro.

So let us now turn to the baroque treatise writers. First of all, there is Ezio Raimondi's anthology *Trattatisti e narratori del Seicento* (Seventeenth-century treatise and narrative prose writers) published by Ricciardi that contains 100 pages of Tesauro's *Cannocchiale aristotelico*, 60 pages of Peregrini, and 60 of Sforza Pallavicino. If I were writing a 30-page term paper instead of a thesis, this anthology would be more than sufficient. But for my thesis, I also want the entire treatises. Among them I need at least: Emanuele Tesauro, *Il cannocchiale aristotelico*; Matteo Peregrini, *Delle acutezze* (On acuities) and *I fonti dell'ingegno ridotti a arte* (The art of wit and its sources); Cardinal Sforza Pallavicino, *Del bene* (On the good) and *Trattato dello stile e del dialogo* (Treatise on style and dialogue). I begin to search for these in the "special collection" section of the author catalog, and I find two editions of the *Cannocchiale*, one from 1670 and the other from 1685. It is a real pity that the first 1654 edition is absent, all the more since I learned that content has been added to the various editions. I do find two nineteenth-century editions of Sforza Pallavicino's complete works, but I do not find Peregrini. (This is unfortunate, but I am consoled by the 60 pages of his work anthologized by Raimondi.)

Incidentally, in some of the critical texts I previously consulted, I found scattered traces of Agostino Mascardi's 1636 treatise *De l'arte istorica* (On the art of history), a work that makes many observations on the art of writing but is not included in these texts among the items of baroque treatise writing. Here in Alessandria there are *five* editions, three from the seventeenth and two from the nineteenth century. Should I write a thesis on Mascardi? If I think about it, this is not such a strange question. If a student cannot travel far from his home, he must work with the material that is locally available. Once, a philosophy professor told me that he had written a book on a specific German philosopher only because his institute had acquired the entire new edition of the philosopher's complete works. Otherwise he would have studied a different author. Certainly not a passionate scholarly endeavor, but it happens.

Now, let us rest on our oars. What have I done here in Alessandria? I put together a critical bibliography that, to be conservative, includes at least 300 titles, if I record all the references I found. In the end, in Alessandria I found more than 30 of these 300 titles, in addition to original texts of at least two of the authors I could study, Tesauro and Sforza Pallavicino. This is not bad for a small city. But is it enough for my thesis?

Let us answer this question candidly. If I were to write a thesis in three months and rely mostly on indirect sources, these 30 titles would be enough. The books I have not found are probably quoted in those I have found, so if I assembled my survey effectively, I could build a solid argument. The trouble would be the bibliography; if I include only the texts that I actually read in their original form, my advisor could accuse me of neglecting a fundamental text. And what if I cheat? We have already seen how this process is both unethical and imprudent.

I do know one thing for certain: for the first three months I can easily work locally, between sessions in the library and at home with books that I've borrowed. I must remember that reference books and very old books do not circulate, nor do volumes of periodicals (but for these, I can work with photocopies). But I can borrow most other kinds of books. In the following months, I could travel to the city of my university for some intensive sessions, and I could easily work locally from September to December. Also, in Alessandria I could find editions of all the texts by Tesauro and Sforza Pallavicino. Better still, I should ask myself if it would not be better to gamble everything on only one of these two authors, by working directly with the original text and using the bibliographical material I found for background information. Afterward, I will have to determine what other books I need, and travel to Turin or Genoa to find them. With a little luck I will eventually find everything I need. And thanks to the fact that I've chosen an Italian topic, I have avoided the need to travel, say, to Paris or Oxford.

Nevertheless, these are difficult decisions to make. Once I have created the bibliography, it would be wise to return to the (hypothetical) advisor and show him what I have. He will be able to suggest appropriate solutions to help me narrow the scope, and tell me which books are absolutely necessary. If I am unable to find some of these in Alessandria, I can ask the librarian if the Alessandria library can borrow them from other libraries. I can also travel to the university library, where I might identify a series of books and articles. I would lack the time to read them but, for the articles, the Alessandria library could write the university library and request photocopies. An important article of 20 pages would cost me a couple of dollars plus shipping costs.

In theory, I could make a different decision. In Alessandria, I have some pre-1900 editions of two major baroque treatise authors, and a sufficient number of critical texts. These are enough to understand these two authors, if not to say something new on a historiographical or philological level. (If there were at least Tesauro's first edition of *Il cannocchiale aristotelico*, I could write a comparison between the three seventeenth-century editions.) Let us suppose that I explore no more than four or five books tracing *contemporary* theories of metaphor. For these, I would suggest: Jakobson's *Preliminaries to Speech Analysis*, the Liège Groupe μ's *A General Rhetoric*, and Albert Henry's *Métonymie et métaphore* (Metonym and metaphor). Here, I have the elements to trace a structuralist history of the metaphor. And they are all books available on the market, they cost about 11 dollars altogether, and they have been translated into Italian. At this point, I could even compare the modern theories of metaphor with the baroque theories. For a work of this kind, I might possibly use Aristotle's texts, Tesauro, 30 or so studies on Tesauro, and the three contemporary reference texts to put together an intelligent thesis, with peaks of originality and accurate references to the baroque, but no claim to philological discoveries. And all this without leaving Alessandria, except to find in Turin or Genoa no more than two or three fundamental books that were missing in Alessandria.

But these are all hypotheses. I could become so fascinated with my research that I choose to dedicate not one but three years to the study of the baroque; or I could take out a loan or look for a grant to study at a more relaxed pace. Do not expect this book to tell you what to put in your thesis, or what to do with your life. What I set out to demonstrate (and I think I did demonstrate) with this experiment is that a student can arrive at a small library with little knowledge on a topic and, after three afternoons, can acquire sufficiently clear and complete ideas. In other words, it is no excuse to say, "I live in a small city, I do not have the books, I do not know where to start, and nobody is helping me."

Naturally the student must choose topics that lend themselves to this game. For example, a thesis on Kripke and Hintikka's logic of possible worlds may not have been a wise choice for our hypothetical student. In fact I did some research on this topic in Alessandria, and it cost me little time. A first look for "logic" in the subject catalog revealed that the library has at least 15 notable books on formal logic, including works by Tarski, Lukasiewicz, Quine, some handbooks, and some studies of Ettore Casari, Wittgenstein, Strawson, etc. But predictably, it has nothing on the most recent theories of modal logic, material that is found mostly in specialized journals and is even absent from some university libraries. However, on purpose I chose a topic that nobody would have taken on during their final year without some kind of previous knowledge, or without already owning some fundamental books on the topic.

I'm not saying that such a topic is only for students who have the resources to purchase books and for frequent travel to larger libraries. I know a student who was not rich, but who wrote a thesis on a similar topic by staying in a religious hostel and purchasing very few books. Admittedly, despite his small sacrifices, his family supported him and he was able to devote himself full time to this project because he didn't have to work. There is no thesis that is intrinsically for rich students, because even the student who chooses "The Variations of Beach Fashion in Acapulco over a Five-Year Period" can always search for a foundation willing to sponsor such a research project. This said, a student should obviously avoid certain topics if he is in a particularly challenging situation. For this reason, I am trying to demonstrate here how to cook a meal with meat and potatoes, if not with gourmet ingredients.

3.2.5   *Must You Read Books? If So, What Should You Read First?*

The examples in this chapter suggest that writing a thesis involves putting together a great number of books. But does a student always write a thesis on books and with books? We have already seen that there are experimental theses that document research in the field, perhaps conducted while observing mice in a maze for many months. Now, I do not feel confident giving precise suggestions on this type of research. Here the method depends on the discipline, and people who embark on this kind of research already live in the laboratory. They work with and learn from other researchers, and they probably do not need this book. However, as I have already said, even in this kind of thesis it is necessary to contextualize the experiment with a discussion of previous scientific literature, and so even here the student must deal with books. The same would be true of a thesis in sociology that required the candidate to spend a long period of time in a real social environment. This student will need books, if nothing else, to understand how others have already carried out similar research projects. There are even thesis projects that require the student to page through newspapers or parliamentary acts, but even these require background literature.

And finally there are the theses that discuss only books, and in general these are in the subjects of literature, philosophy, the history of science, canon law, and formal logic. In Italian universities these are the majority, especially for degrees in the humanities. Consider that an American student who studies cultural anthropology has the Native Americans right around the corner, or finds money to do research in the Congo, while the Italian student usually resigns himself to writing a thesis on Franz Boas's thought. Naturally, more and more students are writing ethnographic theses that involve researching Italian society, but even in these cases the library work is relevant, if only to search previous folklore collections.

Let us say that, for reasons that by now should be easy to understand, this book addresses the vast majority of theses written on books, and using only books. Here we should reiterate that a thesis on books usually employs two kinds: the books it talks about, and the books that help it talk. In other words, the texts that are the object of the study are the primary sources, and the critical literature on those texts constitutes the secondary sources. Regarding our experiment in Alessandria, the original texts of the baroque treatise writers are the primary sources, and all those who wrote about the baroque treatise writers are secondary sources.

The following question therefore arises: should a student deal immediately with the primary sources, or first cover the critical literature? The question may be meaningless for two reasons: (a) because the decision depends on the situation of the student, who may already know his author well and decide to study him in depth, or may be approaching for the first time a very difficult and perhaps seemingly unintelligible author; (b) this is a vicious circle, because the primary source can be incomprehensible without the preliminary critical literature, but it is difficult to evaluate the critical literature without knowing the primary source. However, the question is reasonable when posed by a disoriented student, perhaps our hypothetical student who is dealing with the baroque treatise writers for the first time. He might ask us whether he should begin immediately reading Tesauro, or should first cut his teeth on Getto, Anceschi, Raimondi, and other critics.

It seems to me the most sensible answer is this: approach two or three of the most general critical texts immediately, just to get an idea of the background against which your author moves. Then approach the original author directly, and always try to understand exactly what he says. Afterward, explore the rest of the critical literature. Finally, return to examine the author in the light of the newly acquired ideas. But this advice is quite abstract. In reality, students tend to follow the rhythm of their desire, and often there is nothing wrong with consuming texts in a disorderly way. The student can meander, alternating his objectives, provided that a thick web of personal notes, possibly in the form of index cards, keeps track of these "adventurous" wanderings.

Naturally, the approach depends on the researcher's psychological structure. There are *monochronic* people and *polychronic* people. The monochronic succeed only if they work on one endeavor at a time. They cannot read while listening to music; they cannot interrupt a novel to begin another without losing the thread; at their worst, they are unable to have a conversation while they shave or put on their makeup. The polychronic are the exact opposite. They succeed only if they cultivate many interests simultaneously; if they dedicate themselves to only one venture, they fall prey to boredom. The monochronic are more methodical but often have little imagination. The polychronic seem more creative, but they are often messy and fickle. In the end, if you explore the biographies of great thinkers and writers, you will find that there were both polychronic and monochronic among them.

4 THE WORK PLAN AND THE INDEX CARDS

4.1 The Table of Contents as a Working Hypothesis

After you have conducted your bibliographical research, one of the first things you can do to begin *writing* your thesis is to compose the title, the introduction, and the table of contents—that is, exactly all those things that most authors do *at the end*. This advice seems paradoxical: why start from the end? For one thing, consider that the table of contents usually appears at the beginning of a work, so that the reader can immediately get an idea of what he will find as he reads. Similarly, if you begin writing your thesis by composing the table of contents, it may provide a clearer idea of what you must write. It can function as a working hypothesis, and it can be useful to immediately define the limits of your thesis.

You may object to this idea, realizing that as you proceed in the work, you will be forced to repeatedly revise this hypothetical table of contents, or perhaps rewrite it altogether. This is certainly true, but you will restructure it more effectively if you have a starting point from which to work. Imagine that you have a week to take a 600-mile car trip. Even if you are on vacation, you will not leave your house and indiscriminately begin driving in a random direction. You will make a rough plan. You may decide to take the Milan-Naples highway, with slight detours through Florence, Siena, Arezzo, possibly a longer stop in Rome, and also a visit to Montecassino. If you realize along the way that Siena takes you longer than anticipated, or that it is also worth visiting San Gimignano, you may decide to eliminate Montecassino. Once you arrive in

Arezzo, you may have the sudden, irrational, last-minute idea to turn east and visit Urbino, Perugia, Assisi, and Gubbio. This means that—for substantial reasons—you may change your itinerary in the middle of the voyage. But you will modify *that* itinerary, and not *no* itinerary.

So it happens with your thesis. Make yourself a provisional table of contents and it will function as your work plan. Better still if this table of contents is a summary, in which you attempt a short description of every chapter. By proceeding in this way, you will first clarify for yourself what you want to do. Secondly, you will be able to propose an intelligible project to your advisor. Thirdly, you will test the clarity of your ideas. There are projects that seem quite clear as long as they remain in the author's mind, but when he begins to write, everything slips through his fingers. He may have a clear vision of the starting and ending points, but then he may realize that he has no idea of how to get from one to the other, or of what will occupy the space between. A thesis is like a chess game that requires a player to plan in advance all the moves he will make to checkmate his opponent.

To be more precise, your work plan should include *the title*, *the table of contents*, and *the introduction*. Composing a good title is already a project. I am not talking about the title on the first page of the document that you will deliver to the Registrar's Office many months from now, one that will invariably be so generic as to allow for infinite variations. I am talking of the "secret title" of your thesis, the one that then usually appears as the subtitle. A thesis may have as its "public" title "Radio Commentary and the Attempted Murder of Palmiro Togliatti," but its subtitle (and its true topic) will be "Radio Commentators' Use of Gino Bartali's Tour de France Victory to Distract the Public from the Attempted Murder of Palmiro Togliatti." This is to say that after you have focused on a theme, you must decide to treat only one specific point within that theme. The formulation of this point constitutes a sort of *question*: has there in fact been a deliberate political use of a sport celebrity's victory to distract the public from the attempted murder of the Italian Communist Party leader Palmiro Togliatti? And can a content analysis of the radio news commentary reveal such an effort? In this way the secret title (turned into a question) becomes an essential part of the work plan.

After you have formulated this question, you must subdivide your topic into logical sections that will correspond to chapters in the table of contents. For example:

1. Critical Literature on the Topic
2. The Event
3. The Radio News
4. Quantitative Analysis of the News and Its Programming Schedule
5. Content Analysis of the News
6. Conclusions

Or you can plan a development of this sort:

1. The Event: Synthesis of the Various Sources of Information
2. Radio News Commentary on the Attempted Murder before Bartali's Victory
3. Radio News Commentary on the Attempted Murder over the Three Days Following Bartali's Victory
4. Quantitative Comparison between the Two Sets of News
5. Comparative Content Analysis of the Two Sets of News
6. Sociopolitical Evaluation

Ideally the table of contents should be more detailed than this example, as we have already said. If you wish, you can write it on a large sheet of paper with the titles in pencil, canceling them and substituting others as you proceed, so that you can track the phases of the reorganization.

Another method to compose the hypothetical table of contents is the tree structure:

1. Description of the Event

2. The Radio News ⋯⋯⋯⋯⋯⋯ A. From the Attempted Murder of Togliatti to Bartali's Victory
B. After Bartali's Victory

3. Etc.

This method allows you to add various branches. Whatever method you use, a hypothetical table of contents should contain the following:

1. The state of the issue,
2. The previous research,
3. Your hypothesis,
4. Your supporting data,
5. Your analysis of the data,
6. The demonstration of your hypothesis,
7. Conclusions and suggestions for further research.

The third phase of the work plan is to draft the introduction. The draft should consist of an analytical commentary related to the table of contents: "With this work we propose to demonstrate this thesis. The previous research has left many questions unanswered, and the data gathered is still insufficient. In the first chapter, we will attempt to establish this point; in the second chapter we will tackle this other point. In conclusion, we will attempt to demonstrate a, b, and c. We have set these specific limits for the work. Within these limits, we will use the following method." And so on.

The function of this fictitious introduction (fictitious, because you will rewrite it many times before you finish your thesis) is to allow you to give your ideas a primary direction that will not change, unless you consciously restructure the table of contents. This way, you will control your detours and your impulses. This introduction is also useful for telling your advisor *what you want to do*. But it is even more useful for determining *whether your ideas are organized*. Imagine an Italian student who graduates from high school, where he presumably learned to write because he was assigned an immense quantity of essays. Then he spends four, five, or six years at the university, where he is generally not required to write. When the time comes to write his thesis, he finds himself completely out of practice.[1] Writing his thesis will be a great shock, and it is a bad idea to postpone the writing process until the last minute. Since the student would ideally begin writing as soon as possible, it would be prudent for him to start by writing his own work plan.

Be careful, because until you are able to write a table of contents and an introduction, you cannot be sure that what you are writing is *your* thesis. If you cannot write the introduction, it means that you do not yet have clear ideas on how to begin. If you do in fact have clear ideas on how to begin, it is because you at least suspect where you will arrive. And it is precisely on the basis of this suspicion that you must write your introduction, as if it were a review of the already completed work. Also, do not be afraid to go too far with your introduction, as there will always be time to step back.

At this point, it should be clear that *you will continuously rewrite the introduction and the table of contents as you proceed in your work.* This is the way it is done. The final table of contents and introduction (those that will appear in the final manuscript) will be different from these first drafts. This is normal. If this were not the case, it would mean that all of your research did not inspire a single new idea. Even if you are determined enough to follow your precise plan from beginning to end, you will have missed the point of writing a thesis if you do not revise as you progress with your work.

What will distinguish the first from the final draft of your introduction? The fact that in the latter you will promise much less than you did in the former, and you will be much more cautious. The goal of the final introduction will be to help the reader penetrate the thesis. Ideally, in the final introduction you will avoid promising something that your thesis does not provide. The goal of a good final introduction is to so satisfy and enlighten the reader that he does not need to read any further. This is a paradox, but often a good introduction in a published book provides a reviewer with the right ideas, and prompts him to speak about the book as the author wished. But what if the advisor (or others) read the thesis and noticed that you announced in the introduction results that you did not realize? This is why the introduction must be cautious, and it must promise only what the thesis will then deliver.

The introduction also establishes the *center* and *periphery* of your thesis, a distinction that is very important, and not only for methodological reasons. Your committee will expect you to be significantly more comprehensive on what you have defined as the center than on what you have defined as the periphery. If, in a thesis on the partisan war in Monferrato, you establish that the center is the movements of the *badogliane* formations, the committee will forgive a few inaccuracies or approximations with regard to the *gari-baldine* brigades, but will require complete information on the Franchi and Mauri formations.[2] To determine the center of your thesis, you must make some decisions regarding the material that is available to you. You can do this during the bibliographical research process described in chapter 3, before you compose your work plan in the manner described at the beginning of this chapter.

By what logic should we construct our hypothetical table of contents? The choice depends on the type of thesis. In a historical thesis, you could have a *chronological* plan (for example, "The Persecutions of Waldensians in Italy"), or a *cause and effect* plan (for example, "The Causes of the Israeli-Palestinian Conflict"). You could also choose a *spatial* plan ("The Distribution of Circulating Libraries in the Canavese Geographical Region") or a *comparative-contrastive* plan ("Nationalism and Populism in Italian Literature in the Great War Period"). In an experimental thesis you could have an *inductive* plan, in which you would move from particular evidence to the proposal of a theory. A logical-mathematical thesis might require a *deductive* plan, beginning with the theory's proposal, and moving on to its possible applications to concrete examples. I would argue that the critical literature on your topic can offer you good examples of work plans, provided you use it critically, that is, by comparing the various approaches to find the example that best corresponds to the needs of your research question.

The table of contents already establishes the logical subdivision of the thesis into *chapters*, *sections*, and *subsections*. On the modalities of this subdivision see section 6.4. Here too, a good binary subdivision allows you to make additions without significantly altering the original order. For example:

1 Central Question
   1.1 Subquestions
      1.1.1 Principal Subquestion
      1.1.2 Secondary Subquestion
   1.2 Development of the Central Question
      1.2.1 First Ramification
      1.2.2 Second Ramification

You can also represent this structure as a tree diagram with lines that indicate successive ramifications, and that you may introduce without disturbing the work's general organization:

Table 4.1

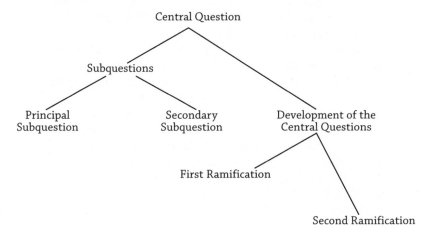

Once you have arranged the table of contents, you must make sure to *always correlate its various points to your index cards and any other documentation you are using.* These correlations must be clear from the beginning, and clearly displayed through abbreviations and/or colors, so that they can help you organize your cross-references. You have already seen examples of cross-references in this book. Often the author speaks of something that has already been treated in a previous chapter, and he refers, in parentheses, to the number of the chapter, section, or subsection. These cross-references avoid unnecessary repetition, and also demonstrate the cohesion of the work as a whole. A cross-reference can signify that the same concept is valid from two different points of view, that the same example demonstrates two different arguments, that what has been said in a general sense is also applicable to a specific point in the same study, and so on. A well-organized thesis should abound in cross-references. If there are none, it means that every chapter proceeds on its own, as if everything that has been said in the previous chapters no longer matters. There are undoubtedly thesis types (for example collections of documents) that can work this way, but cross-references should become necessary at least in their conclusions. A well-written hypothetical table of contents is the numerical grid that allows you to create cross-references, instead of needlessly shuffling through papers and notes to locate a specific topic. This is how I have written the very book you are reading.

So as to mirror the logical structure of the thesis (topic, center and periphery, ramifications, etc.), the table of contents must be articulated in chapters, sections, and subsections. To avoid long explanations, I suggest that you take a look at this book's table of contents. This book is rich in sections and subsections, and sometimes even more minute subdivisions not included in the table of contents. (For example, see section 3.2.3. These smaller subdivisions help the reader understand the argument.) The example below illustrates how a table of contents should mirror the logical structure of the thesis. If a section 1.2.1 develops as a corollary to 1.2, this must be graphically represented in the table of contents:

TABLE OF CONTENTS
1 The Subdivision of the Text
    1.1 The Chapters
        1.1.1 Spacing
        1.1.2 Indentation
    1.2 The Sections
        1.2.1 Different Kinds of Titles
        1.2.2 Possible Subdivision in Subsections
2 The Final Draft
    2.1 Typing Agency or Typing on Your Own
    2.2 The Cost of a Typewriter
3 The Bookbinding

This example also illustrates that the different chapters need not necessarily adhere to the same pattern of subdivision. The nature of the argument may require that one chapter be divided into many sub-subsections, while another can proceed swiftly and continuously under a general title.

A thesis may not require many divisions. Also, subdivisions that are too minute may interrupt the continuity of the argument. (Think, for example, of a biography.) But keep in mind that a detailed subdivision helps to control the subject, and allows readers to follow your argument. For example, if I see that an observation appears under subsection 1.2.2, I know immediately that it is something that refers to section 2 of chapter 1, and that it has the same importance as the observation under subsection 1.2.1.

One last observation: only after you have composed a solid table of contents may you allow yourself to begin writing other parts of your thesis, and at this point you are not required to start with the first chapter. In fact, usually a student begins to draft the part of his thesis about which he feels most confident, and for which he has gathered the best documentation. But he can do this only if, in the background, there is the table of contents providing a working hypothesis.

4.2   Index Cards and Notes

4.2.1   *Various Types of Index Cards and Their Purpose*

Begin to read the material as your bibliography grows. It is unrealistic to think that you will compile a complete bibliography before you actually begin to read. In practice, after putting together a preliminary list of titles, you can immerse yourself in these. Sometimes, before a student even starts a bibliography, he begins by reading a single book, and from its citations he begins to compile a bibliography. In any case, as you read books and articles, the references thicken, and the bibliography file that we have described in chapter 3 grows bigger.

Ideally, when you begin writing your thesis, you would have all the necessary books at home, both new and antique (and you would have a personal library, and a comfortable and spacious working environment where you can divide the books that you will be using into different piles, arranged on many tables). But this ideal condition is very rare, even for a professional scholar. In any case, let us imagine that you have been able to locate and purchase all the books that you need. In principle, the only index cards you will need at this point are the bibliographical cards I have described in section 3.2.2. You will prepare your work plan (i.e., the title, introduction, and table of contents) with your chapters and sections numbered progressively, and as you read the books you will underline them, and you will write in the margins the abbreviations of your table of contents' various chapters. Similarly, you will place a book's abbreviation and the page number near the chapters in your table of contents, so that you will know where to look for an idea or quote when the time comes for writing.

Let us look at a specific example. Suppose you write a thesis on "The Concept of Possible Worlds in American Science Fiction," and that subsection 4.5.6 of your plan is "The Time Warp as a Gateway to Possible Worlds." As you read chapter 21, page 132 of Robert Sheckley's *Mindswap* (New York: Delacorte Press, 1966), you will learn that Marvin's Uncle Max "stumbled into a time warp" while playing golf at the Fairhaven Country Club in Stanhope, and found himself transferred to the planet Celsus V. You will write the following in the margin:

T. (4.5.6) time warp

This note refers to a specific subsection of your thesis (you may in fact use the same book ten years later and take notes for another project, so it is a good idea to know to what project a note refers). Similarly, you will write the following in subsection 4.5.6 of your work plan:

cf. Scheckley, Mindswap, 132

In this area, you will already have noted references to Fredric Brown's *What Mad Universe* and Robert A. Heinlein's *The Door into Summer*.

However, this process makes a few assumptions: (a) that you have the book at home, (b) that you own it and therefore can underline it, and (c) that you have already formulated the work plan in its final form. Suppose you do not have the book, because it is rare and the only copy you can find is in the library; or you have it in your possession, but you have borrowed it and cannot underline it; or that you own it, but it might happen to be an incunabulum of inestimable value; or that, as we have already said, you must continually restructure the work plan as you go. Here you will run into difficulties. This last situation is the most common; as you proceed the plan grows and changes, and you cannot continuously revise the notes you have written in the margins of your books. Therefore these notes should be generic, for example, "possible worlds."

But how can you compensate for the imprecision of such a note? By creating *idea index cards* and keeping them in an *idea file*. You can use a series of index cards with titles such as "Parallelisms between Possible Worlds," "Inconsistencies," "Structure Variations," "Time Warps," etc. For example, the "Time Warps" card will contain a precise reference to the pages in which Sheckley discusses this concept. Afterward you can place all the references to time warps at the designated point of your final work plan, yet you can also move the index card, merge it with the others, and place it before or after another card in the file. Similarly, you might find it useful to create *thematic index cards* and the appropriate file, ideal for a thesis on the history of ideas. If your work on possible worlds in American science fiction explores the various ways in which different authors confronted various logical-cosmological problems, this type of file will be ideal.

But let us suppose that you have decided to organize your thesis differently, with an introductory chapter that frames the theme, and then a chapter for each of the principal authors (Sheckley, Heinlein, Asimov, Brown, etc.), or even a series of chapters each dedicated to an exemplary novel. In this case, you need an *author file*. The *author index card* "Sheckley" will contain the references needed to find the passages in which he writes about possible worlds. And you may also choose to divide this file into sections on "Time Warps," "Parallelisms," "Inconsistencies," etc.

Let us suppose instead that your thesis addresses the question in a much more theoretical way, using science fiction as a reference point but in fact discussing the logic of possible worlds. The science fiction references will be less systematic, and will instead serve as a source of entertaining quotes. In this case, you will need a *quote file*, where you will record on the "Time Warps" index card a particularly apt phrase from Sheckley; and on the "Parallelisms" index card, you will record Brown's description of two perfectly identical universes where the only variation is the lacing pattern of the protagonist's shoelaces. And so on.

But what if Sheckley's book is not currently available, but you remember reading it at a friend's house in another city, long before you envisioned a thesis that included themes of time warps and parallelism? In this case, you fortunately prepared a readings index card on *Mindswap* at your friend's house, including its bibliographical information, a general summary, a series of evaluations addressing its importance, and a series of quotes that at the time seemed particularly apt. (See sections 3.2.2 and 4.2.3 for more information on the readings file.)

So depending on the context, we can create index cards of various types: *connection index cards* that link ideas and sections of the work plan; *question index cards* dealing with how to confront a particular problem; *recommendation index cards* that note ideas provided by others, suggestions for further developments, etc. Each type of index card should have a different color, and should include in the top right corner abbreviations that cross-reference one series of cards to another, and to the general plan. The result is something majestic.

But must you really write all these index cards? Of course not. You can have a simple readings file instead, and collect all your other ideas in notebooks. You can limit yourself to the quote file because your thesis (for example, "The Feminine in Women Writers of the 1940s") starts from a very precise plan, has little critical literature to examine, and simply requires you to collect abundant textual material. As you can see, the nature of the thesis suggests the nature of the index cards.

My only suggestion is that a given file be complete and unified. For example, suppose that you have books by Smith, Rossi, Braun, and De Gomera at home, while in the library you have read books by Dupont, Lupescu, and Nagasaki. If you file only these three, and rely on memory (and on your confidence in their availability) for the other four, how will you proceed when the time comes to begin writing? Will you work half with books and half with index cards? And if you have to restructure your work plan, what materials will you need? Books, index cards, notebooks, or notes? Rather, it will be useful to file cards on Dupont, Lupescu, and Nagasaki in full and with an abundance of quotes, but also to create more succinct index cards for Smith, Rossi, Braun, and De Gomera, perhaps by documenting the page numbers of relevant quotes, instead of copying them in their entirety. At the very least, always work on homogeneous material that is easy to move and handle. This way, you will know at a glance what you have read and what remains to be read.

With that said, in some cases it is convenient and useful to put everything on index cards. Imagine a literary thesis in which you must find and comment on many significant quotes on the same topic, but originating from many different authors. Suppose your topic is "The Concept of Life as Art in Romantic and Decadent Writers." In table 4.2 you will find examples of four index cards that gather useful quotes on this topic. As you can see, each index card bears in the top left corner the abbreviation "QT" to distinguish it from other types of index cards, and then includes the theme "Life as Art." Why do I specify the theme even though I already know what it is? Because the thesis could develop so that "Life as Art" becomes only a part of the work; because this file could also serve me after the thesis and end up merged with a quote file on other themes; because I could find these cards 20 years later and ask myself what the devil they refer to. In addition to these two headings, I have noted the quote's author. In this case, the last name suffices because you are supposed to already have biographical index cards on these authors, or have written about them at the beginning of your thesis. Finally, the body of the index card bears the quote, however short or long it may be. (It could be short or very long.)

Let us look at the index card for Whistler. There is a quote in Italian followed by a question mark. This means that I found the sentence quoted in another author's book, but I am not sure where it comes from, whether it is correct, or whether the original is in English. After I started this card, I happened to find the original text, and I recorded it along

Table 4.2
QUOTE INDEX CARDS

```
    QT
    Life as Art
    Whistler

"Di solito la natura è sbagliata"
                        ?

Original

"Nature is usually wrong"

        J. A. McNeill Whistler

        The Gentle Art of Making Enemies

        xxbxxgxxixxbxx 1890
```

```
    QT
    Life as Art
    Th. Gautier

"In general, when a thing becomes useful, it ceases
to be beautiful"

        Préface des premières poésies (Preface
        to Premières poésies), 1832 ...
```

```
    QT
    Life as Art
    Villiers de l'Isle Adam

"As for living? Our servants will do that for us."

                          Axel ...
```

```
    QT
    Life as Art
    Oscar Wilde

"We can forgive a man for making a useful thing as
long as he does not admire it. The only excuse
for making a useless thing is that one admires it
intensely. All art is quite useless."


        Preface to The Picture of Dorian Gray.
        Edited by Isobel Murray.
        London: Oxford University Press, I974, xxxiv.
```

with the appropriate references. I can now use this index card for a correct citation.

Let us turn to the card for Villiers de l'Isle Adam. I have written the quote from the English translation of the French original.[3] I know what book it comes from, but the information is incomplete. This is a good example of an index card that I must complete. Similarly incomplete is the card for Gautier.[4] Wilde's index card is complete, however, with the original quote in English.

Now, I could have found Wilde's original quote in a copy of the book that I have at home, but shame on me if I neglected writing the index card, because I will forget about it by the time I am finishing my thesis. Shame on me also if I simply wrote on the index card "see page xxxiv" without copying the quote, because when the time comes to write my thesis, I will need all of the texts at hand in order to copy the exact quotations. Therefore, although writing index cards takes some time, it will save you much more in the end.

Table 4.3 shows an example of a connection index card for the thesis on metaphor in seventeenth-century treatise writers that we discussed in section 3.2.4. Here I used the abbreviation "Conn." to designate the type of card, and I wrote a topic that I will research in depth, "The Passage from the Tactile to the Visual." I do not yet know if this topic will become a chapter, a small section, a simple footnote, or even (why not?) the central topic of the thesis. I annotated some ideas that came to me from reading a certain author, and indicated the books to consult and the ideas to develop. As I page through my index cards once the first draft of my thesis is completed, I will see whether I have neglected an idea that was important, and I will need to make some decisions: revise the thesis to make this idea fit; decide that it was not worth developing; insert a footnote to show that I had the idea in mind, but did not deem its development appropriate for that specific topic. Once I have completed the thesis, I could also decide to dedicate my future research precisely to that idea. Remember that an index card file is an investment that you make during your thesis, but if you intend to keep studying, it will pay off years—and sometimes decades—later.

Table 4.3
CONNECTION INDEX CARD

```
Conn.
The Passage from the Tactile to the Visual


See Arnold Hauser, The Social History of Art, vol. 2,
Stanley Godman trans. in collaboration with the author
(New York: Vintage Books, 1951), 175. Here Hauser quotes
Wölfflin regarding the stylistic movement from the
tactile to the visual between the Renaissance and the
baroque: "(I) linear and painterly; (2) plane and
recession; (3) closed and open form; (4) clearness and
unclearness; (5) multiplidity and unity."
These ideas return in Raimondi's Il romanzo senza idillio
(The novel without an idyllic ending), but here they are
related to the recent theories of McLuhan
(The Gutenberg Galaxy) and Walter Ong.
```

I will not elaborate further on the various types of index cards. Let us limit ourselves to discussing how to organize the primary sources, along with the readings index cards of the secondary sources.

4.2.2 *Organizing the Primary Sources*

Readings index cards are useful for organizing critical literature. I would not use index cards, or at least not the same kind of index cards, to organize primary sources. In other words, if you compose a thesis on Joyce, you will naturally write index cards for all the books and articles on Joyce that you are able to find, but it would be strange to create index cards for *Ulysses* or *Finnegans Wake*. The same would apply if you wrote a thesis on articles of the Italian Civil Code, or a thesis in the history of mathematics on Felix Klein's Erlangen Program. Ideally you will always have the primary sources at hand. This is not difficult, as long as you are dealing with books by a classic author available in many good critical editions, or those by a contemporary author that are readily available on the market. In any case, the primary sources are an indispensable investment. You can underline a book or a series of books that *you* own, even in various colors. Let us talk briefly about underlining:

Underlining personalizes the book. The marks become traces of your interest. They allow you to return to the book even after a long period, and find at a glance what originally interested you. But you must underline sensibly. Some people underline everything, which is equivalent to not underlining at all. On the other hand, it is possible that on the same page there is information that interests you on different levels. In that case, it is essential to differentiate the underlining.

Use colors. Use markers with a fine point. Assign a color to each topic, and use the same colors on the work plan and the various index cards. This will be useful when you are drafting your work, because you will know right away that red refers to passages important for the first chapter, and green to those important for the second chapter.

Associate an abbreviation with each color (or use abbreviations instead of the colors). For example, going back to our topic of possible worlds in science fiction, use the abbreviation "TW" to signal everything pertinent to time warps, or "I" to mark inconsistencies between possible worlds. If your thesis concerns multiple authors, assign an abbreviation to each of them.

Use abbreviations to emphasize the relevance of information. A bracket with the annotation "IMP" can signify a *very important* passage, and you will not need to underline each individual line. "QT" will indicate not only that the passage is important, but that you also want to quote it in its entirety. "QT/TW" will indicate that the passage is an ideal quote to illustrate the question of time warps.

Use abbreviations to designate the passages you must reread. Some passages may seem obscure to you when you first read them. You can mark the top margins of these pages with a big "R," so that you know you must review them as you go deeper into the subject, and after other readings have clarified these ideas for you.

When should you not underline? When the book is not yours, obviously, or if it is a rare edition of great commercial value that you cannot modify without devaluing. In these cases, photocopy the important pages and underline those. Or get a small notebook where you can copy the salient passages, with your comments interspersed. Or develop a special file for the primary sources, although this would require a huge effort, because you would have to practically catalog the texts page by page. However, this can work if your thesis is on Alain-Fournier's *Le grand Meaulnes* (*The Wanderer*), a very short little book. But what if it is on Hegel's *The Science of Logic*? And what if, returning to our experiment in Alessandria's library (section 3.2.4), you must catalog the seventeenth-century edition of Tesauro's *Cannocchiale aristotelico*? You will have to resort to photocopies and the aforementioned notebook, annotated throughout with colors and abbreviations.

Supplement the underlining with adhesive page markers. Copy the abbreviations and colors on the portion of the marker that sticks out from the pages.

Beware the "alibi of photocopies"! Photocopies are indispensable instruments. They allow you to keep with you a text you have already read in the library, and to take home a text you have not read yet. But a set of photocopies can become an alibi. A student makes hundreds of pages of photocopies and takes them home, and the manual labor he exercises in doing so gives him the impression that he possesses the work. Owning the photocopies exempts the student from actually reading them. This sort of vertigo of accumulation, a neocapitalism of information, happens to many. Defend yourself from this trap: as soon as you have the photocopy, read it and annotate it immediately. If you are not in a great hurry, do not photocopy something new before you *own* (that is, before you have read and annotated) the previous set of photocopies. There are many things that I *do not know* because I photocopied a text and then relaxed as if I had read it.

If the book is yours and it does not have antiquarian value, do not hesitate to annotate it. Do not trust those who say that you must respect books. You respect books by using them, not leaving them alone. Even if the book is unmarked, you won't make much money reselling it to a bookseller, so you may as well leave traces of your ownership.

4.2.3   The Importance of Readings Index Cards

Among all the types of index cards we have discussed, the most common and the most *indispensable* are the readings index cards. These are where you precisely annotate all the references contained in a book or article, transcribe key quotes, record your evaluation, and append other observations. In short, the readings index card perfects the bibliographical index card described in section 3.2.2. The latter contains only the information useful for tracking down the book, while the former contains all the information on a book or article, and therefore must be *much larger*. You can use standard formats or make your own cards, but in general they should correspond to half a letter-size (or half an A4-size) sheet. They should be made of cardboard, so that you can easily page through them in the index card box, or gather them into a pack bound with a rubber band. They should be made of a material appropriate for both a ballpoint and a fountain pen, so that they do not absorb or diffuse the ink, but instead allow the pen to run smoothly. Their structure should be more or less that of the model index cards proposed in tables 4.4 through 4.11.

Nothing prohibits you from filling up many index cards, and this might actually be a good idea for important books. The cards should be numbered consecutively, and the front of each card should bear abbreviated information about the book or article in question. There are many ways to catalog the book on your readings index card. Your method also depends on your memory, as there are people who have poor memories and need to write everything, and others who only require a quick note. Let us say that the following is the standard method:

1. *Record precise bibliographical information* that is, if possible, more complete than that you have recorded on the bibliographical index card. The latter helped you locate the book, while the readings index card will help you talk about

the book and cite it properly in the final bibliography. You should have the book in your hands when you write the readings index card, so that you can obtain all the available information, such as the edition, the publisher's information, etc.

2. *Record the author's information*, if he is not a well-known authority.

3. *Write a short (or long) summary of the book or article.*

4. *Transcribe the full text of passages you wish to quote* (assuming you are not already using a quote file for this purpose). Use quotation marks and note precisely the page number or numbers. You may also want to record extra quotes to provide context when you are writing. Be sure not to confuse a quote with a paraphrase! (See section 5.3.2.)

5. *Record your personal comments throughout your summary.* To avoid mistaking them for the author's own thoughts, write your comments inside square brackets, and in color.

6. *Mark the card with the appropriate abbreviation or color so that it clearly corresponds to the correct section of your work.* If your card refers to multiple sections, write multiple abbreviations. If it refers to the thesis as a whole, designate this somehow.

So that we can avoid further generalities, let me provide some practical examples. In tables 4.4 through 4.11 you will find some examples of readings index cards. Instead of inventing topics and methods, I retrieved the index cards from my own thesis, "The Aesthetics of Thomas Aquinas." My filing method is not necessarily the best one. These index cards provide an example of *a* method that facilitated different types of index cards. You will see that I was not as precise as I recommend that you be. Much information is missing, while other information is excessively elliptical. In fact I learned some of the lessons in this book later in my career, but it is not a given that you should make the same mistakes that I did. I have not altered the style or obscured the naïveté of these examples, and you can take them for what they are worth. (Notice that I only provide examples of index cards on which an entire work fit. To preserve space, I do *not* provide examples of index cards referring to what became the main sources of my work, because each of these required *ten index cards*.) Let us go over these examples one by one:

Croce index card: This was a short review, important because of the author. Since I had already found the book reviewed, I copied only this single, significant opinion. Look at the final squared brackets: that statement represents exactly what I did in my thesis, two years later.

Biondolillo index card: This is a polemical index card, showing all the irritation of the neophyte who sees his argument scorned. I found it necessary to record my ideas this way, perhaps to insert a polemical note in my work.

Glunz index card: I quickly consulted with a German friend who helped me understand precisely what this thick book discussed. This book did not have immediate relevance to my work, but it was perhaps worthy of a note.

Maritain index card: I already knew *Art and Scholasticism*, this author's fundamental work, but I did not find him very trustworthy. At the end of the card, I made a note that would remind me not to trust the accuracy of his quotes without a subsequent check.

Chenu index card: This is a short essay by a serious scholar on a very important theme in my work, and I squeezed as much juice from it as I could. This essay was the classic case of an indirect source; I noted only what I could then check directly. This card was more of a bibliographical supplement than a readings index card.

Curtius index card: An important book that I consulted only for a particular section. I was in a hurry, so I only skimmed the rest of the book. I did return to it and read it later for other purposes, after I completed my thesis.

Marc index card: An interesting article from which I extracted the juice.

Segond index card: This is what we might call a "disposal" index card, as its purpose was essentially to remind me that I did not need this source for my thesis.

As you can see, I used abbreviations in the top right corner of these cards in the manner I have described above. In fact,

Table 4.4
READINGS
INDEX
CARD

Croce, Benedetto.   Th. Gen. (r)
Recensione a Nelson Sella, Estetica musicale in S. Tommaso d'Aquino (Review of
Nelson Sella's Musical aesthetics in St. Thomas Aquinas).
La critica ~~rivi~~ (1931): 7I. (see index card)

Croce praises Sella's care and the modernity of his aesthetic theories in dealing
with the topic. But moving on to A., Croce states:
"...the fact is that A.'s ideas on beauty and on art are not false, but rather
very general, and therefore it is always possible, in a sense, to accept them or
adopt them. Such are the ideas that assign to pulchritude or beauty the integrity
(or perfection or consonance), and the brightness (that is, the clearity of
colors). Such is the idea that beauty concerns cognitive power, and such is the
doctrine that a creature's beauty is a likeness of the divine beauty shared onto
things. The essential point is that aesthetics did not constitute an object of
interest either for the Middle Ages in general, or in particular for Aquinas, who
labored himself with other questions: whence this satisfaction with generalities.
And therefore it is usually irritating and fruitless to page through critical
works on the aesthetics of Aquinas and other medieval philosophers, unless they are
written with Sella's discreetness and grace (but usually this is not the case)."

[I might refute this thesis for an introductory argument. I might use
the closing words as a claim]

Table 4.5
READINGS
INDEX
CARD

Biondolillo, Francesco.   St. Gen (r)
"L'estetica e il gusto nel Medioevo" (Aesthetics and taste in the Middle Ages).
Chap. 2 in _Breve storia del gusto e del pensiero estetico_ (Short history of taste
and aesthetic thought). Messina: Principato, 1924.

Biondolillo or On Myopic Gentilianism.

Let us pass over the introduction, a vulgarization for young souls of philosopher
Giovanni Gentile's thought. Let us see instead the chapter on the Middle Ages:
Biondolillo dismisses A. on p. 29 in 18 lines. "In the Middle Ages, when
philosophy was considered the handmaiden of theology ... the question of art had
lost the importance originally bestowed upon it by the works of Aristotle and
Plotinus" [Biondolillo's lack of culture or bad faith? His fault or the fault of
his school of thought? Let us proceed:] "We have reached Dante in his maturity who
in the Convivio (2.1) attributed to art as many as four meanings [Biondolillo
expounds the theory of the four senses not knowing that Bede had already done it; he
does not know a thing] ... Dante and others believed that this fourfold meaning
resided in the _Divine Comedy_, but instead the poem has artistic value only when, or
rather only because, it is the pure and disinterested expression of a singular
inner world, and Dante fully loses himself in his vision." [Poor Italy! And poor
Dante! He labors all his life to search for figurative senses, and this guy says
that there were none. Cite this as a historiographic monstrosity.]

Table 4.6
READINGS
INDEX
CARD

Glunz, H. H.   Th.Gen.Lett. (r, b)

Die Literarästhetik des europäischen Mittelalters (The aesthetics of literature in
the European Middle Ages). Bochum-Langendreer: Pöppinghaus, 1937.

Aesthetic sensibility existed in the Middle Ages, and the works of medieval poets
must be seen in light of this sensibility. The center of the study is the poet's
awareness of his own art. It lays out an evolution of medieval literary taste:

7th and 8th c. ← medieval writers first insert Christian doctrines into the empty
                  forms of classical antiquity

9th and 10th c.← medieval writers use ancient tales to illustrate Christian ethics

11th c.   ← the Christian ethos proper appears in liturgical works, in saints'
                   lives, and in paraphrases of the Bible. The concept of the
                   afterlife becomes more prevalent.

12th c.   ← Neoplatonism leads to a more human vision of the world: the idea of
                   God becomes pervasive (in love, professional activities, nature).
                   The allegorical current develops (from Alcuin to the Victorines and
                   beyond).

14th c.   ← Despite remaining at the service of God, poetry changes from moral
                   to aesthetic. As God expresses Himself in the creation, so the poet
                   expresses himself, his thoughts, and feelings (England, Dante, etc.)

De Bruyne reviews this book in Re. néosc. de phil. 1938. He says that this
chronological division of the evolution of medieval sensibility is precarious
because the various stages are always simultaneously present [this is the thesis of
his Études: I should distrust his lack of historical awareness; he believes too
much in the Philosophia Perennis] The medieval artistic civilization is polyphonic.

ℱℓ Glunz 2

De Bruyne criticizes Glunz because he mostly ignoredᴜ the formal pleasure of
poetry; medieval writers had a very keen sense of this, as the poetic arts show.
Also according to De Bruyne, this literary aesthetics was part of a more
general aesthetic vision that Glunz neglected, an aesthetics where the
Pythagorean theory of proportions, Augustinian qualitative aesthetics (modus,
species, and ordo), and Dionysian aesthetics (claritas, lux) converged. The
whole theory was sustained by the psychology of the Victorines and the Christian
vision of the universe.

Table 4.7
READINGS
INDEX
CARD

Maritain, Jacques.
"Signe et symbole" (Sign and Symbol).

Th. Simb (v)

Revue Thomiste (April 1938): 299-330.

Hoping that an in-depth study of the topic (from the Middle Ages to the present) will appear sometime in the future, Maritain intends to deal with the philosophical theory of the sign and the reflections on the magical sign. [Unbearable as usual: he modernizes without doing philology. So for example, he does not go back to A., but rather to John of St. Thomas!] He develops John's theory (see my index card), "Signum est id quod repraesentat aliud a se potentiae cognoscenti" (Log. 2.P.21.I). "(Signum) essentialiter consistit in ordine ad signatum"

But the sign is not always the image, and vice versa (the Son is the image and not the sign of the Father, and a scream is the sign and not the image of pain). John adds, "Ratio ergo imaginis consistit in hoc quod procedat ab alio ut a principio, et in similitudine ejus, ut docet St. Thomas I.35 and XCXIII" (???)
Then Maritain says that the symbol is a sign-image: "quelque chose de sensible signifiant un objet en raison d'une rélation presupposée d'analogie" (303).
He suggests I check A., De Ver. 8.5 and C.G. 3.49.
Maritain then develops some ideas on the formal sign, the instrumental sign, and the practical sign, etc.; and on the sign as an act of magic (a very well documented part).
He barely touches on art [but here there are already the hints at the unconscious and deep roots of art that will return in his later work, Creative Intuition].
What follows is interesting for a Thomistic interpretation: "... dans l'oeuvre

Maritain 2

d'art se rencontrent le signe spéculatif (l'oeuvre manifeste autre chose
qu'elle) et le signe poétique (elle communique un ordre, un appel); non
qu'elle soit formellement signe pratique, mais c'est un signe spéculatif qui
par surabondance est virtuellement pratique: ▬ et elle-même, sans le
vouloir, et à condition de ne pas le vouloir, est aussi une sorte de signe
magique (elle séduit, elle ensorcelle)" (329).

NB Do not trust Maritain's quotes without checking them!

Table 4.8
READINGS
INDEX
CARD

Chenu, M.D.   Th. Im. fant. (s)

"Imaginatio: Note de lexicographie philosophique" (Imaginatio: A note on philosophical
lexicography). In Miscellanea Mercati, vol. 2, 593-602. Vatican City, 1946.

Various senses of the term imaginatio, first and foremost the Augustinian one:
"Imaginatio est vis animae, quae per figuram corporearum rerum absente corpore sine
exteriori sensu dignoscit" (chap. 38 of the De ▶ spiritu et anima that we can
attribute in part to Isaac of Stella, and in part to Hugh of Saint Victor and others).
In his De unione corporis et spiritus (PL 227.285), Hugh discusses how the imaginatio
accomplishes the sublimation of sensory data into intelligible data. In this mystical
perspective the spiritual enlightenment and the dynamic series of the powers are
called formatio. The role of the imaginatio in this process of mystical formatio also
returns in Bonaventure's Itinerarium: sensus, imaginatio (= sensualitas), ratio,
intellectus, intelligentia, apex mentis. Imaginatio participates in the formation of
the intelligible, the object of the intellectus, whereas the intelligentia,
completely free of sensible bonds, grasps the intellectibile.
Boethius adopts the same distinction. The intelligibile is the tangible world,
whereas the intellectibile is God, the ideas, the hyle (matter), and the first
principles. See Comm. in Isag. Porph. I.3. Hugh of Saint Victor in the Didasc.
summarizes this position. Gilbert de la Porrée mentions that many use the term opinio
to refer to imaginatio and intellectus, as does William of Conches. The imago is
forma immersed in matter, not pure form.

Chenu 2

And now Aquinas!

For him, in agreement with the Arabs (De ver. I4.I), the imago is apprehensio
quidditatis simplicis, quae alio nomine formatio dicitur (in I Sent. I9.5.I ad 7).
[But then it is the simplex apprehensio!!!] Imaginatio is a translation of the Arab
term "taṣawor." The latter is derived from "ṣurat" (image), a term that also means
form, and that comes from the verb "ṣawara" (to form, to forge; also to paint and
to conceive). [Very important, I must review!!!]
Aristotle's νόησις becomes formatio: the act of forming in oneself the
representation of the thing.

For this reason in A. (I Sent. 8.I.9), "Primo quod cadit in imaginatione intellectus
est ens." Then Aristotle's De Anima introduces the well-known definition of phantasia
(imagination). But ~~~~ ~~~~~~ for medieval people, phantasia meant sensus
communis, and imaginatio was the virtus cogitativa.
Only Gundissalinus tries to argue: sensus communis = virtus imaginativa = phantasia.
[What a mess! Check everything]

Table 4.9
READINGS
INDEX
CARD

Th. gen

Curtius, Ernst Robert.
European Literature and the Latin Middle Ages. Translated by Willard R. Trask.
New York: Pantheon Books, 1953. Originally published as Europäische Literatur und lateinisches Mittelalter (Bern: Franke, 1948).
(in particular chap. 12, sec. 3)

Great book. For now I only need p. 224.
It attempts to demonstrate that a concept of poetry in all its dignity, revelatory capacity, and capacity to investigate truth was unknown to the Scholastics, but was alive in Dante and in the fourteenth-century writers. [Here he is correct.]
For example, in Albert the Great the scientific mode (modus definitionis, divisivus, collectivus) is opposed to the poetic mode of the bible (stories, parables, metaphors). The modus poeticus is considered the weakest of the philosophical modes. [There is something similar in A., go check!!!]
In fact, Curtius refers to A. (I.I.9 ad I) and to the distinction of poetry as infima doctrina. (See index cards.)
In short, scholasticism has never been interested in poetry and has never produced any poetics [although this is true for scholasticism, it is not true for the Middle Ages in general] or any art theory [this is not true]. Attempting to draw from it an aesthetic theory of literature and the plastic arts is therefore senseless and useless.
The author condemns this attempt on p. 224n20: "When Scholasticism speaks of beauty, the word is used to indicate an attribute of God. The metaphysics of beauty

Curtius 2

(e.g., in Plotinus) and theories of art have nothing whatever to do with each other. [This is true, but they meet on the neutral grounds of a theory of form!] 'Modern' man immeasurably overvalues art because he has lost the sense of intelligible beauty that Neoplatonism and the Middle Ages possessed. 'Sero te amavi, pulchritudo tam antiqua et tam nova, sero te amavi,' says Augustine to God (Conf., X.27.38). Here beauty is meant of which aesthetics knows nothing." [Indeed, but what about the question of the divine beauty's participation in beings?]

[Attention: this guy is not like Biondolillo! He does not know certain connecting philosophical texts, but he knows what he is talking about. Refute him with respect.]

Table 4.10
READINGS
INDEX
CARD

Marc, A.

"La methode d'opposition en ontologie thomiste" (The method of opposition in

Thomistic ontology). Revue Néoscolastique 33 (1931): 149-169.

Th. Tom Gen Trasc (r)

Despite being a theoretical article, it contains useful hints.

The Thomistic system is structured like a game of oppositions that gives it life. From

the primal idea of being (in which the spirit and the real meet in a cognitive act

attaining the first reality which exceeds them both), to the transcendentals seen in

mutual opposition: identity and diversity, unity and multiplicity, contingency and

necessity, being and not-being become Unity. Being in relation to the intelligence as

inner experience is Truth, in relation to the truth as exterior appetibility is Good:

"une notion synthétique concilie en elle divers aspects et révèle l'être rélatif à la

fois à l'intelligence et à la volonté, interieur et exterieur à l'esprit: c'est
                                    ces

le Beau. A la simple connaissance il ajoute la complaisance et la joie, tout comme

il ajoute au bien la connaissance: il est la bonté du vrai, le verité du bien;

la splendeur de tous les transcendentaux reunis"—quoted from Maritain (154).

The demonstration continues with this line of development:

Marc 2

Being:

   a. Transcendentals

   2. Analogy as the composition of multiplicity into unity

       Act and potency   [here he is very close to Grenet, or vice versa]

       Being and essence

   3. Predicaments: Being is in the measure in which we affirm it—and we affirm it

       in the measure in which it is

       Substance: individuation etc.

       <u>The relation</u>

Unity is reached through the opposition and the composition of all the opposites.

What was a scandal for thought nevertheless made it systematic.

[Use this text for some ideas on the transcendentals. Use Marc's ideas on joy and

pleasure for my chapter on the concept of aesthetic vision, according to which

pulchra dicuntur quae visa placent]

Segond, Joseph.
"Esthétique de la lumière et de l'ombre" (The aesthetics of light and shadow).   Th. Lux, Clar. (g)
Revue Thomiste 45 (1939): 743-748

A study on light and shadow intended in a physical sense. No references to
the Thomistic doctrine.
Of no interest to me.

Table 4.11
READINGS
INDEX
CARD

the lower-case letters in parentheses replace colored points that were on the original cards. There is no need for me to explain exactly to what these referred; it is only important to note that I used them to organize my cards.

4.2.4 *Academic Humility*

Do not let this subsection's title frighten you. It is not an ethical disquisition. It concerns reading and filing methods.

You may have noticed that on one of the cards, as a young scholar, I teased the author Biondolillo by dismissing him in a few words. I am still convinced that I was justified in doing so, because the author attempted to explain the important topic of the aesthetics of Thomas Aquinas in only 18 lines. This case was extreme, but I filed the card on the book, and I noted the author's opinion anyway. I did this not only because we must record all the opinions expressed on our topic, but also because *the best ideas may not come from the major authors*. And now, to prove this, I will tell you the story of the abbot Vallet.

To fully understand this story, I should explain the question that my thesis posed, and the interpretive stumbling block that obstructed my work for about a year. Since this problem is not of general interest, let us say succinctly that for contemporary aesthetics, the moment of the perception of beauty is generally an intuitive moment, but for St. Thomas the category of intuition did not exist. Many contemporary interpreters have striven to demonstrate that he had somehow talked about intuition, and in the process they did violence to his work. On the other hand, St. Thomas's moment of the perception of objects was so rapid and instantaneous that it did not explain the enjoyment of complex aesthetic qualities, such as the contrast of proportions, the relationship between the essence of a thing and the way in which this essence organizes matter, etc. The solution was (and I arrived at it only a month before completing my thesis) in the discovery that aesthetic contemplation lay in the much more complex act of judgment. But St. Thomas did not explicitly say this. Nevertheless, the way in which he spoke of the contemplation of beauty could only lead to this conclusion. Often this is precisely the scope of interpretive research: to bring an author to say explicitly what he did not say, but that he could not have avoided saying had the question been posed to him. In other words, to show how, by comparing the various statements, that answer must emerge, in the terms of the author's scrutinized thought. Maybe the author did not give the answer because he thought it obvious, or because—as in the case of St. Thomas—he had never organically treated the question of aesthetics, but always discussed it incidentally, taking the matter for granted.

Therefore, I had a problem, and none of the authors I was reading helped me solve it (although if there was anything original in my thesis, it was precisely this question, with the answer that was to come out of it). And one day, while I was wandering disconsolate and looking for texts to aid me, I found at a stand in Paris a little book that attracted me at first for its beautiful binding. I opened it and found that it was a book by a certain abbot Vallet, titled *L'idée du Beau dans la philosophie de Saint Thomas d'Aquin* (The idea of beauty in the philosophy of St. Thomas Aquinas) (Louvain, 1887). I had not found it in any bibliography. It was the work of a minor nineteenth-century author. Naturally I purchased it (and it was even inexpensive). I began to read it, and I realized that the abbot Vallet was a poor fellow who repeated preconceived ideas and did not discover anything new. If I continued to read him, it was not for "academic humility," but for pure stubbornness, and to recoup the money I had spent. (I did not know such humility yet, and in fact I learned it reading that book. The abbot Vallet was to become my great mentor.) I continued reading, and at a certain point—almost in parentheses, said probably unintentionally, the abbot not realizing his statement's significance—I found a reference to the theory of judgment linked to that of beauty. Eureka! I had found the key, provided by the poor abbot Vallet, who had died a hundred years before, who was long since forgotten, and yet who still had something to teach to someone willing to listen.

This is academic humility: the knowledge that anyone can teach us something. Perhaps this is because we are so clever that we succeed in having someone less skilled than us teach us something; or because even someone who does not seem

very clever to us has some hidden skills; or also because
someone who inspires us may not inspire others. The reasons are many. The point is that we must listen with respect
to anyone, without this exempting us from pronouncing our
value judgments; or from the knowledge that an author's
opinion is very different from ours, and that he is ideologically very distant from us. But even the sternest opponent
can suggest some ideas to us. It may depend on the weather,
the season, and the hour of the day. Perhaps, had I read the
abbot Vallet a year before, I would not have caught the hint.
And who knows how many people more capable than I had
read him without finding anything interesting. But I learned
from that episode that if I wanted to do research, as a matter
of principle I should not exclude any source. This is what I
call academic humility. Maybe this is hypocritical because it
actually requires pride rather than humility, but do not linger
on moral questions: whether pride or humility, practice it.

5   WRITING THE THESIS

5.1   The Audience

To whom do you speak when you write your thesis? To your advisor? To all the students or scholars who will have the chance to consult the work in the future? To the general public of nonspecialists? Should you conceive the thesis as a book that will find its way into the hands of thousands of readers, or as a learned report to an academic institution? These are important questions because they concern first and foremost the expository form that you will give to your work, but they also concern the level of internal clarity that you hope to achieve.

Let us immediately eliminate a misunderstanding: it is a common belief that a popular work, where the topic is explained so that anyone can understand it, requires less skill than a specialized scientific report that expresses itself through formulas intelligible only to a few privileged readers. This is not completely true. Certainly the discovery of Einstein's equation $E = mc^2$ required much more ingenuity than, for example, even the most brilliant physics textbook. But usually works that do not affably explain the terms they use (and that rely instead on winks and nods) reveal authors who are more insecure than those who make every reference and every step explicit. If you read the great scientists or the great critics you will see that, with a few exceptions, they are quite clear and are not ashamed of explaining things well.

Let us then say that a thesis is a work that, for pragmatic reasons, you should address to your advisor, but that is also meant to be read and consulted by others, even scholars who are not well versed in that particular discipline. So, in a philosophy thesis, it will certainly not be necessary to begin by explaining what philosophy is, and similarly it will not be necessary to explain what a volcano is in a thesis on volcanology. But immediately below this level of obvious knowledge, you should provide the readers with all the information they need to understand your thesis.

First of all, *it is necessary to define your terms*, unless they are irrefutable canonical terms of the discipline. In a thesis on formal logic, I will not have to define the term "implication," but in a thesis on the philosopher Clarence Irving Lewis's notion of "strict implication," I will have to define the difference between this term and "material implication." In a thesis in linguistics, I will not have to define the notion of "phoneme," unless my topic is the definition of the term as used by the linguist Roman Jakobson. Yet if I use the word "sign" in this same thesis in linguistics, it might not be a bad idea to define this term, because different authors use it to define different entities. Therefore, as a general rule, *define all the technical terms used as key categories in your argument*.

Secondly, we must not necessarily presume that the readers have done the work that we have done. If we have written a thesis on Cavour, one of the major figures in the unification of Italy, our readers may already be familiar with him. But if our thesis is on a less widely known patriot like Felice Cavallotti, it may not be a bad idea to remind the readers, if only succinctly, when he lived, when he was born, and how he died. As I write, I have in front of me two theses in the humanities: one on Giovanni Battista Andreini and the other on Pierre Rémond de Sainte-Albine. I would be willing to wager that, in a group of 100 university professors that includes many experts in the humanities, only a small percentage would be familiar with these two minor authors. Now, the first thesis gets off to a bad start with the following sentence:

> The history of studies on Giovan Battista Andreini begins with a list of his works compiled by Leone Allacci, theologian and scholar of Greek origin (Chios 1586–Rome 1669) who contributed to the history of theater. ...

You can imagine the disappointment of readers expecting an introduction to Andreini, and who instead must wade through biographical information about Allacci. But the author of the thesis may respond, "Andreini is the hero of my thesis!" Exactly, and if he is your hero, hurry up and introduce him to your readers, and do not trust the fact that the advisor knows who he is. This is not simply a private letter to the advisor, it is potentially a book meant for humanity. The second thesis begins more appropriately:

> The object of our thesis is a text that appeared in France in 1747, written by an author who left very few other traces of himself, Pierre Rémond de Sainte-Albine. ...

It then proceeds to introduce the text and its importance. To me, this seems like the correct way to begin. I know that Sainte-Albine lived in the eighteenth century and that, if I don't know much about him, I am excused by the fact that he left few traces of his life.

5.2   How to Write

Once we have decided *to whom* to write (to humanity, not to the advisor), we must decide *how* to write, and this is quite a difficult question. If there were exhaustive rules, we would all be great writers. I could at least recommend that you rewrite your thesis many times, or that you take on other writing projects before embarking on your thesis, because writing is also a question of training. In any case, I will provide some general suggestions:

You are not Proust. Do not write long sentences. If they come into your head, write them, but then break them down. Do not be afraid to repeat the subject twice, and stay away from too many pronouns and subordinate clauses. Do not write,

> The pianist Wittgenstein, brother of the well-known philosopher who wrote the *Tractatus Logico-Philosophicus* that today many consider the masterpiece of contemporary philosophy, happened to have Ravel write for him a concerto for the left hand, since he had lost the right one in the war.

Write instead,

> The pianist Paul Wittgenstein was the brother of the philos-
> opher Ludwig Wittgenstein. Since Paul was maimed of his
> right hand, the composer Maurice Ravel wrote a concerto for
> him that required only the left hand.

Or,

> The pianist Paul Wittgenstein was the brother of the famous
> philosopher, author of the *Tractatus*. The pianist had lost his
> right hand in the war. For this reason the composer Maurice
> Ravel wrote a concerto for him that required only the left
> hand.

Do not write,

> The Irish writer had renounced family, country, and church,
> and stuck to his plans. It can hardly be said of him that he
> was a politically committed writer, even if some have men-
> tioned Fabian and "socialist" inclinations with respect to
> him. When World War II erupted, he tended to deliberately
> ignore the tragedy that shook Europe, and he was preoccu-
> pied solely with the writing of his last work.

Rather write,

> Joyce had renounced family, country, and church. He stuck
> to his plans. We cannot say that Joyce was a "politically com-
> mitted" writer even if some have gone so far as describing
> a Fabian and "socialist" Joyce. When World War II erupted,
> Joyce deliberately ignored the tragedy that shook Europe.
> His sole preoccupation was the writing of *Finnegans Wake*.

Even if it seems "literary," please do not write,

> When Stockhausen speaks of "clusters," he does not have in
> mind Schoenberg's series, or Webern's series. If confronted,
> the German musician would not accept the requirement to
> avoid repeating any of the twelve notes before the series has
> ended. The notion of the cluster itself is structurally more
> unconventional than that of the series. On the other hand
> Webern followed the strict principles of the author of *A
> Survivor from Warsaw*. Now, the author of *Mantra* goes well

beyond. And as for the former, it is necessary to distinguish between the various phases of his oeuvre. Berio agrees: it is not possible to consider this author as a dogmatic serialist.

You will notice that, at some point, you can no longer tell who is who. In addition, defining an author through one of his works is logically incorrect. It is true that lesser critics refer to Alessandro Manzoni simply as "the author of *The Betrothed*," perhaps for fear of repeating his name too many times. (This is something manuals on formal writing apparently advise against.) But the author of *The Betrothed* is not the biographical character Manzoni in his totality. In fact, in a certain context we could say that there is a notable difference between the author of *The Betrothed* and the author of *Adelchi*, even if they are one and the same biographically speaking and according to their birth certificate. For this reason, I would rewrite the above passage as follows:

> When Stockhausen speaks of a "cluster," he does not have in mind either the series of Schoenberg or that of Webern. If confronted, Stockhausen would not accept the requirement to avoid repeating any of the twelve notes before the end of the series. The notion of the cluster itself is structurally more unconventional than that of the series. Webern, by contrast, followed the strict principles of Schoenberg, but Stockhausen goes well beyond. And even for Webern, it is necessary to distinguish among the various phases of his oeuvre. Berio also asserts that it is not possible to think of Webern as a dogmatic serialist.

You are not e. e. cummings. Cummings was an American avant-garde poet who is known for having signed his name with lower-case initials. Naturally he used commas and periods with great thriftiness, he broke his lines into small pieces, and in short he did all the things that an avant-garde poet can and should do. But you are not an avant-garde poet. Not even if your thesis is on avant-garde poetry. If you write a thesis on Caravaggio, are you then a painter? And if you write a thesis on the style of the futurists, please do not write as a futurist writes. This is important advice because nowadays many tend to write "alternative" theses, in which the rules of critical discourse are not respected. But the language of the thesis is a *metalanguage*, that is, a language that speaks of other languages. A psychiatrist who describes the mentally ill does not express himself in the manner of his patients. I am not saying that it is wrong to express oneself in the manner of the so-called mentally ill. In fact, you could reasonably argue that they are the only ones who express themselves the way one should. But here you have two choices: either you do not write a thesis, and you manifest your desire to break with tradition by refusing to earn your degree, perhaps learning to play the guitar instead; or you write your thesis, but then you must explain to everyone *why* the language of the mentally ill is not a "crazy" language, and to do it you must use a metalanguage intelligible to all. The pseudo-poet who writes his thesis in poetry is a pitiful writer (and probably a bad poet). From Dante to Eliot and from Eliot to Sanguineti, when avant-garde poets wanted to talk about their poetry, they wrote in clear prose. And when Marx wanted to talk about workers, he did not write as a worker of his time, but as a philosopher. Then, when he wrote *The Communist Manifesto* with Engels in 1848, he used a fragmented journalistic style that was provocative and quite effective. Yet again, *The Communist Manifesto* is not written in the style of *Capital*, a text addressed to economists and politicians. Do not pretend to be Dante by saying that the poetic fury "dictates deep within," and that you cannot surrender to the flat and pedestrian metalanguage of literary criticism.[1] Are you a poet? Then do not pursue a university degree. Twentieth-century Italian poet Eugenio Montale does not have a degree, and he is a great poet nonetheless. His contemporary Carlo Emilio Gadda (who held a degree in engineering) wrote fiction in a unique style, full of dialects and stylistic idiosyncrasies; but when he wrote a manual for radio news writers, he wrote a clever, sharp, and lucid "recipe book" full of clear and accessible prose.[2] And when Montale writes a critical article, he writes so that all can understand him, including those who do not understand his poems.

Begin new paragraphs often. Do so when logically necessary, and when the pace of the text requires it, but the more you do it, the better.

Write everything that comes into your head, but only in the first draft. You may notice that you get carried away with your inspiration, and you lose track of the *center* of your topic. In this case, you can remove the parenthetical sentences and the digressions, or you can put each in a note or an *appendix* (see section 6.3). Your thesis exists to prove the hypothesis that you devised at the outset, not to show the breadth of your knowledge.

Use the advisor as a guinea pig. You must ensure that the advisor reads the first chapters (and eventually, all the chapters) far in advance of the deadline. His reactions may be useful to you. If the advisor is busy (or lazy), ask a friend. Ask if he understands what you are writing. Do not play the solitary genius.

Do not insist on beginning with the first chapter. Perhaps you have more documentation on chapter 4. Start there, with the nonchalance of someone who has already worked out the previous chapters. You will gain confidence. Naturally your working table of contents will anchor you, and will serve as a hypothesis that guides you (see section 4.1).

Do not use ellipsis and exclamation points, and do not explain ironies. It is possible to use language that is *referential* or language that is *figurative.* By referential language, I mean a language that is recognized by all, in which all things are called by their most common name, and that does not lend itself to misunderstandings. "The Venice-Milan train" indicates in a referential way the same object that "The Arrow of the Lagoon" indicates figuratively. This example illustrates that "everyday" communication is possible with partially figurative language. Ideally, a critical essay or a scholarly text should be written referentially (with all terms well defined and univocal), but it can also be useful to use metaphor, irony, or litotes. Here is a referential text, followed by its transcription in figurative terms that are at least tolerable:

> [*Referential version:*] Krasnapolsky is not a very sharp critic of Danieli's work. His interpretation draws meaning from the author's text that the author probably did not intend. Consider the line, "in the evening gazing at the clouds." Ritz interprets this as a normal geographical annotation, whereas

Krasnapolsky sees a symbolic expression that alludes to poetic activity. One should not trust Ritz's critical acumen, and one should also distrust Krasnapolsky. Hilton observes that, "if Ritz's writing seems like a tourist brochure, Krasnapolsky's criticism reads like a Lenten sermon." And he adds, "Truly, two perfect critics."

[*Figurative version*:] We are not convinced that Krasnapolsky is the sharpest critic of Danieli's work. In reading his author, Krasnapolsky gives the impression that he is putting words into Danieli's mouth. Consider the line, "in the evening gazing at the clouds." Ritz interprets it as a normal geographical annotation, whereas Krasnapolsky plays the symbolism card and sees an allusion to poetic activity. Ritz is not a prodigy of critical insight, but Krasnapolsky should also be handled with care. As Hilton observes, "if Ritz's writing seems like a tourist brochure, Krasnapolsky's criticism reads like a Lenten sermon. Truly, two perfect critics."

You can see that the figurative version uses various rhetorical devices. First of all, the litotes: saying that you are not convinced that someone is a sharp critic means that you are convinced that he *is not* a sharp critic. Also, the statement "Ritz is not a prodigy of critical insight" means that he is a modest critic. Then there are the *metaphors*: putting words into someone's mouth, and playing the symbolism card. The tourist brochure and the Lenten sermon are two *similes*, while the observation that the two authors are perfect critics is an example of *irony*: saying one thing to signify its opposite.

Now, we either use rhetorical figures effectively, or we do not use them at all. If we use them it is because we presume our reader is capable of catching them, and because we believe that we will appear more incisive and convincing. In this case, we should not be ashamed of them, and *we should not explain them*. If we think that our reader is an idiot, we should not use rhetorical figures, but if we use them and feel the need to explain them, we are essentially calling the reader an idiot. In turn, he will take revenge by calling the author an idiot. Here is how a timid writer might intervene to neutralize and excuse the rhetorical figures he uses:

[*Figurative version with reservations:*] We are not convinced that Krasnapolsky is the "sharpest" critic of Danieli's work. In reading his author, Krasnapolsky gives the impression that he is "putting words into Danieli's mouth." Consider Danieli's line, "in the evening gazing at the clouds." Ritz interprets this as a normal geographical annotation, whereas Krasnapolsky "plays the symbolism card" and sees an allusion to poetic activity. Ritz is not a "prodigy of critical insight," but Krasnapolsky should also be "handled with care"! As Hilton ironically observes, "if Ritz's writing seems like a vacation brochure, Krasnapolsky's criticism reads like a Lenten sermon." And he defines them (again with irony!) as two models of critical perfection. But all joking aside ...

I am convinced that nobody could be so intellectually *petit bourgeois* as to conceive a passage so studded with shyness and apologetic little smiles. Of course I exaggerated in this example, and here *I say that I exaggerated* because it is didactically important that the parody be understood as such. In fact, many bad habits of the amateur writer are condensed into this third example. First of all, the use of quotation marks to warn the reader, "Pay attention because I am about to say something big!" Puerile. Quotation marks are generally only used to designate a direct quotation or the title of an essay or short work; to indicate that a term is jargon or slang; or that a term is being discussed in the text as a word, rather than used functionally within the sentence. Secondly, the use of the exclamation point to emphasize a statement. This is not appropriate in a critical essay. If you check the book you are reading, you will notice that I have used the exclamation mark only once or twice. It is allowed once or twice, if the purpose is to make the reader jump in his seat and call his attention to a vehement statement like, "Pay attention, never make this mistake!" But it is a good rule to speak softly. The effect will be stronger if you simply say important things. Finally, the author of the third passage draws attention to the ironies, and apologizes for using them (even if they are someone else's). Surely, if you think that Hilton's irony is too subtle, you can write, "Hilton states with subtle irony that we are in the presence of two perfect critics." But the irony must be *really* subtle to merit such a statement. In the quoted text, after Hilton has mentioned the vacation brochure and the Lenten sermon, the irony was already evident and needed no further explanation. The same applies to the statement, "But all joking aside." Sometimes a statement like this can be useful to abruptly change the tone of the argument, but only if you were *really* joking before. In this case, the author was not joking. He was attempting to use irony and metaphor, but these are serious rhetorical devices and not jokes.

You may observe that, more than once in this book, I have expressed a paradox and then warned that it was a paradox. For example, in section 2.6.1, I proposed the existence of the mythical centaur for the purpose of explaining the concept of scientific research. But I warned you of this paradox not because I thought you would have believed this proposition. On the contrary, I warned you because I was afraid that you would have doubted too much, and hence dismissed the paradox. Therefore I insisted that, despite its paradoxical form, my statement contained an important truth: that research must clearly define its object so that others can identify it, even if this object is mythical. And I made this absolutely clear because this is a didactic book in which I care more that everyone understands what I want to say than about a beautiful literary style. Had I been writing an essay, I would have pronounced the paradox without denouncing it later.

Always define a term when you introduce it for the first time. If you do not know the definition of a term, avoid using it. If it is one of the principal terms of your thesis and you are not able to define it, call it quits. You have chosen the wrong thesis (or, if you were planning to pursue further research, the wrong career).

Do not explain the location of Rome without then explaining the location of Timbuktu. It gives me chills to read sentences like, "Guzzo defined the Jewish-Dutch pantheist philosopher Spinoza ..." Stop! Either you are writing a thesis on Spinoza, and in this case your reader already knows who Spinoza is, and also you will already have informed the reader that Augusto Guzzo wrote a book on Spinoza; or you are quoting this statement tangentially in a thesis on nuclear physics, and in this case you should presume that the reader is aware of Spinoza but not of Guzzo; or you are writing a thesis on post-Gentilian philosophy in Italy,[3] and you can expect your reader to know both Guzzo and Spinoza. Even in a thesis on history, do not write "T. S. Eliot, an English poet ..." Take it for granted that T. S. Eliot is universally known (and also consider that he was born in the United States). At most, if you wish to emphasize that it was precisely an English poet who said something particular, you will write, "It was an English poet, Eliot, who said that ..." But if you write a thesis on Eliot, have the humility to provide all the information about him in the text. If not in the text, at least provide it in a note near the beginning, and be honest and precise enough to condense all of his necessary biographical information into ten lines. The reader, as much as he may know the subject, will not necessarily have memorized Eliot's birthday. Take this into consideration when you write a work on a minor author of past centuries. Do not presume that everyone knows of him. One never knows. Immediately introduce him, his cultural context, and so on. But even if the author was Molière, how much will it cost you to insert a note with a couple of dates?

I or we?[4] Should the student introduce his opinions in the first person? Should he state, "I think that ... "? Some believe that this is more honest than using the majestic plural. I disagree. A writer says "we" because he presumes that his readers can share what he is saying. Writing is a social act. I write so that you as the reader accept what I propose to you. At the most, I think, the student can try to avoid personal pronouns by adopting more impersonal expressions such as, "therefore one should conclude that," "it then seems granted that," "one should say at this point," "one should presume," "therefore one infers that," "in examining this text one sees that," etc. It is not necessary to say, "the article that we previously quoted," when it suffices to say, "the article previously quoted." But I think the student can write, "the article previously quoted shows *us* that," because these types of expressions do not imply any personalization of the academic discourse.

5.3   Quotations

5.3.1   *When and How to Quote: 10 Rules*

Generally speaking, you will quote many texts by other
authors in your thesis: the textual object of your work, or
the primary source or sources; and the critical literature on
your topic, or the secondary sources. Therefore, practically
speaking, there are two kinds of quotes: (a) quotes from a
text that you will interpret; (b) quotes from a text that you
will use to support your interpretation. It is difficult to say
abstractly whether you should quote abundantly or sparingly. It depends on the type of thesis you are writing. A
critical analysis of a writer obviously requires that large passages of his works be quoted and analyzed. In other cases, a
quote can be a manifestation of laziness, for example if the
candidate is unwilling or unable to summarize a collection of
data and prefers to let someone else do it for him. Hence, we
provide the following ten rules:

> *Rule 1*: Quote the object of your interpretive analysis with
> reasonable abundance.

> *Rule 2*: Quote the critical literature only when its author-
> ity corroborates or confirms your statements.

These two rules imply some obvious corollaries. First,
if the passage you wish to analyze exceeds half a page, it
means something is wrong. Either your analysis is too
general and you will not be able to comment on the text
point by point; or you are discussing an entire text rather
than a passage, and presenting a global criticism rather
than an analysis. In these cases, if the text is important
but too long, present it in full *in an appendix,* and quote
only short passages over the course of your chapters.
Second, when quoting or citing critical literature, be sure
that it says something new, or that it confirms *authorita-
tively* what you have said. The following illustrates a *useless* quote and a *useless* citation:

> Mass communication constitutes, as McLuhan says,
> "one of the central phenomena of our time." We should
> not forget that, in our country alone, two out of three

individuals spend a third of their day in front of the TV, according to Savoy.

What is wrong or naïve in this example? First, that mass communication is a central phenomenon of our time is a banality that anyone could have said. I do not exclude the possibility that McLuhan himself may have said it (I did not check—I invented this quote), but it is not necessary to refer to an authority to prove something so obvious. Second, it is possible that the data on the TV audience is accurate, but Savoy does not constitute an *authority*. (In fact, it is a name I also invented.) The author of the thesis should have cited the data of the Italian Central Institute of Statistics, a sociological research project signed by renowned scholars who are beyond suspicion, or the results of his own inquiry backed up by an appendix of tables that present his data, rather than citing just any old Savoy.

Rule 3: If you don't want readers to presume that you share the opinion of the quoted author, you must include your own critical remarks before or after the passage.

Rule 4: Make sure that the author and the source (print or manuscript) of your quote are clearly identifiable. You can do this by including one of the following: (a) a superscript number and a corresponding note (see section 5.4.2), especially when you mention the author for the first time; (b) the author's name and the work's publication date, in parentheses after the quote (see section 5.4.3); (c) the page number in parentheses, but only when the entire chapter (or the entire thesis) centers on the same work by the same author. Table 5.1 illustrates how you could structure a page of a thesis with the title "Epiphany in James Joyce's *Portrait*." In this case, once you have clarified to which edition you refer, cite your primary source with the page number in parentheses in the text, and cite the critical literature in the note.[5]

Rule 5: Quote your primary source from the critical edition, or the most canonical edition. In a thesis on Balzac, avoid quoting the pages from the paperback Livre de

Table 5.1

EXAMPLE OF THE CONTINUOUS ANALYSIS OF A SINGLE TEXT

The text of *Portrait* is rich with these moments of ecstasy that Joyce had already defined in *Stephen Hero* as epiphanic:

> Glimmering and trembling, trembling and unfolding, a breaking light, an opening flower, it spread in endless succession to itself, breaking in full crimson and unfolding and fading to palest rose, leaf by leaf and wave of light by wave of light, flooding all the heavens with its soft flushes, every flush deeper than other. (151)

It is immediately evident that the "submarine" vision changes to the vision of a flame, in which red tones and sensations of brightness prevail. Now, we know that metaphors of fire frequently recur in *Portrait*, and that the word "fire" appears at least 59 times and variations of the word "flame" appear 35 times.[1] Here we can see the association between fire and the epiphanic experience, and this illuminates the relations between *Portrait* and Gabriele D'Annunzio's *The Flame*. Let us examine this passage from *Portrait*:

> Or was it that, being as weak of sight as he was shy of mind, he drew less pleasure from the reflection of the glowing sensible world through the prism of a language manycoloured and richly storied … (146)

Here we find a stunning reference to a passage in D'Annunzio's *The Flame*,

> She was compelled into that blazing environment *as though into a forge* …

....

1 Leslie Hancock, *Word Index to James Joyce's Portrait of the Artist* (Carbondale: Southern Illinois University Press, 1976).

Poche edition, and at least quote from the Pléiade edition of Balzac's complete works. In general, for ancient and classical authors it is sufficient to cite sections, chapters, and lines according to current usage (see section 3.2.3). Regarding contemporary authors, if various editions are available, it is better to cite either from the first, or from the most recent if it is revised and corrected. The first edition is preferable if the following editions are simply reprints, and the last edition is preferable if it contains revisions, additions, or updates. In any case, your reference should specify both the first edition and the most recent edition, and should clarify from which one you are quoting (see section 3.2.3).

Rule 6: When your primary source is foreign, quote it in the original language. This rule is mandatory for literary works. In these cases, adding a translation in parentheses or in a note may be useful, but follow your advisor's suggestions on this. Even if you are not analyzing the literary style of an author, if the exact expression of his thought, in all of its linguistic shades, has a certain weight (for example a philosopher's commentary), then you should work with the text in the original language if possible. However, I recommend that you add the translation in parentheses or in a note, because the translation itself also constitutes an interpretive exercise on your part. If you are taking from a foreign author only a piece of information, statistical or historical data, or a general criticism, you can simply use a good translation, or even translate the passage yourself. In this case you do not want to submit the reader to continuous jumps from one language to the other, and it is sufficient to precisely cite the original title and to clarify which translation you are using. Finally, you may find yourself discussing the texts of a foreign author who happens to be a poet or a writer of fiction, but you only wish to examine his philosophical ideas and not his literary style. Here, if there are numerous long quotes, you may also decide to refer to a good translation to render the argument more fluid, and simply insert some short passages *in the original language*

when you want to emphasize the revealing use of a particular word. (See also rule 4, point c.)

Rule 7: The reference to the author and the work must be
clear. The following (incorrect) example should illustrate
our point:

> We agree with Vasquez when he claims that "the problem
> under scrutiny is far from being solved,"[1] and, despite
> Braun's well-known opinion[2] that "light has been defin-
> itively shed on this age-old question," we believe with our
> author that "we have a long way to go before we reach a
> satisfying stage of knowledge."

The first quote is certainly from Vasquez and the second from Braun, but is the third really from Vasquez, as
the context implies? And since we have indicated in footnote 1 that Vasquez's first quote comes from page 160
of his work, should we also assume that the third quote
comes from the same page in the same book? And what if
Braun was the source of the third quote?

Here is how we should have drafted the same passage:

> We agree with Vasquez when he claims that "the problem
> under scrutiny is far from being solved,"[1] and, despite
> Braun's well-known opinion that "light has been defini-
> tively shed on this age-old question,"[2] we believe with our
> author that "we have a long way to go before we reach a
> satisfying stage of knowledge."[3]

Notice that footnote 3 indicates "Vasquez 1976, 161."
If the quote had still been from p. 160, and if it had
immediately followed the previous Vasquez quote without being interrupted by the Braun quote, we could have
written "ibid." But shame on us if we had written "ibid."

---

1 Roberto Vasquez, *Fuzzy Concepts* (London: Faber, 1976), 160.
2 Richard Braun, *Logik und Erkenntnis* (Munich: Fink, 1968), 345.

---

1 Roberto Vasquez, *Fuzzy Concepts* (London: Faber, 1976), 160.
2 Richard Braun, *Logik und Erkenntnis* (Munich: Fink, 1968), 345.
3 Vasquez 1976, 161.

in this case, since the two Vasquez quotes are separated by the quote from Braun. Had we done this, "ibid." would have lead the reader to believe that Vasquez's sentence was from p. 345 of Braun's previously cited book. "Ibid." means "in the same place," and should only be used to repeat *verbatim* the reference of the previous note.

Rule 8: When a quote does not exceed two or three lines, you can insert it into the body of the text enclosed in quotation marks. I will do this now as I quote from Campbell and Ballou, who state, "Direct quotations not over three typewritten lines in length are enclosed in quotation marks and are run into the text."[1] When the quote is longer, it is better to set it off as a block quotation. In this case the quotation marks are not necessary, because it is clear that all set-off passages are quotes, and we must commit to a different system for our observations. (Any secondary developments should appear in a note.) Here is an example of two consecutive block quotations:[6]

> If a direct quotation is more than three typewritten lines in length, it is set off from the text in a separate paragraph, or paragraphs, and single-spaced. …
>
> The paragraphing of the original source should be retained in direct quotations. Paragraphs that were consecutive in the original are separated by a single space, as are the lines within each paragraph; paragraphs that are quoted from two different sources and that are not separated by intervening text should be separated by a double space.[2]

> Indenting is used to indicate quotations, especially in factual writing involving numerous quotations of some length. … No quotation marks are used.[3]

---

1 William G. Campbell and Stephen V. Ballou, *Form and Style*, 4th ed. (Boston: Houghton Mifflin, 1974), 40.

2 Ibid.

3 Porter G. Perrin, *An Index to English*, 4th ed. (Chicago: Scott, Foresman, 1965), 338.

This method is quite convenient because it immediately reveals the quoted texts; it allows the reader to skip them if he is skimming, to linger if he is more interested in the quoted texts than in our commentary, and finally, to find them immediately when need be.

Rule 9: Quotes must be *accurate*. First, transcribe the words exactly as they appear. (To this end, it is always a good idea to check the quotes against the original in your final draft, because errors or omissions may have occurred when you copied them by hand or typed them.) Second, do not omit text from a quote without indicating your omission with an *ellipsis*, three consecutive periods with or without brackets, in place of the omitted part. Third, do not make interpolations without clearly signaling them; each of our comments, clarifications, and specifications must appear enclosed in brackets. Finally, we must also indicate emphases that are ours rather than the author's by adding, after the quote and enclosed in brackets, a formula such as "emphasis mine."

If the author that you quote, despite his worthiness of mention, makes an evident mistake, you must respect his mistake, but you must indicate it to the reader.[7] At the very least, indicate the mistake with the following expression enclosed in square brackets: [*sic*], literally meaning "so." Thus you should write that Savoy states that, "in 1820 [*sic*], after Napoleon Bonaparte's death, Europe was in a grim situation with many shadows and few lights." But, if I were you, I would stay away from this mysterious Savoy.

Rule 10: Quotes are like testimony in a trial, and you must always be able to track down the witnesses and demonstrate their reliability. For this reason, the reference must be *exact and accurate* (do not quote from an author without indicating the book and page number), and it must be *verifiable*. If this is the case, how should you proceed if important information or criticism comes from a personal communication, a letter, or a manuscript? In a note, you can use one of these expressions:

1. Personal communication with the author, June 6, 1975.
2. Personal letter to author, June 6, 1975.

3. Recorded statements, June 6, 1975.
4. C. Smith, "The Sources of Snorri Sturluson's *Edda*" (manuscript).
5. C. Smith, Paper presented at the XII Physiotherapy Conference (manuscript, forthcoming from Mouton, The Hague).

You will notice that for sources 2, 4, and 5 there are related documents that you can exhibit. Source 3 is vague because the term "recording" does not specify whether you are talking about a magnetic audio recording or stenographic notes. As for source 1, only the source of the information could disprove you (but he may have died in the meantime). In these extreme cases, it is always good practice, after you have given a final form to the quote, to send a letter to the author with a copy of the text, and to ask for a letter of authorization in which he acknowledges the ideas you have attributed to him. If you are dealing with *enormously* important unpublished information (e.g., a new formula resulting from secret research), you should put a copy of the letter of authorization in the thesis's appendix. Naturally, do so only if the author of the information is a well-known scholarly authority, and not any old Joe.

Minor rules: If you want to be precise about text you have omitted, consider punctuation marks as you insert the ellipsis (the three ellipsis periods with or without the square brackets):

If we omit a section of little importance, ... the ellipsis must follow the punctuation mark of the complete section. If we omit a central part ... , the ellipsis precedes the commas.

When you quote poetry, follow the usage of the critical literature on your topic. In any case, you can quote a single line by inserting it in the text: "la donzelletta vien dalla campagna."[8] You can quote two lines by inserting them into the text and separating them with a slash: "I cipressi che a Bolgheri alti e schietti / van da San Guido in duplice filar."[9] If instead you are dealing with a longer poetic passage, it is better to use the indentation system:

> And when we are married,
> How happy we'll be.
> I love sweet Rosie O'Grady
> And Rosie O'Grady loves me.[10]

Also use the indentation system if you are dealing with a single line that will be the object of a long analysis, for example if you want to draw out the fundamental elements of Verlaine's poetics from the line

> De la musique avant toute chose [11]

In cases like this, I would say that it is not necessary to italicize the line even if it is in a foreign language. This especially would be the case with a thesis on Verlaine; otherwise you would have hundreds of pages all in italics. Rather, write,

> De la musique avant toute chose
> *Et pour cela préfère l'Impair*
> Plus vague et plus soluble dans l'air,
> Sans rien en lui qui pèse ou qui pose. ...[12]

And indicate "emphasis mine" if the center of your analysis is the notion of *l'impair*.

5.3.2   *Quotes, Paraphrases, and Plagiarism*

When you created your readings index cards, you summarized the various points of the author in question. That is to say that you *paraphrased* the author, rewording the author's thought. In other instances you quoted entire passages enclosed in quotation marks. When you then begin writing your thesis, you no longer have the text in front of you, and perhaps you will copy entire passages from your index cards into your thesis. In this case, you must be sure that the passages that you copy are really paraphrases and not *quotes without quotation marks*. Otherwise, you will have committed *plagiarism*.

This form of plagiarism is very common. The student has a clean conscience because, in a footnote, he says he is referring to that given author. But the reader becomes suspicious of your thesis when he notices by chance that the page is not paraphrasing the original text, but in fact *copying* it without using quotation marks. And here we are not only talking about the advisor, but anyone else who will see your thesis in the future, either to publish it or to evaluate your competencies.

How can you make sure that you are paraphrasing and not plagiarizing? First of all, a paraphrase is generally much shorter than the original. But there are cases in which the author of a sentence or fairly short paragraph says very juicy things. In this case, your paraphrase should be very long, probably longer than the original passage. Here you do not have to worry neurotically about each of your words being different from the author's, and in fact sometimes it is inevitable or even useful that some of the author's terms remain unchanged. The most reassuring test of your paraphrases will come when you are able to paraphrase the text without looking at it. This will mean not only that you have avoided plagiarism, but also that you have understood the text you are paraphrasing.

To better illustrate this point, I will reproduce a passage from Norman Cohn's *The Pursuit of the Millennium* in the first paragraph below. Then I will provide an example of a reasonable paraphrase in the second paragraph, and an example of a faulty paraphrase that constitutes plagiarism in the third paragraph. In the fourth paragraph, I will give an example of a paraphrase almost identical to the third, but in which I have avoided plagiarism through an honest use of quotation marks.

> [*The original text:*] "The coming of Antichrist was even more tensely awaited. Generation after generation lived in constant expectation of the all-destroying demon whose reign was indeed to be lawless chaos, an age given over to robbery and rapine, torture and massacre, but was also to be the prelude to the longed-for consummation, the Second Coming and the Kingdom of the Saints. People were always on the watch for the 'signs' which, according to the prophetic tradition, were to herald and accompany the final 'time of troubles'; and since the 'signs' included bad rulers, civil discord, war, drought, famine, plague, comets, sudden deaths

of prominent persons and an increase in general sinfulness, there was never any difficulty about finding them."[1]

[*An honest paraphrase*:] Cohn is very explicit on this topic. He outlines the state of tension typical of this period, in which the wait for Antichrist is at the same time a wait for the demon's reign, characterized by pain and disorder; and a prelude to the so-called Second Coming, the Parousia, Christ's triumphant return. And in an age dominated by sorrowful events including plunders, lootings, famines, and plagues, there was no lack of "signs" that the prophetic texts had always announced as typical of the coming of Antichrist.[1]

[*Plagiarism*:] On the other hand, we should not forget that the coming of Antichrist was even more tensely awaited. The generations lived in the constant expectation of the all-destroying demon whose reign was indeed to be lawless chaos, an age given over to robbery and rapine, torture and massacre, but was at the same time to be the prelude to the Second Coming or the Kingdom of the Saints. People were always on the watch for the "signs" which, as stated by the prophets, were to accompany and herald the final "time of troubles"; and since these "signs" included the bad rulers, the civil discord, the war, the drought, the famine, the plagues and the comets, and also the sudden deaths of important persons (in addition to an increase in general sinfulness), there was never any difficulty about finding them.[1]

[*A paraphrase with quotes*:] On the other hand, Cohn reminds us that "the coming of Antichrist was even more tensely awaited." People greatly anticipated the "demon whose reign was indeed to be lawless chaos, an age given over to robbery and rapine, torture and massacre, but was also to be the

1 Norman Cohn, *The Pursuit of the Millennium*, 2nd ed. (New York: Harper & Row, 1961), 20–21.

1 Norman Cohn, *The Pursuit of the Millennium*, 2nd ed. (New York: Harper & Row, 1961), 20–21.

1 Norman Cohn, *The Pursuit of the Millennium*, 2nd ed. (New York: Harper & Row, 1961), 20–21.

prelude to the longed-for consummation, the Second Coming and the Kingdom of the Saints." Now, Cohn concludes, given the dreadful variety of events identified by the prophetic texts as presages of the "time of troubles," in an age marked by plunders, lootings, famines, and plagues "there was never any difficulty about finding them."[1]

Now, if you make the effort to compose a paraphrase as detailed as the fourth one, you may as well quote the entire passage. But to do so, your readings index card should have reproduced the passage verbatim, or paraphrased it beyond suspicion. Since, when you write your thesis, you will not be able to remember what you did during the research phase, it is necessary that you proceed correctly from the very beginning. If there are no quotation marks on the index card, you must be able to trust that the card contains an honest paraphrase that avoids plagiarism.

5.4 Footnotes

5.4.1 The Purpose of Footnotes

According to a fairly common opinion, a thesis or a book with copious notes exhibits erudite snobbism, and often represents an attempt to pull the wool over the reader's eyes. Certainly we should not rule out the fact that many authors abound in notes to confer a tone of importance on their work; and that others stuff their notes with nonessential information, perhaps plundering with impunity the critical literature they have examined. Nevertheless, when used appropriately, notes are useful. It is hard to define in general what is appropriate, because this depends on the type of thesis. But we will try to illustrate the cases that require notes, and how the notes should be formatted.

1. *Use a note to indicate the source of a quote.* Too many bibliographical references in the text can interrupt your argument and make your text difficult to read. Naturally there are ways to integrate essential references into the

---

1 Norman Cohn, *The Pursuit of the Millennium*, 2nd ed. (New York: Harper & Row, 1961), 20–21.

text, thus doing away with the need for notes, such as the author-date system (see section 5.4.3). But in general, notes provide an excellent way to avoid burdening the text with references. If your university doesn't mandate otherwise, use a *footnote* for bibliographical references rather than an *endnote* (that is, a note at the end of the book or the chapter), because a footnote allows the reader to immediately spot the reference.

2. *Use notes to add additional supporting bibliographical references on a topic you discuss in the text.* For example, "on this topic see also so-and-so." Also in this case, footnotes are more convenient than endnotes.

3. *Use notes for external and internal cross-references.* Once you have treated a topic, you can include the abbreviation "cf." (for the Latin *confer,* meaning "to bring together") in the note to refer the reader to another book, or another chapter or section of your text. If your internal cross-references are essential, you can integrate them into the text. The book you are reading provides many examples of internal cross-references to other sections of the text.

4. *Use notes to introduce a supporting quote that would have interrupted the text.* If you make a statement in the text and then continue directly to the next statement for fluidity, a superscript note reference after the first statement can refer the reader to a note in which a well-known authority backs up your assertion.[1]

5. *Use notes to expand on statements you have made in the text.*[2] Use notes to free your text from observations that, however important, are peripheral to your argument or

---

1 "All important statements of fact that are not common knowledge … must be supported by evidence of their validity. This may be done in the text, in the footnotes, or in both." William G. Campbell and Stephen V. Ballou, *Form and Style,* 4th ed. (Boston: Houghton Mifflin, 1974), 50.

2 Use *content notes* to discuss or expand on points in the text. For example, Campbell and Ballou note that it is useful to transfer to notes "technical discussions, incidental comments, corollary materials, and additional information" (ibid.).

do nothing more than repeat from a different point of view what you have essentially already said.

6. *Use notes to correct statements in the text.* You may be sure of your statements, but you should also be conscious that someone may disagree, or you may believe that, from a certain point of view, it would be possible to object to your statement. Inserting a partially restrictive note will then prove not only your academic honesty but also your critical spirit.[3]

7. *Use notes to provide a translation of a quote, or to provide the quote in the original language.* If the quote appears in its original language in the main body of the text, you can provide the translation in a note. If however you decide for reasons of fluidity to provide the quote in translation in the main text, you can repeat the quote in its original language in a note.

8. *Use notes to pay your debts.* Citing a book from which you copied a sentence is paying a debt. Citing an author whose ideas or information you used is paying a debt. Sometimes, though, you must also pay debts that are more difficult to document. It is a good rule of academic honesty to mention in a note that, for example, a series of original ideas in your text could not have been born without inspiration from a particular work, or from a private conversation with a scholar.

Whereas notes of types 1, 2, and 3 are more useful as footnotes, notes of types 4 through 8 can also appear at the end of the chapter or of the thesis, especially if they are very long. Yet we will say that *a note should never be too long*;

---

3 In fact, after having said that notes are useful, we must specify that, as Campbell and Ballou also mention, "the use of footnotes for the purpose of elaboration calls for considerable discretion. Care should be taken not to lose force by transferring valuable and significant facts to the footnotes; directly relevant ideas and information should be included in the text" (ibid.). On the other hand, as the authors themselves say, "Each footnote must in practice justify its existence" (ibid.). There is nothing more irritating than notes that seem inserted only to impress, and that do not say anything important to the argument.

otherwise it is not a note, it is an *appendix,* and it must be inserted and numbered as such at the end of the work. At any rate, be consistent: use either all footnotes or all endnotes. Also, if you use short footnotes and longer appendices at the end of the work, do this consistently throughout your thesis.

And once again, remember that if you are examining a homogeneous source, such as the work of only one author, the pages of a diary, or a collection of manuscripts, letters, or documents, you can avoid the notes simply by establishing abbreviations for your sources at the beginning of your work. Then, for every citation, insert the relevant abbreviation and the page or document number in parentheses. For citing classics, follow the conventions in section 3.2.3. In a thesis on medieval authors who are published in Jacques-Paul Migne's *Patrologia Latina,* you can avoid hundreds of notes by putting in the text parenthetical references such as this: (*PL* 30.231). Proceed similarly for references to charts, tables, or illustrations in the text or in the appendix.

5.4.2   *The Notes and Bibliography System*

Let us now consider the note as a means for citation. If in your text you speak of an author or quote some of his passages, the corresponding note should provide the necessary documentation. This system is convenient because, if you use footnotes, the reader knows immediately what author and work you are citing. Yet this process imposes duplication because you must repeat in the final bibliography the same reference you included in the note. (In rare cases in which the note references a work that is unrelated to the specific bibliography of the thesis, there is no need to repeat the reference in the final bibliography. For example, if in a thesis in astronomy I were to cite Dante's line, "the Love that moves the sun and all the other stars," the note alone would suffice.)[1] The presence of the references in the note certainly does not

---

1   *Par.* XXXIII.145. [The English translation is from Dante Alighieri, Paradiso, trans. Jean Hollander and Robert Hollander, with an introduction and notes by Robert Hollander (New York: Anchor Books, 2007), 917. —Trans.]

invalidate the need for a final bibliography. In fact, the final bibliography provides the material you have consulted at a glance, and it also serves as a comprehensive source for the literature on your particular topic. It would be impolite to force the reader to search the notes page by page to find all the works you have cited.

Moreover, the final bibliography provides more complete information than do the notes. For example, in citing a foreign author, the note provides only the title in the original language, while the bibliographical entry will also include a reference to the translation. Furthermore, while usage suggests citing an author by *first name* and *last name* in a note, the bibliography presents authors in alphabetical order by last name. Additionally, if the first edition of an article appeared in an obscure journal, and the article was then reprinted in a widely available miscellaneous volume, the note may reference only the miscellaneous volume with the page number of the quote, while the bibliography will also require a reference to the first edition. A note may also abbreviate certain data or eliminate subtitles, while the bibliography should provide all this information.

Table 5.2 provides an example of a thesis page with various footnotes, and table 5.3 shows the references as they will appear in the final bibliography.[13] Notice the differences between the two. You will see that the notes are more casual than the bibliography, that they do not cite the first edition, and that they aim only to give enough information to enable a reader to locate the text they mention, reserving the complete documentation for the bibliography. Also, the notes do not mention whether the volume in question has been translated. After all, there is the final bibliography in which the reader can find this information.

What are the shortcomings of this system? Take for example footnote 6 of table 5.2. It tells us that Lakoff's article is in the previously cited miscellaneous volume *Semantics*. Where was it cited? Luckily, in the same paragraph, and the reference appears in the table's footnote 5. What if it had been cited ten pages earlier? Should we repeat the reference for convenience? Should we expect the reader to check the

Table 5.2

EXAMPLE OF THE NOTES AND BIBLIOGRAPHY SYSTEM

Even though Chomsky[1] accepts the principle of Katz and Fodor's interpretive semantics[2] that derives the meaning of a sentence from the sum of the meanings of its elementary constituents, he does not renounce his belief that deep syntactic structure primarily determines meaning.[3]

Naturally, Chomsky eventually developed a more articulated stance, as his first works already foretold.[4] He develops this stance through discussions that he describes in the essay "Deep Structure, Surface Structure and Semantic Interpretation,"[5] placing the semantic interpretation at the intersection between the deep structure and the surface structure. Other authors, for example Lakoff,[6] attempt to build a generative semantics in which the logical-semantic form generates the syntactic structure itself.[7]

1 Noam Chomsky, *Aspects of the Theory of Syntax* (Cambridge, MA: MIT Press, 1965), 162.

2 Jerrold J. Katz and Jerry A. Fodor, "The Structure of a Semantic Theory," in *The Structure of Language*, ed. J. J. Katz and J. A. Fodor (Englewood Cliffs, NJ: Prentice-Hall, 1964), 479–518.

3 For a satisfactory overview of this position see Nicolas Ruwet, *An Introduction to Generative Grammar* (Amsterdam: North-Holland, 1973).

4 Noam Chomsky, "Persistent Topics in Linguistic Theory," *Diogenes* (Fall 1965): 13–20.

5 Noam Chomsky, "Deep Structure, Surface Structure and Semantic Interpretation," in *Semantics: An Interdisciplinary Reader in Philosophy, Linguistics and Psychology*, ed. Danny D. Steinberg and Leon A. Jakobovits (Cambridge, UK: Cambridge University Press, 1971), 183–216.

6 George Lakoff, "On Generative Semantics," in Steinberg and Jakobovits, *Semantics*, 232–296.

7 In line with this approach cf. James McCawley, "Where Do Noun Phrases Come From?," in Steinberg and Jakobovits, *Semantics*, 217–231.

Table 5.3

EXAMPLE OF A CORRESPONDING STANDARD BIBLIOGRAPHY

Chomsky, Noam. *Aspects of the Theory of Syntax.* Cambridge, MA: MIT Press, 1965.

———. "Deep Structure, Surface Structure and Semantic Interpretation." In Steinberg and Jakobovits, *Semantics*, 183–216. Originally published in *Studies in General and Oriental Linguistics*, ed. Roman Jakobson, 52–91 (Tokyo: TEC Corporation for Language and Education Research, 1970).

———. "Persistent Topics in Linguistic Theory." *Diogenes* (Fall 1965): 13–20. Originally published as "De quelques constantes de la théorie linguistique." *Diogène* 51 (July-September 1965): 4–21.

Katz, Jerrold J., and Jerry A. Fodor. "The Structure of a Semantic Theory." In *The Structure of Language*, ed. J. J. Katz and J. A. Fodor, 479–518. Englewood Cliffs, NJ: Prentice-Hall, 1964. Originally published as "The Structure of a Semantic Theory." *Language* 39, no. 2 (April-June 1963): 170–210.

Lakoff, George. "On Generative Semantics." In Steinberg and Jakobovits, *Semantics*, 232–296.

McCawley, James. "Where Do Noun Phrases Come From?" In Steinberg and Jakobovits, *Semantics*, 217–231.

Ruwet, Nicolas. *An Introduction to Generative Grammar.* Trans. Norval S. H. Smith. Amsterdam: North-Holland, 1973. Originally published as *Introduction à la grammaire générative* (Paris: Plon, 1967).

Steinberg, Danny D., and Leon A. Jakobovits, eds. *Semantics: An Interdisciplinary Reader in Philosophy, Linguistics and Psychology.* Cambridge, UK: Cambridge University Press, 1971.

bibliography? In this instance, the author-date system is more convenient.

5.4.3 The Author-Date System

In many disciplines (and with increasing frequency) authors use a system that allows them to eliminate all reference notes, preserving only content notes and cross-references. This system presupposes that the final bibliography is organized by authors' names, and includes the date of publication of the first edition of the book or article. Here is an example of a bibliographical entry in a thesis that uses the author-date system:

Chomsky, Noam. 1965. *Aspects of the Theory of Syntax*. Cambridge, MA: MIT Press.

What does this bibliography entry allow you to do? When you must discuss this book in the text, you can eliminate the entire footnote (the superscript note reference number in the text, the footnote itself, and the reference in the footnote) and proceed as follows:

As Chomsky wrote, "mathematical study of formal properties of grammars is, very likely, an area of linguistics of great potential" (1965, 62).

or

"It is quite apparent that current theories of syntax and semantics are highly fragmentary and tentative, and that they involve open questions of a fundamental nature" (Chomsky 1965, 148).

When the reader checks the final bibliography, he understands that "(Chomsky 1965, 148)" indicates "page 148 of Noam Chomsky's 1965 book *Aspects of the Theory of Syntax*, ..."

This system allows you to prune the text of the majority of the notes. In addition, it means that, at the writing stage, you only need to document a book *once*. For this reason, this system is especially appropriate when the student must constantly cite many books, or cite the same book often, allowing him to avoid annoying little notes full of "Ibid." This system is indispensable even for a student writing a condensed review of the critical literature on a particular topic. For example, consider a sentence like this:

> Stumpf (1945, 88–100), Rigabue (1956), Azzimonti (1957), Forlimpopoli (1967), Colacicchi (1968), Poggibonsi (1972), and Gzbiniewsky (1975) have extensively treated the issue, while Barbapedana (1950), Fugazza (1967), and Ingrassia (1970) have completely ignored it.

If you had to insert a reference note for each of these citations, you would have quite a crowded page. In addition, the reader would be deprived of the temporal sequence that clearly illustrates the chronological record of interest in the issue.

However, the author-date system works only under certain conditions:

1. The bibliography must be *homogeneous* and *specialized*, and readers of your work should already be familiar with your bibliography. If the condensed literature review in the example above referred, suppose, to the sexual behavior of the order of amphibians known as *Batrachia* (a most specialized topic), it would be presumed that the reader knows at a glance that "Ingrassia 1970" means the volume *Birth Control among the Batrachia* (or that he knows, at least intuitively, that it is one of Ingrassia's most recent works, structured differently from his well-known works of the 1950s). If instead you are writing, for example, a thesis on Italian culture in the first half of the twentieth century, in which you will cite novelists, poets, politicians, philosophers, and economists, the author-date system no longer works well because few readers can recognize a book by its date of publication alone (although they can refer to the bibliography for this information). Even if the reader is a specialist in one field, he will probably not recognize works outside that field.

2. The bibliography in question must be *modern,* or at least of the last two centuries. In a study of Greek philosophy it is not conventional to cite a book by Aristotle by its year of publication, for obvious reasons.

3. The bibliography must be scholarly/academic. It is not conventional to write "Moravia 1929" to indicate Alberto Moravia's best-selling Italian novel *The Indifferent Ones*.

In table 5.4 you will see the same page presented in table 5.2, but reformulated according to the author-date system. You will see immediately that it is *shorter*, with only one note instead of six. The corresponding reference list (table 5.5) is

Table 5.4
EXAMPLE OF THE AUTHOR-DATE SYSTEM

Even though Chomsky (1965a, 162) accepts Katz and Fodor's principle of interpretive semantics (1963) that derives the meaning of a sentence from the sum of the meanings of its elementary constituents, he does not renounce his belief that deep syntactic structure primarily determines meaning.[1]

Naturally, as his first works already foretold (1965b, 163), Chomsky eventually developed a more articulated stance, placing the semantic interpretation at the intersection of deep structure and surface structure (1970). Other authors (Lakoff 1971) attempt to build a generative semantics in which the logical-semantic form generates the syntactic structure itself (cf. McCawley 1971).

[1] For a satisfactory overview of this position, see Ruwet 1967.

slightly longer, but also clearer. It is easy to see the temporal sequence of an author's works (you may have noticed that when two works by the same author appear in the same year, they are distinguished by adding lowercase letters to their year of publication), and the internal references require less information and are more direct.

Also, notice how I have dealt with multiple articles that appear in the same miscellaneous volume: I have recorded a

Table 5.5
EXAMPLE OF A CORRESPONDING REFERENCE LIST

Chomsky, Noam. 1965a. *Aspects of the Theory of Syntax*. Cambridge, MA: MIT Press.

———. 1965b. De quelques constantes de la théorie linguistique. *Diogène* 51:4–21. Reprinted as Persistent Topics in Linguistic Theory. *Diogenes* (Fall 1965): 13–20.

———. 1970. Deep Structure, Surface Structure and Semantic Interpretation. In *Studies in General and Oriental Linguistics*, ed. Roman Jakobson, 52–91. Tokyo: TEC Corporation for Language and Education Research. Now available in Steinberg and Jakobovits 1971, 183–216.

Katz, Jerrold J., and Jerry A. Fodor. 1963. The Structure of a Semantic Theory. *Language* 39, no. 2 (April-June): 170–210. Now available in *The Structure of Language*, ed. J. J. Katz and J. A. Fodor, 479–518. Englewood Cliffs, NJ: Prentice-Hall, 1964.

Lakoff, George. 1971. On Generative Semantics. In Steinberg and Jakobovits 1971, 232–296.

McCawley, James. 1971. Where Do Noun Phrases Come From? In Steinberg and Jakobovits 1971, 217–231.

Ruwet, Nicolas. 1967. *Introduction à la grammaire générative*. Paris: Plon. Trans. Norval S. H. Smith as *An Introduction to Generative Grammar* (Amsterdam: North-Holland, 1973).

Steinberg, Danny D., and Leon A. Jakobovits, eds. 1971. *Semantics: An Interdisciplinary Reader in Philosophy, Linguistics and Psychology*. Cambridge, UK: Cambridge University Press.

single entry for each of these, but also a separate entry for the miscellaneous volume itself. For example, in addition to entries for the articles by Chomsky, Lakoff, and McCawley, I have included a separate entry for the volume edited by Steinberg and Jakobovits in which these articles appear. But sometimes my thesis cites only one of many articles in a miscellaneous volume. In this case, I have integrated that volume's reference into the entry for the single article I cite in my thesis. For example, I have integrated the reference to *The Structure of Language* edited by Katz and Fodor into the entry of the article "The Structure of a Semantic Theory" by the same authors, because the latter is the only article I cite from the former.

You will also notice that the author-date system shows at a glance when a particular text was published for the first time, even if we usually encounter this text in the form of more recent editions. For this reason, this system is useful in homogeneous treatments of a topic in specific disciplines, since in these fields it is often important to know who proposed a certain theory for the first time, or who completed certain empirical research for the first time.

There is a final reason to use the author-date system when possible. Suppose you have finished writing your thesis, and you have typewritten the final draft with many footnotes. Even if you started numbering your notes over again at the beginning of each chapter, a particular chapter may require as many as 100 notes. Suddenly you notice that you have neglected to cite an important author whom you cannot afford to ignore, and whom you must cite at the beginning of this chapter. You must now insert the new note and change 100 numbers. With the author-date system, you do not have this problem; simply insert the name and the date of publication in parentheses, and then add the item to the general bibliography (in pen, or by retyping only a single page). Even if you have not finished typewriting your thesis, inserting a note that you have forgotten still requires renumbering and often presents other annoying formatting issues, whereas with the author-date system you will have few troubles in this area.

If you use the author-date system in a thesis with a homogeneous bibliography, you can be even more succinct by using multiple abbreviations for journals, manuals, and conference proceedings. Below are two examples from two bibliographies, one in the natural sciences, the other in medicine. (Do not ask me what these bibliographical entries mean. Presumably readers in these fields will understand them.)

Mesnil, F. 1896. Etudes de morphologie externe chez les Annélides. *Bull. Sci. France Belg.* 29:110–287.

Adler, P. 1958. Studies on the eruption of the permanent teeth. *Acta Genet. Stat. Med.* 8:78–94.

5.5   Instructions, Traps, and Conventions

The tricks of academic work are innumerable, and innumerable are the traps into which you can fall. Within the limits of this short treatment, we can only provide, in no particular order, a series of instructions to help you avoid such traps. Although these instructions may not help you navigate the Bermuda Triangle that you must cross in writing your thesis, they will at least alert you to the existence of such perils, and that you must ultimately face them on your own.

Do not credit or cite notions of common knowledge. Nobody would think of writing "Napoleon who, as Ludwig states, died in Saint Helena," but this kind of naïveté happens often. It is easy to say, "The mechanical looms, as Marx says, marked the advent of the industrial revolution," though this was a universally accepted notion even before Marx.

Do not attribute to an author an idea that he cites as belonging to someone else. Not only because you will appear to have used an indirect source unmindfully, but also because that author might have cited the idea without accepting it. In a little semiotics manual of mine, I cited, among the various possible classifications of signs, one that divides them into expressive and communicative versions. I then found in a student paper the assertion that, "according to Eco, signs are divided between the expressive and communicative." However, I have always been opposed to this coarse subdivision. I had cited it for objectivity, but I did not appropriate it.

Do not add or delete notes only to force the numbering to add up. When you have already typewritten your thesis (or even if you have simply written it legibly for the typist), it may happen that you must eliminate a note that turned out to be incorrect, or that you must add a new one at any cost. As a result the numbering of the following notes does not add up, and good for you if you have numbered notes by chapter and not from the very beginning of your thesis. (It is one thing to correct notes from 1 to 10, another to correct them from 1 to 150.) To avoid changing all the note reference numbers, you will be tempted to insert a filler note or eliminate another note. This temptation is human. But in these cases it is better to insert an additional superscript sign, such as a plus (+) sign, to refer the reader to the inserted note. However, this is surely a makeshift solution that may displease some advisors, so rearrange the numbering if you can.

There is a method for citing from indirect sources while still observing the rules of academic honesty. It is always better not to cite secondhand information, but sometimes this is impossible to avoid. Two systems are common, depending on the situation. First, let us suppose that Sedanelli quoted from Smith the statement that "The language of bees is translatable in terms of transformational grammar." In this case, we wish to highlight that Sedanelli assumes responsibility for this statement. We will then say in a note, using a not-so-elegant formula:

1. C. Sedanelli, *Il linguaggio delle api* (Milan: Gastaldi, 1967), 45, quoting C. Smith, *Chomsky and Bees* (Chattanooga: Vallechiara Press, 1966), 56.

In the second case we wish to highlight that the statement belongs to Smith, and we quote Sedanelli only to assuage our conscience, since we are taking Smith's quote from a second-hand source. We will then write the note:

1. C. Smith, *Chomsky and Bees* (Chattanooga: Vallechiara Press, 1966), 56, as quoted in C. Sedanelli, *Il linguaggio delle api* (Milan: Gastaldi, 1967), 45.

Always give precise information on critical editions, revisions, and the like. Specify if an edition is a critical edition and indicate its editor. Specify if a second or more recent edition is revised, enlarged, or corrected. Otherwise you risk misrepresenting the opinions that an author expressed in the 1970 revised edition of his 1940 work as if he had actually expressed them in 1940, when some discoveries had perhaps not yet been made.

Pay attention when you quote a pre-1900 author from foreign sources. Different cultures name the same figures differently. For instance, while we Italians refer to "Pietro Ispano" and the French to "Scot Erigène," in English you will find "Peter of Spain" and "Scotus Eriugena." In an Italian text you will encounter "Nicholas of Cusa" in the form of "Niccolò Cusano," and you should easily recognize personalities like "Petrarque" or "Petrarca," "Michel-Ange," "Vinci," and "Boccace." "Roberto Grossatesta" in Italian appears as "Robert Grosseteste" in English, "Alberto Magno" as "Albert the Great," and "San Tommaso d'Aquino" as simply "Aquinas." The person known in Italian as "Anselmo d'Aosta" appears in English as "Anselm of Canterbury." Do not speak of two painters when you refer to "Roger van der Wayden" and "Rogier de la Pasture," because they are one and the same. "Giove" is "Jupiter," naturally. Also, pay attention when you are copying Russian names from an old French source. You would probably avoid writing "Staline" or "Lenine," but you may still fall for "Ouspensky," when you should instead transliterate "Uspenskij." The same applies to names of cities: "Den Haag," "La Haye," and "L'Aia" all refer to "The Hague."

How do we learn these naming conventions, of which there are many hundreds? We read various texts in various languages on the same topic. We join the club. Music lovers know "the King" is Elvis Presley, sports fans know that "Doctor J" is Julius Erving, and American high school students know that "Mark Twain" is Samuel Clemens. Those who do not know these things are considered naïve or provincial. A literature student who discusses in his thesis the relationship between Arouet and Voltaire after reading a few secondary sources might be considered "ignorant" instead of merely provincial.[14]

Pay attention when you find numbers in foreign texts. For instance, in an Italian book you will find 2.625 for two thousand six hundred twenty-five, while 2,25 means two and twenty-five hundredths.

Pay attention to references to centuries in foreign sources. For instance, in Italian you will find references to *Cinquecento*, *Settecento*, *Novecento* and not the XVI (sixteenth), XVIII (eighteenth), and XX (twentieth) centuries. However, in a French or English book the Italian word *Quattrocento* indicates a precise period of Florentine culture. Do not make facile equivalencies among different languages. The Italian *Rinascimento* covers a different period than the Renaissance, since it excludes seventeenth-century authors. *Manierismo* is another tricky term because it refers to a specific period in Italian art history, and not to what is known in English as mannerism, or in German as *Manierismus*.

Acknowledgments. If someone other than your advisor provided verbal suggestions, lent you rare books, or gave you similar kinds of help, it is good practice to acknowledge them in a section at the beginning or end of your thesis. It also shows that you were diligent enough to consult knowledgeable people. However, it is bad taste to thank your advisor. If he helped you, he has simply done his job.

Additionally, you may happen to thank and to declare your debt to a scholar that your advisor hates, abhors, and despises. This is a serious academic incident, and it is your fault. You should have trusted your advisor, and if he told you that someone is an imbecile, you should not have consulted that person. Or, if your advisor is open-minded and he accepts that his student has used resources with which he disagrees, this incident will simply become a matter of civil discussion at your thesis defense. If instead your advisor is an old capricious baron, spiteful and dogmatic, you have probably made the wrong choice for an advisor. However, if, despite these flaws, you truly wanted this advisor because you believed that he would treat you like a protégé, then you must be coherently dishonest and ignore this other person in your acknowledgments, because you have chosen to become the same kind of person that your mentor is.

5.6   Academic Pride

In section 4.2.4 we discussed academic humility, which concerns the research method and the interpretation of texts. Now let us discuss academic pride, which concerns confidence in writing.

There is nothing more annoying than a thesis in which the author continuously gives unsolicited excuses (and this sometimes even happens in published books):

> We are not qualified to deal with such a topic. Nevertheless we would like to venture a guess that ...

What do you mean, you are not qualified? You have devoted months and maybe years to the topic you have chosen, you have presumably read everything there was to read on it, you have reflected on it, taken notes, and now you say that you are not qualified? But what have you been doing all this time? If you do not feel qualified, do not defend your thesis. If you defend it, it is because you feel ready, and in this case you have no right to make excuses. So, once you have illustrated other scholars' opinions, once you have illuminated the particular difficulties of the issue, and once you have clarified that there can be alternative answers to a specific question, *jump in at the deep end*. Have no qualms about saying, "we think that ..." or, "it is possible to think that ..." When you speak, *you* are the expert. If you are to be exposed as a fraud because you have not done rigorous work, shame on you, but you have no right to hesitate if you have done good work. On your specific topic, you are humanity's functionary who speaks in the collective voice. Be humble and prudent before opening your mouth, but once you open it, be dignified and proud.

By writing a thesis on topic X, you assume that nobody has discussed this topic so exhaustively or clearly before you. Throughout this book I have shown that you must be cautious in choosing a topic, that you must be wary enough to settle on a topic that is extremely limited, perhaps very easy, and perhaps despicably specialized. But on the topic you have chosen, be it even "Variations in Newspaper Sales at the Newsagent on the Corner of Washington and State during the First Week of August 1976," on that topic you must be *the utmost living authority*. And even if you have chosen a litera-ture survey in which you summarize all that has been said on a topic without adding anything new, you are the authority on what has been said by the other authorities. Nobody must know better than you *all* that has been said on that topic. Naturally, you must work with a clear conscience. But this is another story. Here I am discussing a matter of style. Do not whine and be complex-ridden, because it is annoying.

Attention: the following chapter is not printed but instead type-written. It provides a model of the thesis's final draft. The final draft entails two specific documents: the final written draft, and the final typewritten draft. It may first seem like writing the final draft is your responsibility and that this is wholly a conceptual issue, whereas typing is a manual matter that is the responsibility of the typist. But this is not really the case. Giving a typewritten form to a thesis also means making some method-ological choices. If the typist makes them for you, following certain standards, your thesis will still have a specific graphic-expository format that also affects its content. It is more desir-able that you make these choices yourself, and in this case, any kind of draft you have adopted (writing by hand, typing with a single finger, or—horror!—using the tape recorder) must con-tain formatting instructions for the typist.

For these reasons, you will find formatting instructions in this chapter that will help you impose a conceptual order as well as a "communicative façade" on your thesis. Also, you may or may not use the services of a typist. You could type it yourself, especially if your work requires special graphic conventions. You may be able to type at least a first typewritten draft on your own, and the typ-ist will have only to clean up what you have already formatted. The question here is whether you can type, or can learn to type. If the answer is yes to either, remember that a used typewriter costs less than paying a typist to type your thesis.

6. THE FINAL DRAFT

6.1. <u>Formatting the Thesis</u>
6.1.1. Margins and Spaces

   This chapter begins with its title, in full
capitals, with left-hand justification (but it
could also be centered on the page). The chapter bears a number, in this case an Arabic
numeral (below we will see the available alternatives). Then, after three or four blank
lines, the title of the section appears flush
left, underlined, and preceded by the Arabic
numeral of the chapter and that of the section.
Then the title of the subsection appears two
lines below (or double-spaced). The title of
the subsection is not underlined, so as to distinguish it from that of the section. The text
begins three lines under this title, and the
first word is indented two spaces.
   You can decide to indent the text only at the
beginning of a section or at the beginning of
each paragraph, as we are doing on this page.
The indentation for a new paragraph is important
because it shows at a glance that the previous
paragraph has ended, and that the argument
restarts after a pause. As we have already seen,
it is good to begin a new paragraph often, but
not randomly. The new paragraph means that a
logical period, comprised of various sentences,
has organically ended and a new portion of the
argument is beginning. It is as if we were to
pause while talking to say, "Understood? Agreed?

Good, let us proceed." Once all have agreed, we
begin a new paragraph and proceed, exactly as we
are doing in this case.

Once the section is finished, leave three
lines between the end of the text and the title
of the new section. (This is triple spacing.)
Although this chapter is double-spaced, a thesis
may be triple-spaced, so that it is more read-
able, so that it appears to be longer, and so
that it is easier to substitute a retyped page.
When the thesis is triple-spaced, the distance
between the title of a chapter, the title of
a section, and any other subhead increases by
one line.

If a typist types the thesis, the typist
knows how much margin to leave on all four
sides of the page. If you type it, consider
that the pages will have some sort of binding
which will require some space between binding
and text, and the pages must remain legible on
that side. (It is also a good idea to leave
some space on the other side of the page.)

This chapter on formatting, as we have
already established, takes the form of typewritten pages of a thesis, insofar as the
format of this book allows. Therefore, while
this chapter refers to your thesis, it also
refers to itself. In this chapter, I underline
terms to show you how and when to underline;
I insert notes to show you how to insert notes;
and I subdivide chapters, sections, and subsections to show you the criteria by which to subdivide these.

6.1.2. Underlining and Capitalizing

The typewriter does not include italic type, only roman type. Therefore, in a thesis you must <u>underline</u> what in a book you would italicize. If the thesis were the typescript for a book, the typographer would then compose in italics all the words you underlined.

What should you then underline? It depends on the type of thesis, but in general, underline the following:

1. Foreign words of uncommon use (do not underline those that are already anglicized or currently in use, like the Italian words "ciao" and "paparazzi," but also "chiaroscuro," "manifesto," and "libretto"; in a thesis on particle physics, do not underline words common in that field such as "neutrino");
2. Scientific names such as "<u>felis catus</u>," "<u>euglena viridis</u>," "<u>clerus apivorus</u>";
3. Technical terms: "the method of <u>coring</u> in the processes of oil prospecting ...";
4. Titles of books (not of book chapters or journal articles);
5. Titles of dramatic works, paintings, and sculptures: "In her essay 'La théorie des mondes possibles dans l'étude des textes: Baudelaire lecteur de Brueghel' (The theory of possible worlds in the study of texts: Baudelaire as reader of Brueghel), Lucia Vaina-Pusca refers to Hintikka's <u>Knowledge and Belief</u> in demonstrating that

Baudelaire's poem 'The Blind' is inspired
by Pieter Bruegel the Elder's painting
<u>The Parable of the Blind</u>";

6. Names of newspapers, magazines, and journals: "see the article 'E dopo le elezioni?'
   (What is next after the election?) that
   appeared in <u>L'Espresso</u> on June 24, 1976";

7. Titles of films, published musical scores,
   and lyric operas.

<u>Do not underline other authors' quotes</u>.
Instead, follow the rules given in section 5.3.
Underlining too much is like crying wolf: if
you do it too many times, nobody will take
notice. An underline must always correspond to
that special intonation you would give to your
voice if you were to read the text. It must
attract the attention of your listeners, even
if they are distracted.

You can decide to underline (sparingly)
single terms of particular technical importance, such as your work's keywords. Here is
an example:

> Hjelmslev uses the term <u>sign function</u>
> for the correlation between two <u>func-</u>
> <u>tives</u> belonging to the two otherwise
> independent planes of <u>expression</u> and
> <u>content</u>. This definition challenges the
> notion of the sign as an autonomous
> entity.

Let it be clear that every time you introduce
an underlined technical term you must define it
immediately before or after. Do not underline

for emphasis ("We believe what we have discovered <u>decisively</u> proves our argument that ...").
In general, avoid emphasis of any kind, including exclamation points. Also avoid ellipsis
points used for anything other than to indicate
a specific omission from a text you have
quoted. Exclamation points, ellipses used to
suspend a thought or sentence, and underlined
nontechnical terms are typical of amateur writers and appear only in self-published books.

6.1.3. Sections

A section can have a number of subsections,
as in this chapter. If you underline the title
of a section, not underlining the title of a
subsection will suffice to distinguish the two,
even if their distance from the text is the
same. On the other hand, as you can see, stra-
tegic numbering can also help distinguish a
section from a subsection. Readers will understand that the first Arabic numeral indicates
the chapter, the second Arabic numeral indicates the section, and the third indicates the
subsection.
<u>6.1.3.Sections</u> Here I have repeated the title
of this subsection to illustrate another system
for formatting it. In this system, the title is
underlined and run in to the first paragraph of
text. This system is perfectly fine, except it
prevents you from using the same method for a
further subdivision of the subsection, something that may at times be useful (as we shall
see in this chapter). You could also use a

numbering system without titles. For example,
here is an alternative way to introduce the
subsection you are reading:
6.1.3. Notice that the text begins immediately
after the numbers; ideally, two blank lines
would separate the new subsection from the previous one. Notwithstanding, the use of titles
not only helps the reader but also requires
coherence on the author's part, because it
obliges him to define the section in question
(and consequently, by highlighting its essence,
to justify it).

With or without titles, the numbers that
identify the chapters and the paragraphs can
vary. See section 6.4 for more suggestions on
numbering. Remember that the structure of the
table of contents (the numbers and titles of
the chapters and sections) must mirror the
exact structure of the text.

6.1.4. Quotation Marks and Other Signs

Use quotation marks in the following cases:

1. To quote another author's sentence or sentences in the body of the text, as I will do
   here by mentioning that, according to
   Campbell and Ballou, "direct quotations not
   over three typewritten lines in length are
   enclosed in quotation marks and are run into
   the text."[1]

---

1. William Giles Campbell and Stephen
   Vaughan Ballou, Form and Style, 4th ed.
   (Boston: Houghton Mifflin, 1974), 40.

2. To quote another author's individual terms,
   as I will do by mentioning that, according
   to the already-cited Campbell and Ballou,
   there are two types of footnotes: "content"
   and "reference." After the first use of the
   terms, if we accept our authors' terminology
   and adopt these technical terms in our
   thesis, we will no longer use quotation
   marks when we repeat these terms.

3. To add the connotation of "so-called" to
   terms of common usage, or terms that are
   used by other authors. For example, we can
   write that what idealist aesthetics called
   "poetry" did not have the same breadth that
   the term has when it appears in a publisher's catalog as a technical term opposed to
   fiction and nonfiction. Similarly we will
   say that Hjelmslev's notion of sign function
   challenges the current notion of "sign." We
   do not recommend, as some do, using quotation marks to emphasize a word, as an underline better fulfills this function.

4. To quote lines in a dramatic work. When
   quoting a dramatic work, it is not incorrect
   to write that Hamlet pronounces the line,
   "To be or not to be, that is the question,"
   but instead we recommend the following:

   Hamlet: To be or not to be, that is the
   question.

   Use the second format unless the critical
   literature that you are consulting uses
   other systems by tradition.

And how should you indicate a quote within
another quote? Use single quotation marks for
the quote within a quote, as in the following
example, in which according to Smith, "the
famous line 'To be or not to be, that is the
question' has been the warhorse of all
Shakespearean actors." And what if Smith said
that Brown said that Wolfram said something?
Some writers solve this problem by writing
that, according to Smith's well-known statement, "all who agree with Brown in 'refusing
Wolfram's principle that "being and not being
coincide"' incur an unjustifiable error." But if
you refer to rule 8 of section 5.3.1, you will
see that, by setting off Smith's quote from the
main text, you will avoid the need for a third
level of quotation marks.

Some European writers use a third kind of
quotation marks known as <u>guillemets</u>, or French
quotation marks. It is rare to find them in an
Italian thesis because the typewriter cannot
produce them. Yet recently I found myself in
need of them in one of my own texts. I was
already using double quotation marks for short
quotes and for the "so-called" connotation, and
I had to distinguish the use of a term as
a /signifier/ (by enclosing it in slashes) and
as a «signified» (by enclosing it in guille-
mets). Therefore, I was able to write that the
word /dog/ means «carnivorous and quadruped
animal, etc.», and similar statements. These
are rare cases, and you will have to make a
decision based on the critical literature that
you are using, working by hand with a pen in

the typewritten thesis, just as I have done in
this page.

Specific topics require other signs. It is not
possible to give general instructions for these,
although we can provide some examples here. For
some projects in logic, mathematics, or non-
European languages, you can only write these
signs by hand (unless you own an IBM Selectric
electric typewriter, into which you can insert
different typeballs that allow you to type different alphabets). This is certainly difficult
work. However, you may find that your typewriter
can produce alternative graphemes. Naturally,
you will have to ask your advisor if you can
make these substitutions, or consult the critical literature on your topic. As an example,
table 6.1 gives a series of logic expressions
(on the left) that can be transcribed into the
less laborious versions on the right.

Table 6.1

p ⊃ q	becomes	p → q
p ∧ q	"	p . q
p ∨ q	"	p v̲ q
☐ p	"	Lp
◇ p	"	Mp
∿ p	"	– p
(∀ x)	"	(Ax)
(∃ x)	"	(Ex)

The first five substitutions are also acceptable in print; the last three are acceptable in
the context of a typewritten thesis, although
you should perhaps insert a note that justifies
your decision and makes it explicit.

You may encounter similar issues if you are
working in linguistics, where a phoneme can be
represented as [b] but also as /b/. In other
kinds of formalization, parenthetical systems
can be reduced to sequences of parentheses. So,
for example, the expression

$$\{[(p \supset q) \wedge (q \supset r)] \supset (p \supset r)\}$$

can become

$$(((p \rightarrow q) \cdot (q \rightarrow r)) \rightarrow (p \rightarrow r))$$

Similarly, the author of a thesis in transformational linguistics knows that he can use
parentheses to represent syntactic tree branch-
ing. In any case, anyone embarking on these
kinds of specialized projects probably already
knows these special conventions.

6.1.5. Transliterations and Diacritics

To <u>transliterate</u> is to transcribe a text
using the closest corresponding letters from an
alphabet that is different from the original.
Transliteration does not attempt to give a phonetic interpretation of a text, but reproduces
the original letter by letter so that anyone
can reconstruct the text in its original spelling if they know both alphabets.

Transliteration is used for the majority of
historic geographical names, as well as for
words that do not have an English-language
equivalent. Table 6.2 shows the rules of transliteration of the Greek alphabet (which can be
transliterated, for example, for a thesis in
philosophy) and the Cyrillic alphabet (for
Russian and some other Slavic languages).

Table 6.2
HOW TO TRANSLITERATE NON-LATIN ALPHABETS

ANCIENT GREEK ALPHABET

Capital letters	Small letters	Transliteration
A	α	a
B	β	b
Γ	γ	g
Δ	δ	d
E	ε	ĕ
Z	ζ	z
H	η	ē
Θ	θ	th
I	ι	i
K	κ	c
Λ	λ	l
M	μ	m
N	ν	n
Ξ	ξ	x
O	ο	ŏ
Π	π	p
P	ρ	r
Σ	σ ς	s
T	τ	t
Y	υ	ü
Φ	φ	ph
X	χ	ch
Ψ	ψ	ps
Ω	ω	ō

Note: γγ = ng
       γκ = nc
       γξ = ncs
       γχ = nch

RUSSIAN ALPHABET

Capital/small	Transl.	Capital/small	Transl.
А а	a	П п	p
Б б	b	Р р	r
В в	v	С с	s
Г г	g	Т т	t
Д д	d	У у	u
Е е	e	Ф ф	f
Ё ё	ё	Х х	kh
Ж ж	zh	Ц ц	ts
З з	z	Ч ч	ch
И и	i	Ш ш	sh
Й й	y	Щ щ	shch
К к	k	Ы ы	y
Л л	l	Ь ь	´
М м	m	Э э	e
Н н	n	Ю ю	yu
О о	o	Я я	ya

<u>Diacritics</u> are signs that modify normal let-
ters of the alphabet to give them a particular
phonetic value. Italian accents are diacritics.
For example, the acute accent "´" on the final
"e" of the Italian <u>perché</u> gives it its closed
pronunciation. Other diacritics include the
French cedilla of "ç," the Spanish tilde of "ñ,"
the German dieresis of "ü," and also the less-
known signs of other alphabets, such as the
Czech "č" or c with haček, the Danish "ø" or o
with stroke, and the Polish "ł" or l with
stroke. In a thesis (on something other than
Polish literature) you can eliminate, for example, the stroke on the l and the acute accents
on the o and z: instead of writing <u>Łódź</u> you can
write <u>Lodz</u>. Newspapers also do this. However,
for the Latin languages there are stricter
rules. Let us look at some specific examples:

Respect the use of all diacritics that appear
in the French alphabet, such as the cedilla in
<u>Ça ira</u>. Respect the particular signs of the
Spanish alphabet: the vowels with the acute
accent and the n with tilde "ñ." Respect the
particular signs of the Portuguese alphabet
such as the vowels with the tilde, and the "ç."

Also, always respect the three particular
signs of the German alphabet: "ä," "ö," and
"ü." And always write "ü," and not "ue" (<u>Führer</u>,
not <u>Fuehrer</u>).

For all other languages, you must decide case
by case, and as usual the solution will differ
depending on whether you quote an isolated word
or are writing your thesis on a text that is
written in that particular language.

6.1.6. Punctuation, Foreign Accents,
and Abbreviations

There are differences in the use of punctuation and the conventions for quotation marks,
notes, and accents, even among the major
presses. A thesis can be less precise than a
typescript ready for publication. Nevertheless,
it is useful to understand and apply the general criteria for punctuation. As a model, I
will reproduce the instructions provided by
Bompiani Editore, the press that published the
original Italian version of this book, but we
caution that other publishers may use different
criteria. What matters here are not the criteria themselves, but the coherence of their
application.

Periods and commas.[1] When periods and commas
follow quotes enclosed in quotation marks, they
must be inserted inside the quotation marks,
provided that the quoted text is a complete
sentence. For example, we will say that, in
commenting on Wolfram's theory, Smith asks
whether we should accept Wolfram's opinion that
"being is identical to not being from any possible point of view." As you can see, the final
period is inside the quotation marks because
Wolfram's quote also ended with a period. On
the other hand, we will say that Smith does not
agree with Wolfram's statement that "being is
identical to not being". Here we put the period
after the quotation mark because only a portion
of Wolfram's sentence is quoted. We will do the

same thing for commas: we will say that Smith,
after quoting Wolfram's opinion that "being is
identical to not being", very convincingly
refutes it. And we will proceed differently
when we quote, for example, the following sentence: "I truly do not believe," he said, "that
this is possible." We can also see that a comma
is omitted before an open parenthesis.
Therefore, we will <u>not</u> write, "he loved variegated words, fragrant sounds, (a symbolist
idea), and velvety pulses" but instead "he loved
variegated words, fragrant sounds (a symbolist
idea), and velvety pulses".

<u>Superscript note reference numbers</u>. Insert the
superscript note reference number after the
punctuation mark. You will therefore write for
example:

> The best literature review on the topic,
> second only to Vulpius',[1] is the one
> written by Krahehenbuel.[2] The latter does
> not satisfy Pepper's standards of
> "clarity",[3] but is defined by Grumpz[4] as
> a "model of completeness."

<u>Foreign accents</u>. In Italian, if the vowels "a,"
"i," "o," and "u" are accented at the end of a

---

1. This is a dummy note, inserted to illustrate
   the correct format; the author is fictional.
2. Fictional author.
3. Fictional author.
4. Fictional author.

word, the accent is <u>grave</u> (e.g. <u>accadrà</u>, <u>così</u>, <u>però</u>, <u>gioventù</u>). Instead the vowel "e" at the end of a word almost always requires the <u>acute</u> accent (e.g. <u>perché</u>, <u>poiché</u>, <u>trentatré</u>, <u>affinché</u>, <u>né</u>, <u>poté</u>) with a few exceptions: è, <u>cioè</u>, <u>caffè</u>, <u>tè</u>, <u>ahimè</u>, <u>piè</u>, <u>diè</u>, <u>stiè</u>, <u>scimpanzè</u>. All Italian words of French origin also contain grave accents, such as <u>gilè</u>, <u>canapè</u>, <u>lacchè</u>, <u>bebè</u>, <u>bignè</u>, proper nouns such as <u>Giosuè</u>, <u>Mosè</u>, <u>Noè</u>, and others.(When in doubt, consult a good Italian dictionary.) Also in Italian, tonic accents (<u>subìto</u>, <u>princìpi</u>, <u>mèta</u>, <u>èra</u>, <u>dèi</u>, <u>sètta</u>, <u>dài</u>, <u>dànno</u>, <u>follìa</u>, <u>tintinnìo</u>) are omitted, with the exception of <u>subìto</u> and <u>princìpi</u> in ambigious sentences:

<u>Tra prìncipi e princìpi incerti fallirono i</u> <u>moti del 1821.</u>(Between uncertain princes and principles, the uprisings of 1821 failed.)

Also remember that Spanish words have <u>only</u> acute accents: <u>Hernández</u>, <u>García Lorca</u>, <u>Verón</u>.

<u>Abbreviations.</u> Table 6.3 provides a list of common abbreviations. Specific subjects (paleography, classical and modern philology, logic, mathematics, etc.) have separate series of abbreviations that you will learn by reading the critical literature on your thesis topic.

Table 6.3
COMMON ABBREVIATIONS

anon.	anonymous
art.	article (for parts of a law, not for newspaper or magazine articles)
bk.	book (for example, "vol. 1, bk. 1")
cf.	*confer*, compare
chap.	chapter (plural "chaps.")
col.	column (plural "cols.")
ed.	edition (first, second, etc.); editor (plural "eds."); edited by; editor's note
e.g.	*exempli gratia*, for example
ex.	example
ff.	and following (e.g. pp. 34ff.)
fig.	figure (plural "figs.")
fol.	folio (plural "fols.")
ibid.	*ibidem*, on the same page in the previously cited work
i.e.	*id est*, that is
inf.	*infra*, below
MS	manuscript (plural "MSS")
n.	note (plural "nn.") (for example, "cf. n. 3")
NB, n.b.	*nota bene*, pay attention to
n.d.	no date of publication

no.	number
n.p.	no place of publication
n.s.	new series
p.	page (plural "pp.")
par.	paragraph
passim	throughout (use this abbreviation when the author treats the concept throughout the work, instead of on a particular page)
pseud.	pseudonym (do not confuse this abbreviation with "pseudo," a term that indicates instead that the authorship of a work is uncertain)
r.	recto, one of the odd-numbered pages of a book
sec.	section (also §)
[sic]	thus, written in this manner by the author I am quoting
trans.	translated by; translator(s) (this abbreviation is followed by the name of the translator and, sometimes, of the original language; it can also indicate a translator's note)
v.	*vide*, see; verse (plural "vv."); verso (one of the even-numbered pages of a book, as opposed to recto); versus (in some contexts)
viz.	*videlicet*, that is to say, namely
vol.	volume (plural "vols.")
vs.	versus, as opposed to

6.1.7. Some Miscellaneous Advice

Do not capitalize general concepts, and pay
attention when you capitalize proper nouns. You
can certainly write "Love" and "Hate" if you are
examining two precise philosophical notions of
an ancient author, but a contemporary author
who talks about "the Cult of the Family" uses
the capitals only with irony. In a thesis in
the field of cultural anthropology, if you wish
to dissociate yourself from a concept that you
attribute to others, it is preferable to write,
"the cult of the family." For historical periods, refer to the "Revolutionary" period and the
"Tertiary" era. Here are some more examples that
are generally accepted: write "North America,"
"Black Sea," "Mount Fuji," "World Bank,"
"Federal Reserve," "Sistine Chapel," "House of
Representatives," "Massachusetts General
Hospital," "Bank of Labor," "European Economic
Community," and sometimes "Central Station."
(Only capitalize the word "station" if it is
part of the proper noun. Write "Grand Central
Station" for Chicago's famous central railway
station that was recently demolished; but if
you are commuting to Boston University from out
of state, your train arrives at "Back Bay
station.") Also, write "Magna Carta," "Bulla
Aurea," and "St. Mark's Basilica." Refer to "the
Letters of St. Catherine," "the Monastery of St.
Benedict" and "the Rule of St. Benedict;" and in
French, use "Monsieur Teste," and "Madame
Verdurin." Italians write "piazza Garibaldi" and
"via Roma"; but Americans write "Washington

Square Park" and "Wall Street." Capitalize
German common names, as Germans do:
"Ostpolitik," "Kulturgeschichte." You must capitalize proper nouns such as "Italians,"
"Congolese," "the Pulitzer Prize," and "the Holy
Father," but you may write "the bishop," "the
doctor," "the colonel," "the president," "the
north," and "the south." Generally speaking, you
should put everything you can into lower-case
letters, as long as you can do so without compromising the intelligibility of the text. For
more precise usages, follow the critical literature in the specific discipline you are studying, but be sure to model your text after those
published in the last decade.

<u>When you open quotation marks of any kind,
always close them</u>. This seems like an obvious
recommendation, but it is one of the most
common oversights in typewritten texts. A quote
begins, and nobody knows where it ends.

<u>Use Arabic numerals in moderation</u>. Obviously
this advice does not apply if you are writing a
thesis in mathematics or statistics, or if you
are quoting precise data and percentages.
However, in the middle of a more general argument, write that an army had "50,000" (and not
"fifty thousand") soldiers, but that a work is
"comprised of three volumes," unless you are
writing a reference, in which you should use "3
vols." Write that the losses have "increased by
ten percent," that a person has "lived until the
ripe old age of 101," that a cultural revolution

occurred in "the sixties," and that the city was
"seven miles away."

Whenever possible, write complete dates such
as "May 17, 1973," and not "5/17/73." Naturally
you can use abbreviated dates when you must
date an entire series of documents, pages of a
diary, etc.

Write that a particular event happened at
"half past eleven," but write that during the
course of an experiment, the water had risen
approximately "9.8 inches at 11:30 a.m." Write
the matriculation number "7535," the home at "30
Daisy Avenue," and "page 144" of a certain book.

Underline only when necessary. As we have
said, underline foreign terms that have not
been absorbed by English, such as "borgata" or
"Einfühlung." But do not underline "ciao,"
"pasta," "ballerina," "opera," and "maestro." Do
not underline brand names or famous monuments:
"the Vespa sped near the Colosseum." Usually,
foreign philosophical terms are not pluralized
or declined, even if they are underlined:
"Husserl's Erlebnis" or "the universe of the
various Gestalt." However, this becomes prob-
lematic if in the same text you use Latin terms
and decline them: "we will therefore analyze
all the subiecta and not only the subiectum
that is the object of the perceptual experience." It is better to avoid these difficult
situations by using the corresponding English
term (usually one adopts the foreign term
simply to show off his erudition), or by
rephrasing the sentence.

<u>Wisely alternate ordinal and cardinal num-</u>
<u>bers, Roman and Arabic numerals</u>. Although the
practice is becoming less common, Roman numerals can indicate the major subdivision of a
work. A reference like "XIII.3" could indicate
either volume thirteen, book (or issue) three;
or canto thirteen, line three. You can also
write "13.3" and the reader will understand you,
but "3.XIII" will look strange. You can write
"<u>Hamlet</u> III, ii, 28" and it will be clear that
you are referring to line twenty-eight of the
second scene of the third act of Hamlet, or you
can write "<u>Hamlet</u> III, 2, 28" (or "<u>Hamlet</u>
3.2.28"). But do not write "Hamlet 3, II,
XXVIII." Indicate images, tables, or maps as
"fig. 1.1" and "table 4.1."

<u>Reread the typescript</u>! Do this not only to
correct the typographical errors (especially
foreign words and proper nouns), but also to
check that the note numbers correspond to the
superscript numbers in the text, and that the
page numbers in the works you have cited are
correct. Be absolutely sure to check the
following:

<u>Pages</u>: Are they numbered consecutively?
<u>Cross-references</u>: Do they correspond to the
right chapter or page?
<u>Quotes</u>: Are they enclosed in quotation marks,
and have you closed all quotations? Have you
been consistent in using ellipses, square
brackets, and indentations? Is each quote properly cited?

Notes: Does the superscript note reference number in the text correspond to the actual note number? If you are using footnotes, is the note appropriately separated from the body of the text? Are the notes numbered consecutively, or are there missing numbers?
Bibliography: Are authors in alphabetical order? Did you mix up any first and last names? Are all the bibliographical references complete? Did you include accessory details (e.g. the series title) for some entries, but not for others? Did you clearly distinguish books from journal articles and book chapters? Does each entry end with a period?

6.2. The Final Bibliography

Had we not already discussed this topic at length at least twice, this would be a very long and detailed section. In section 3.2.3 we discussed how to record bibliographical information for books and articles, and in sections 5.4.2 and 5.4.3 we discussed both how to reference a work in the text and in a note, and how to format references so they work with the final bibliography. If you return to these three sections, you will find everything you need to write a good final bibliography.

Additionally, let us say first of all that a thesis must have a final bibliography, notwithstanding the detail and precision of the references in the notes. You cannot force your reader to shuffle through pages of text to find needed information. For some theses, the final

bibliography is a useful if not essential addition. For others, the final bibliography may
constitute the most interesting part: studies
on the critical literature of a given topic; a
thesis on all the published and unpublished
works of a given author; or a thesis centered
on bibliographical research, such as "Studies
on Fascism from 1945 to 1950," where obviously
the final bibliography is not an aid but the
primary goal.

Finally, we just need to add a few instructions on how to structure a bibliography. Let
us imagine, for example, a thesis on Bertrand
Russell. We will divide the bibliography into
"Works by Bertrand Russell" and "Works on
Bertrand Russell." (We could also have a more
general section called "Works on the History of
Philosophy in the Twentieth Century.") Russell's
works will appear in <u>chronological</u> order while
the critical literature on Russell will appear
in <u>alphabetical</u> order, unless the topic of the
thesis is "Studies on Bertrand Russell from
1950 to 1960 in England," in which case the
critical literature should also appear in
chronological order. In a thesis about
Watergate, we could divide the bibliography as
follows: excerpts from the Nixon White House
tapes, court transcripts and other court documents, official statements, media coverage, and
critical literature. (We might also include a
section of relevant works on contemporary
American politics.) As you can see, the format
will change according to the thesis type, and
the goal is to organize your bibliography so

that it allows readers to identify and distinguish between primary and secondary sources,
rigorous critical studies and less reliable
secondary sources, etc.

   In essence, and based on what we have said in
the previous chapters, the aims of a bibliography are: (a) to clearly identify a source; (b)
to enable the reader to find the source if
needed; (c) to demonstrate the author's familiarity with the chosen discipline. Demonstrating
familiarity with the discipline entails demonstrating both knowledge of all the literature on
your topic and a command of the discipline's
bibliographical conventions. Regarding the
latter, it may be that the standard conventions
described in this book are not the best for your
situation, and for this reason you should model
your work on the critical literature in your
specific field. Regarding the former, you will
need to decide whether to include only the works
you have consulted or all those that exist on a
particular topic. The most obvious answer is
that the bibliography of a thesis must list only
the works you have consulted, and that any other
solution would be dishonest. But here too, it
depends on the type of thesis you are writing.
For example, the specific aim of your research
project may include compiling all the written
texts on a specific topic, even though it may be
humanly impossible to read them all before you
graduate. In this case you should clearly state
that you did not consult all the works in the
bibliography, and should indicate those you did
read, perhaps with an asterisk. But such a

project is valid only where there are no existing complete bibliographies, so that your work consists precisely of compiling references that were once scattered. If by chance there is already a complete bibliography, it is better to refer the reader to it, and to include in your bibliography only the works you have actually consulted.

Often the reliability of a bibliography is evident from its title. Readers will have very different expectations from titles such as "Bibliographical References," "Works Cited," and "General Bibliography on Topic X." You cannot use the title "Bibliography on the Second World War" for a meager bibliography of thirty titles in English. Instead, simply call it "Works Cited" and hope for the best.

And no matter how meager your bibliography is, at least make an effort to put it in the correct alphabetical order. There are some rules: begin with the last name, and obviously titles of nobility like "de" and "von" do not belong to the last name, while capitalized prepositions do. So include "D'Annunzio" under D, but "Ferdinand de Saussure" under S, as "Saussure, Ferdinand de." Write "De Amicis, Edmondo," "Du Bellay, Joachim," "La Fontaine, Jean de"; but write "Beethoven, Ludwig van." Here too, keep an eye on the critical literature and follow its conventions. For example, for ancient authors (and until the fourteenth century), alphabetize by the first name. Do not alphabetize by what might seem to be the last name but is actually a patronymic or an indication of place of birth.

In conclusion, below is a standard division
for the final bibliography of a generic thesis:

Primary sources
Bibliographical indexes
Secondary sources on the topic or the author
(perhaps divided into sections for books and
articles)
Additional material (interviews, documents,
statements).

6.3. The Appendices

In some cases, the appendix or appendices are
indispensable. If you are writing a thesis in
philology and discussing a rare text that you
have found and transcribed, you can present
this text in the appendix, and this may be the
most original contribution of the entire work.
In a thesis in history in which you often refer
to a certain document, you could present it in
the appendix, even if it has already been
published. A thesis in law that discusses a law
or a body of laws should present these in the
appendix (unless they are part of current,
widely accessible codes). Place tables, diagrams, and statistical data in the appendix,
unless they are short examples that you can
insert into the main text.
In general, place particular materials in the
appendix to prevent long and boring quotes in
the body of the text, and to facilitate quick
reference. Place in the appendix all the data
and documents that would burden the text and

make reading difficult. On the other hand,
numerous references to the appendix can also
make reading difficult, especially if they force
the reader to constantly page back and forth
between the section he is reading and the end of
the thesis. In these cases you should follow
common sense, if nothing else, by doing everything you can to make the text clear, inserting
short citations, and summarizing the content of
the material which appears in the appendix.

If you think it is fitting to develop a certain theoretical point, yet you realize that it
interferes with the development of your overall
argument because it is an accessory to or an
extension of your topic, you can place the
treatment of that point in the appendix. Suppose
you are writing a thesis on the influence of
Aristotle's <u>Poetics</u> and <u>Rhetoric</u> on Renaissance
thought, and you discover that, in the twentieth
century, the Chicago School has offered contemporary reinterpretations of these texts. If the
observations of the Chicago School are useful to
clarify the relationship between Aristotle and
Renaissance thought, you will cite them in the
text. But it may be interesting to go deeper
into the topic in a separate appendix, where you
can use the example of the Chicago School's
reinterpretations to illustrate how not only
Renaissance scholars but also scholars in our
century have made an effort to revitalize the
Aristotelian texts. Similarly, you may find
yourself writing a thesis in Romance philology
on the character of Tristan, and dedicating an
appendix to the myth's use by the Decadent

movement, from Wagner to Thomas Mann. This topic
is not immediately relevant to the philological
topic of your thesis, but you may wish to argue
that Wagner's interpretation provides interesting suggestions to the philologist or, on the
contrary, that it represents a model of flawed
philology, perhaps suggesting further reflection
and investigation. This kind of appendix is not
recommended for a thesis, because it better
suits the work of a mature scholar who can take
the liberty of venturing into erudite digressions and various modes of criticism. However, I
am suggesting it for psychological reasons.
Inspired by your enthusiasm, you will sometimes
discover complementary or alternative avenues of
research, and you will not resist the temptation
to discuss these insights. By reserving these
insights for the appendix, you will be able to
satisfy your need to express them without compromising the rigor of your thesis.

6.4. The Table of Contents

In the table of contents, you must record
all the chapters, sections, and subsections of
the text, and you must exactly match their
numbering, pages, and wording. This may seem
like obvious advice, but before handing in the
thesis, you should carefully verify that you
have met these requirements.

The table of contents is an indispensable service that you provide both to the reader and to
yourself, as it helps one to quickly locate a
particular topic. Generally in English and also

in many German books, it appears at the beginning; in Italian and French books, it appears at the end. (Recently, some Italian publishers have also begun placing the table of contents at the beginning.) I think the table of contents is more convenient at the beginning of a work. You can find it after a few pages, whereas you have to exert more energy to consult it at the end. But if it is at the beginning, it should truly be at the beginning. Some English books place it after the preface; but often after the preface comes an introduction to the first edition, then an introduction to the second edition. This is an outrage. They may as well place the table of contents in the middle of the book.

An alternative is to place a table of contents proper (listing only the chapters) at the very beginning of a work, and a more detailed version with exhaustive subdivisions at the end. Another alternative is to place the table of contents with the chapters at the beginning, and an index of subjects at the end, generally accompanied by an index of names. However, this is not necessary in a thesis. It is sufficient to write a detailed table of contents, and preferably to place it at the beginning of the thesis, right after the title page.

The structure of the table of contents must mirror that of the text, as must the format. This means that if in the text section 1.2 is a section of chapter 1, you must make this evident in the layout of the table of contents. To clarify, we will provide two models of a table of contents in table 6.4, but you could organize

Table 6.4

MODELS OF A TABLE OF CONTENTS: Example 1

THE WORLD OF CHARLIE BROWN

MODELS OF A TABLE OF CONTENTS: Example 2

THE WORLD OF CHARLIE BROWN

the chapters and sections differently, using
Roman and Arabic numerals, letters, etc.

You could number the table of contents shown
in table 6.4 as follows:

A. FIRST CHAPTER
    A.1. First Section
    A.2. Second Section
        A.2.1. First Subsection
        A.2.2. Second Subsection
        Etc.

Or you could present it this way:

I. FIRST CHAPTER
    I.1. First Section
    I.2. Second Section
        I.2.1. First Subsection
        I.2.2. Second Subsection
        Etc.

You can even choose other criteria, as long as
they provide the same immediate clarity and
evidence.

As you can see, it is not necessary to conclude the titles with a period. Also, it is a
good rule to align the numbers to the right of
the column and not the left, as follows:

       7.
       8.
       9.
     10.

Not:

       7.
       8.
       9.
       10.

The same applies to Roman numerals.

Sophistication? No, cleanliness. If your tie is crooked, you straighten it, and even a hippie does not like to have pigeon droppings on his shoulder.

7 CONCLUSIONS

I would like to conclude with two observations. First, writing a thesis should be fun. Second, writing a thesis is like cooking a pig: nothing goes to waste.

If you lack research experience and are afraid to begin your thesis, you may be terrorized after reading this book. Confronted with all these rules and instructions, you may feel that it is impossible to get out alive. But remember this: for the sake of completeness, I wrote this book for a hypothetical student without *any* experience. But you have probably already read some pertinent books, and you have probably already acquired many of the techniques described in this book. My book can then serve as a reminder, bringing to awareness what many of you have already absorbed without realizing it. A driver, when he is confronted with a record of his own actions, realizes that he is a prodigious machine that makes vital decisions within a fraction of a second, with no margin for error. And still, almost everyone drives a car, and (as the moderate number of car accident victims indicates) the vast majority of drivers and passengers get out alive.

What really matters is that you write your thesis with gusto. If you choose a topic that interests you, and if you truly dedicate to your thesis the time you have allotted, however short (we have set a minimum of six months), you will experience the thesis as a game, as a bet, or as a treasure hunt. There is the satisfaction of competitive sports in hunting a text that is difficult to find; and there is the satisfaction of solving an enigma in discovering, after long reflection, the solution to an apparently insoluble problem. You must experience the thesis as a challenge. You are the challenger. At the beginning you posed a question which you did not yet know how to answer. The challenge is to find the solution in a finite number of moves. Sometimes, you can experience the thesis as a game between you and your author; he seems to conceal his secret from you, and you must trick him, question him gently, compel him to say what he does not want to say, but what he should have said. Sometimes, the thesis is a game of solitaire; you have all the pieces, and the challenge is to make them fall into place.

If you play the game with competitive gusto, you will write a good thesis. But if you begin with the idea that it is a meaningless ritual in which you have no interest, you have lost before you have begun. If this is the case, as I have already told you (and I do not wish repeat this illegal advice), have someone else write it for you. Or copy it. Do not waste your time, or that of your advisor, the person who must aid you and read your thesis from beginning to end.

If you write the thesis with gusto, you will be inspired to continue. Usually, while a student begins working on his thesis, he thinks only about finishing it, and he dreams of the vacation that will follow. But if you work rigorously, it is not abnormal for you to become obsessed with your work, unable to stop. You want to explore in depth all the points that you have omitted, you want to chase all the tangential ideas that struck you but that you eliminated for brevity, you want to read other books, and you want to write essays. This is the sign that the thesis has activated your intellectual metabolism, and that it has been a positive experience. It is the sign that you are the victim of a compulsion to research, somewhat like Charlie Chaplin's character in *Modern Times*, a factory worker who keeps tightening screws even after a long day of work. Like Chaplin, you will have to make an effort to restrain yourself.

But once you have temporarily contained this urge, you may realize that you have a calling for research, that the thesis was not simply the means to a degree, and the degree was not simply the means to career advancement, or to please your parents. However, your motivation to continue research does not necessarily have to translate into a university career. It also does not preclude you from accepting a job offer upon graduation. You can dedicate a reasonable amount of time to research while working another job, without expecting a university appointment. In many fields, a good professional must also continue to study.

If you devote yourself to your research, you will find that a thesis done well is a product of which nothing goes to waste. You can convert your finished thesis into one or more scholarly articles, or maybe even a book (with some revision). But in time, you may return to your thesis to find material to quote for other projects, or to reuse your readings index cards, maybe using parts that did not make it to the final draft of your first work. The marginal parts of your thesis may present themselves anew, as the beginning of new research projects. You may even decide to return to your thesis after decades. Your thesis is like your first love: it will be difficult to forget. In the end, it will represent your first serious and rigorous academic work, and this is no small thing.

NOTES

Translators' Foreword

1. Umberto Eco, *Dire quasi la stessa cosa: Esperienze di traduzione* (Milan: Bompiani, 2003), 364. Our translation. [Trans.]

2. All currency conversions are based on the actual June 15, 1977, exchange rate of Italian *lire* to US dollars. "Convertitore storico delle valute," Banca d'Italia, http://cambi.bancaditalia.it/cambi/cambi.do ?lingua=it&to=convertitore (accessed May 2013). [Trans.]

Introduction to the Original 1977 Edition

1. One could ask why I do not use the female pronoun "she" when referring to a student, candidate, professor, or advisor. It is because I drew on personal memories and experiences, and I identify better with the male counterpart.

Chapter 1

1. At the time of this book's publication, Italians who held *laurea* degrees enjoyed preferential access to public-sector jobs and automatic career advancement, even if their degree was in a field unrelated to their employment. [Trans.]

2. We could add a fifth rule: "The professor should be the appropriate fit for the topic." In fact, there are candidates who wish to work with the professor of Subject A, because they feel an affinity with him or because they are simply lazy, despite the fact that their thesis would be better served by the professor of Subject B. Often the professor accepts (out of predilection, vanity, or carelessness) and then is unable to effectively direct the thesis.

Chapter 2

1. C. W. Cooper and E. J. Robins, *The Term Paper: A Manual and Model*, 4th ed. (Stanford: Stanford University Press, 1967), 3.

2. In 1968, Italian university students rebelled against what they perceived as an antiquated curriculum, an elitist system that favored privileged applicants, and an unjust distribution of power between students and faculty. [Trans.]

3. Although isolated "free radio" stations emerged in Italy in the late 1960s, they became a nationwide phenomenon between 1975 and 1979. These private, local radio stations were illegal until 1976 because they broke the frequency monopoly of RAI, Italy's national broadcasting company. The Constitutional Court sentence no. 202 (July 28, 1976) restricted the monopoly of RAI to national programming, and opened local programming to the private sector. However, the Italian parliament failed to provide specific legislation to regulate the activity of the local stations, which is why Eco designates them as "semilegal" in 1977. See Stefano Dark, *Libere! L'epopea delle radio italiane degli anni '70* (Viterbo: Stampa alternativa/Nuovi Equilibri, 2009), 87–88. [Trans.]

4. ARCI, or Associazione Ricreativa Culturale Italiana (Italian Recreational and Cultural Association), was officially constituted in Florence on May 26, 1957, by a national convention of cultural, recreational, and athletic clubs fostering democratic and antifascist ideals. "L'Associazione. Storia," *Arci Bologna*, http://www.arcibologna .it/lassociazione/storia (accessed April 22, 2013). [Trans.]

5. Lotta Continua ("The Fight Continues" or "Continuous Fight") was a far-left extraparliamentary movement active in Italy from 1969 to 1976. [Trans.]

Chapter 3

1. "Maritain's interpretation of the expression *visa placent* is extremely popular with neo-Thomists, many of whom take his definition of beauty as *id quod visum placet*—namely, the definition 'Beauty is that which pleases when it is seen'—to be a correct quotation from Aquinas. In fact what Aquinas actually wrote was 'Pulchra enim dicuntur quae visa placent'—that is, 'things are called beautiful which please when they are seen.' Aquinas's words refer to what we

might call a sociological fact, whereas Maritain's version amounts to a metaphysical definition." Umberto Eco, *The Aesthetics of Thomas Aquinas*, trans. Hugh Bredin (Cambridge, MA: Harvard University Press, 1988), 240n22. [Trans.]

2. So that Eco's documentation guidelines will be useful to English-speaking students, we have adapted his preferred reference formats (examples numbers 1 and 5) to those recommended by *The Chicago Manual of Style*, 15th ed. (Chicago: University of Chicago Press, 2003). We have similarly adapted Eco's references throughout this book. [Trans.]

3. William Giles Campbell and Stephen Vaughan Ballou, *Form and Style*, 4th ed. (Boston: Houghton Mifflin, 1974), 69. [Trans.]

4. Although searching under the terms "seventeenth century," "baroque," and "aesthetics" seems fairly obvious, "poetics" is a slightly more subtle choice. My justification is that a student cannot have formulated this subject from scratch, but in fact a professor, a friend, or a preliminary reading must have prompted him. So he may well have heard the term "baroque poetics" or have encountered mentions of poetics (that is, literary theories) in general. So let us assume that the student has this preliminary knowledge.

5. Our translation. [Trans.]

Chapter 4

1. Unlike Italian universities, universities in other countries (including the United States) generally do not require oral exams. Instead, they require papers, that is, an essay or a "mini thesis" of 10 to 20 pages for each course. This is a useful system that some Italian professors have also adopted. (Italian regulations do not exclude this system; and the oral exam, primarily focusing on factual knowledge, is only one of the methods available to the professor to assess the student's abilities.)

2. The partisan war in Monferrato (Piedmont, Italy) was part of the larger partisan liberation movement known as the *Resistenza* (Resistance) that took place during the latter years of World War II (September 1943–May 1945) in opposition to both the Nazi forces occupying Italy and the fascist forces of the Italian Social Republic. While allied against the same enemies, partisans in the *garibaldine* brigades were generally associated with the Italian Communist Party

(PCI), while those in the *badogliane* formations were politically moderate and loyal to King Vittorio Emanuele III and Marshal Pietro Badoglio. The *Franchi* and *Mauri* were two important *badogliane* formations, respectively headed by Edgardo Sogno del Vallino and Enrico Martini, aka Mauri. See Giorgio Bocca, *Storia dell'Italia partigiana* (Bari: Laterza, 1970). [Trans.]

3. Auguste Villiers de l'Isle-Adam, *Axel*, trans. Marilyn Gaddis Rose (Dublin: Dolmen Press, 1970), 170. [Trans.]

4. The index card includes our translation from Théophile Gautier, "Préface," in *Poésies completes*, vol. 1, *Premières poésies, 1830–1832, Albertus, 1832, Poésies diverses, 1833–1838*, ed. Maurice Dreyfous (Paris: G. Charpentier, 1884), 4, http://gallica.bnf.fr/ark:/12148/bpt6k62191411/f22.image. [Trans.]

Chapter 5

1. *Purg.* XXIV. 53–54. The English translation is from Dante Alighieri, *Purgatorio*, trans. Jean Hollander and Robert Hollander, with an introduction and notes by Robert Hollander (New York: Anchor Books, 2004), 531. [Trans.]

2. First published anonymously as *Norme per la redazione di un testo radiofonico* (Turin: Edizioni Radio italiana, 1953), then enlarged in Carlo Emilio Gadda, *Norme per la redazione di un testo radiofonico* (Turin: ERI—Edizioni Rai Radiotelevisione italiana, 1973). [Trans.]

3. Eco is referring to the Italian idealist philosopher Giovanni Gentile (1875–1944). [Trans.]

4. Despite Eco's compelling argument regarding this topic, his advice in this paragraph does not necessarily reflect current English usage. [Trans.]

5. In our translation in table 5.1 we quoted from James Joyce, *A Portrait of the Artist as a Young Man: Authoritative Text, Backgrounds and Contexts, Criticism,* ed. John Paul Riquelme, text ed. Hans Walter Gabler with Walter Hettche (New York: W. W. Norton, 2007), and from Gabriele D'Annunzio, *The Flame,* trans. Susan Bassnett (New York: Marsilio Publishers, 1991), 10. [Trans.]

6. There are various ways to format block quotations on the printed page. They can be set in a smaller font size (an option that the typewriter *does not* have), or indented, or single-spaced if the rest of the

text is double-spaced. When typing your thesis, you should follow the formatting guidelines set by your institution.

7. This is not always the case in current English usage. Different manuals recommend different practices in this situation. [Trans.]

8. "The country girl is coming from the fields." Giacomo Leopardi, "The Village Saturday," in *The Canti, with a Selection of His Prose*, trans. J. G. Nichols (Manchester: Carcanet, 1994), 106. [Trans.]

9. "The cypresses that to Bolgheri go tall and straight from San Guido in double lines." Giosue Carducci, "The Cypresses of San Guido," in *The New Lyrics of Giosue Carducci*, trans. William Fletcher Smith (Colorado Springs, CO: privately printed, 1942), 66. [Trans.]

10. Maude Nugent, "Sweet Rosie O'Grady, 1896," in *500 Best-Loved Song Lyrics*, comp. and ed. Roland Herder (Mineola, NY: Dover, 1998), 336. [Trans.]

11. "Music, music before all things, / Uneven rhythm suits it well / In air more vague and soluble / With nothing there that weighs or clings." Paul Verlaine, "Art poétique," in *Selected Verse: A Bilingual Edition*, trans. and ed. Doris-Jeanne Gourévitch (Waltham, MA: Blaisdell Publishing, 1970), 136–137. [Trans.]

12. Ibid. [Trans.]

13. Note that I fabricated this example ad hoc to contain references of different kinds, and I would not swear to its reliability or conceptual clarity. Also note that, for reasons of simplicity, I have limited the bibliography to the essential data, neglecting the requirements of accuracy and completeness listed in section 3.2.3. And finally, what we define as a standard bibliography in table 5.3 can take various forms, depending on the citation style you adopt.

14. The French writer François-Marie Arouet is better known by his pen name Voltaire. [Trans.]

Chapter 6

1. Despite the cleverness of the following system, it is rarely used by contemporary English writers. [Trans.]